The Good Teacher

The Good Teacher will help teachers, student teachers, teacher trainers and others interested in the sociology and psychology of education to explore and make better sense of professional practice by examining that practice in the context of popular views as to what constitutes good teaching.

The book identifies and elaborates three dominant discourses of good teaching:

- the competent craftsperson, currently favoured by central governments
- the reflective practitioner, who continues to get widespread support among teacher trainers and educators
- the charismatic subject, whose popular appeal is evidenced in filmic and other media representations of teaching.

All of these discourses are critiqued on the basis of their capacity both to help and to hinder improved practice and understandings of practice. In particular, it is argued that the discourses all have a tendency, if not checked, to over-emphasise the individual teacher's or student teacher's responsibility for successful and unsuccessful classroom encounters, and to understate the role of the wider society and education systems in such successes and failures.

The Good Teacher will be of interest to all those in the teaching profession and those considering teaching as a career. It offers advice and support, and directs teachers towards a better understanding of the self-as-practitioner.

Alex Moore is currently a Senior Lecturer in Curriculum Studies at the Institute of Education, University of London.

The Good Teacher

Dominant discourses in teaching
and teacher education

Alex Moore

RoutledgeFalmer
Taylor & Francis Group

LONDON AND NEW YORK

First published 2004
by RoutledgeFalmer
11 New Fetter Lane, London EC4P 4EE

Simultaneously published in the USA and Canada
by RoutledgeFalmer
29 West 35th Street, New York, NY 10001

RoutledgeFalmer is an imprint of the Taylor & Francis Group

© 2004 Alex Moore

Typeset in Sabon by BC Typesetting Ltd, Bristol
Printed and bound in Great Britain by
Biddles Ltd, King's Lynn

British Library Cataloguing in Publication Data
A catalogue record for this book is available from the British Library

Library of Congress Cataloging in Publication Data
A catalog record for this book has been requested

ISBN 0–415–33564–7 (hbk)
ISBN 0–415–33565–5 (pbk)

BK
₹ 32.00

For Anna

Contents

Acknowledgements

My deepest thanks to all those friends, colleagues and loved ones who have supported me in various ways through the painful business of attempting to transfer some of my ideas from their secure haven in the mind to the turbulent waters of the public domain – a transference I have never found easy. In particular, to Dennis Atkinson for his unendingly interesting and stimulating commentaries on life educational; to Andy Ash, my co-researcher on the London University-funded study *Developing Reflective Practice in Beginning Teachers*, for his wisdom, friendship and support through difficult times and for his generosity in allowing me to make use of shared data for my own ends; to my long-suffering wife and children for putting up with the grumpiness and absenteeism that invariably accompany this sort of activity; to Anna Clarkson at RoutledgeFalmer for asking me to write the book in the first place, for encouraging me, with habitual good humour and reasonableness, to stick at it when the going got tough, and for helping to turn my initial, confused attempts into a more readable text; to the teachers and student teachers without whose articulate testimonies this book would never have been written; to the ESRC and the University of London, whose grants made possible two of the three research projects on which I have drawn in support of my argument; to David Halpin, Gwyn Edwards and Rosalyn George for being critical friends and for allowing me to use data collected and analysed as a team on the *Professional Identities Project*; and to all my other wonderful colleagues and students at the Institute of Education and at Goldsmiths College for their support, inspiration, tolerance and wisdom over the years.

Some of the material in this book has appeared elsewhere in other guises, and I am additionally grateful to various editors for approving reproduction of this, albeit in modified form. Specifically, some of my suggestions regarding charisma, competence, reflective practice and reflexivity appear in a condensed form in Chapter 8 of M. Hammersley (ed.) *Researching School Experience* (Falmer Press, 1999) and in Chapter 5 of A. Moore, *Teaching and Learning: Pedagogy, Curriculum and Culture* (RoutledgeFalmer, 2000); some of the material and examples I have used in relation to teacher effectiveness and pedagogical pragmatism first appeared in the co-authored article A. Moore, G. Edwards, D. Halpin and R. George, 'Compliance, Resistance and Pragmatism: The (Re)construction of Schoolteacher Identities in a Period of Intensive Educational Reform', *British Educational Research Journal* 28(4) (2002) 551–65; and the ideas concerning reflexivity and the O/other had their first public airing in the co-authored article A. Moore and D. Atkinson, 'Charisma, Competence and Teacher Education', *Discourse* 19(2) (1998) 171–82, subsequently to be revised in the paper A. Moore and A. Ash, 'Developing Reflective Practice in Beginning Teachers: Helps, Hindrances and the Role of the Critical o/Other', British Educational Research Association Annual Conference, University of Exeter, 2002; *Education-line, BEI*).

Part I

The good teacher

Themes and issues

1 Being a good teacher – influences and calls

The question 'What makes a good teacher?' is just about the most important in education. . . . We do know some of the answers to the question . . . and our most urgent objective should be to establish the conditions under which the best existing practice can be spread more widely.

(Lord Boyle, Introduction to Kemble 1971, pp. 9, 11)

Revealed: the ideal teacher.

(Headline in the *Times Educational Supplement*, 16 June 2000, p. 5, announcing the publication of Hay McBer 2000)

Being a good teacher: competent and reflective practitioners

The last three decades have seen a plethora of publications about how to teach and about how to teach teachers. While many of these have concentrated on the organisation and broad content of courses of teacher education (NUT 1976; DES 1981; Alexander *et al.* 1984), others have fallen into the category of the teaching *guide*, offering tips and advice to inexperienced teachers on such matters as managing pupils' learning and behaviour, marking and assessing pupils' work, and long- and short-term lesson planning (e.g. Cohen and Manion 1977; Stephens and Crawley 1994). Such publications may be said to support a particular model of teaching and of initial and continuing teacher education that prioritises the notion of the teacher as trained 'craftsperson' (Marland 1975).

These publications sit not uncomfortably with another model of teaching and teacher education that has recently enjoyed a resurgence of popularity with government agencies in Britain and elsewhere: that of the 'competent' teacher (Council for the Accreditation of Teacher Education 1992; Department for Education and Employment 1997a, 1997b; Teacher Training Agency 1998). According to this model, teachers are trained in the acquisition of certain *competences* related to aspects of classroom management, long-term, medium-term and short-term planning, developing and sharing subject knowledge, and assessing, recording and reporting students' work –

leading to the achievement of prescribed, assessable and (presumably) acquired-for-life '*standards*'.

Together, these models have come to represent what I shall call the *competent craftsperson* discourse of teaching and teacher education, wherein the teacher is configured and understood as one who 'works upon' the raw material of their students, improving the extent and quality of learning and skills through the application and development of identified skills of their own. (I use the term 'discourse' – more of which later – in the Foucauldian sense, to denote the constructed linguistic, conceptual and ethical parameters within which our perceptions of the social world and our actions within it are framed: parameters essentially introduced and sustained *by* language and 'knowledge', and controlled and patrolled by ideologies that tend to serve specific interests at the expense of others.)

Other publications have moved beyond what might be called the skills-based approach to teaching, to offer advice about underlying perceptions, procedures and approaches in what is recognised as a highly complex set of activities and interrelations. Such publications, eschewing the notion that teaching is reducible to discrete and finite lists of skills and practices, have focused on the importance of informed *reflection* on what one does in the classroom. This notion of 'reflective practice', which places as much emphasis on teachers' own evaluations of their practice (in specific contexts) as on the planning and management skills into which such evaluations feed, though already current under different names in the early 1970s (see, for instance, Combs 1972; Wragg 1974), really came to the fore in the 1980s and early 1990s in Britain through the work of such writers as Schon (1983, 1987), Valli (1992) and Elliott (1993a, 1993b). Today, what has evolved into a reflective practitioner *discourse* continues to show its popular appeal on bookshop shelves (e.g. Loughran 1996; Loughran and Russell 1997; Mitchell and Weber 1996; Pollard 2002a, 2002b), even as it becomes increasingly marginalised by government-sponsored publications favouring the 'competent craftsperson' discourse (Ofsted/TTA 1996; DfEE 1997a, 1997b) – a discourse with which it might, at first glance, appear to be at odds.

Popular conceptualisations of good teachers: charismatic and caring subjects

In addition to these two 'official' discourses of good teaching (official, that is, in terms of their representation and validation in policy documentation and in books aimed at teachers and teacher educators) there exists a third discourse that has great *popular* appeal: that of the teacher as charismatic subject. Within the terms of this discourse the key to good teaching is conceived as having less to do with education and training, and more to do with the inherent or intrinsic qualities of character or personality of the teacher, typically coupled with a deeply 'caring' orientation aimed very specifically at 'making a difference' to pupils' lives. Within this discourse, successful teachers are perceived not as having been 'made' (not, at least, through processes of teacher training and education), but as simply possessing 'the right stuff' – the capacity to command enthusiasm, respect and even love through the sheer force of their classroom presence.

If there are fewer published materials on being charismatic than on being competent or reflective, it is precisely because of this underpinning principle of the charismatic subject discourse that charisma cannot be 'acquired': that is to say, no amount of training or education can turn a 'dull', uncharismatic teacher into a lively, charismatic one, any more than one can train, teach or compel someone to be enthusiastic or caring. The concept of the charismatic teacher – which continues to haunt large numbers of teachers and student teachers – is, however, continually popularised and hegemonised in filmic and other fictive representations of successful teaching, where it can have the effect not so much of complementing as of undermining both the competent craftsperson and the reflective practitioner discourses. As we shall see in Chapter 3, the successful, charismatic teachers portrayed in (for example) feature films tend to have had little or no teacher education or training, to know nothing about theories of teaching and learning, and to eschew reflection on practice in favour of instinctive or opportunistic responses and reactions to classroom events.

The charismatic subject discourse, despite its somewhat peripheral status in the official discourses of good teaching, remains a very powerful one, not least because it is itself founded on and supported by a series of what Britzman (1991) refers to as 'cultural myths' and what Bruner (1996) calls 'folk pedagogy': that is to say, particular 'common-sense' convictions and suppositions about teaching and learning that act as supporters and perpetuators of the discourse. For Britzman, 'cultural myths' include such everyday platitudes as 'everything depends on the teacher', 'the teacher as expert' and 'the teacher as self-made' (Britzman 1991, pp. 6–8, 222–37) – platitudes which provide 'a set of ideal images, definitions, justifications, and measures for thought, feeling, and agency that work to render as unitary and certain the reality [they seek] to produce'. For Bruner, 'folk pedagogies' are, in essence, also cultural myths, this time supporting convictions that, for example, children are 'empty vessels to be filled with knowledge that only adults can provide' and 'pupils should be presented with facts, principles and rules of action [to be] remembered, and then applied' (Bruner 1996, pp. 49, 55: see also Watkins and Mortimore 1999, p. 15).

Britzman's suggestion that cultural myths contribute to the construction of something called reality through the over-simplification and universalisation of social life and experience points up the attraction both of myths and of the discourses they shape and support. Myths, after all, 'provide a semblance of order, control, and certainty in the face of the uncertainty and vulnerability of the teacher's world' (ibid.). However, the universalising discourses they help to construct, Britzman argues, have the effect of heaping too much attention on the actions of the individual and too little on the social structures in which the individual's actions are situated, having consequently a fundamentally conservative function, encouraging a symptomatic rather than a causal explanation of failure, and supporting individual at the expense of collective responsibility. As Britzman suggests:

> In the case of student teachers, cultural myths *structure a particular discourse* about power, authority, and knowledge that heightens individual effort as it trivializes school structure and the agency of students. The problem is that when the power of individual effort becomes abstracted from the dynamics of the social, student teachers cannot effectively intervene in the complex conditions that push them to take up the normative practices that discourage their desires for change.
>
> (1991, p. 222, my italics)

Britzman argues that teacher education has traditionally been dogged by a persistent common-sense belief – often, in the past, operationalised in policy and practice – that, if not necessarily 'born' rather than 'made', teachers do 'make themselves'. This particular cultural myth, she suggests,

> functions to devalue any meaningful attempt to make relevant teacher education, educational theory, and the social process of acknowledging the values and interests one brings to and constructs because of the educational encounter.
>
> (1991, p. 230)

In a curious way (curious, since the concept of good teachers being 'born' seems to stand in direct opposition to the concept of good teachers being 'made'), the charismatic discourse serves a similar function in relation to teacher education and training to that identified by Britzman regarding teachers as self-made professionals. That is, the discourse not only undermines the discourses of the competent craftsperson and the reflective practitioner, but it also undermines the very project of teacher education and training itself – including the belief that productive teaching cannot be achieved in the absence of genuine *understanding* (understanding, for example, of theories related to teaching and learning; of the part played by the teacher's and pupil's own histories, dispositions, perceptions and experiences in the teaching and learning situation; and of the wider social and cultural relations within which all forms of classroom practice are inevitably located). It is precisely this emphasis on understanding – which can be promoted and developed through constructive and instructive dialogues both among teachers and between student teachers and their more experienced colleagues – that lies at the heart of everything else that I wish to argue and promote in this book.

Dominant discourses: the dangers of reductionsim

One of the suggestions I shall make in the pages that follow is that the two discourses of the competent craftsperson and the reflective practitioner not only remain the dominant 'official' discourses in teacher education, but have the capacity – if not always the intention – both to weaken one another and to marginalise alternative teacher-education discourses, including discourses which seek to prioritise the idiosyncratic, contingent aspects of teaching and learning (Maguire 1995; Moore 1996) as opposed to those which may be perceived and presented as 'universal'. I shall argue that all these discourses, though typically perceived and presented in apparent opposition to one another, are often similarly characterised by and rooted in psychological notions of the ideal, unified 'self' (Lacan 1977, 1979; Walkerdine 1982, 1990) and in a 'modernist' or 'scientific' view of teaching and learning that is circumscribed by a notion of closure and the naming of parts (Hamilton 1993; Reid 1993). This is a view which, I am aware, will initially surprise, disappoint and perhaps anger some proponents of reflective practice but which will, I hope, become more acceptable as I declare my own allegiance not only to reflective practice itself but to a particular *form* of reflective practice which I shall refer to as *reflexivity*. As for the charismatic subject discourse, I shall suggest that although this features far less prominently in the taught elements of pre-service (and indeed early and continuing professional development) courses for schoolteachers, it is a discourse that student teachers 'bring with them' into their courses, where it often conflicts with the two other discourses or at best sits in a state of uneasy tolerance with them. Furthermore, the continuing championing of the charismatic discourse 'outside' the training/development discourse – in films and in newspapers, certainly, but also on the street or in conversations with family and friends – can, unless it is dealt with and contextualised via the taught course, lead to considerable discomfort and even self-imposed failure on the student teacher's part (Moore and Atkinson 1998).

None of this means that I believe the competent craftsperson, reflective practitioner or charismatic subject discourses to be wholly or inevitably 'bad' or to be avoided (in fact, they are unavoidable), or that I shall be suggesting that teachers do not need to be competent or reflective, or that they should not be perceived at times as 'charismatic' or at all times as 'caring' (though, as will become clear, I shall be using these latter terms in very particular ways). Indeed, I have spent a great part of the past fifteen years of my professional life trying to help teachers and student teachers to become both more competent at and more constructively reflective about what they do, as well as foregrounding their own enthusiasm and passion in the classroom encounter – and I shall no doubt continue to do so. There is much of merit in the competent craftsperson and reflective practitioner discourses, not least in the oppositional stance they may help to provide in relation to some other dominant discourses (*like* the charismatic subject discourse) which unhelpfully mystify the teaching process or which threaten to exclude the majority of the population from the possibility of ever successfully pursuing teaching as a career. Conversely, the charismatic subject discourse itself can, depending on how we address and internalise it, act as a useful counter to some of the more mechanistic, technicist tendencies of the competent practitioner discourse (and, more recently, of the reflective practice discourse), reminding us that teaching is an art as well as a science, that good communication skills are at the heart of good teaching, and that what is communicat-*ed* should not restrict itself to facts, knowledge or skills alone.

The problem with all these discourses occurs when they are adopted not in concert with one another or with other, equally instructive discourses, but in a way which affords them too great a dominance: we might say, when they evolve from being merely beliefs or views about teaching to discourses through which teaching is fundamentally perceived, experienced, spoken about and understood. When this happens, they revert, I shall suggest, to their Cartesian roots, becoming sucked down into the same essentialist positions that Britzman correctly identifies and challenges in the 'teachers-make-themselves' discourse and that may be seen as implicit in the *Times Educational Supplement* quotation with which this chapter opened – in the case of the competent craftsperson and charismatic subject discourses, inevitably so if the discourse refuses to open its borders to other traffic; in the case of the reflective practitioner discourse, potentially (and too often actually) so if its parameters are too closely confined or if it allows itself to become taken over or 'colonized' (Kress 1989, p. 7) by technicist discourses like that of the competent craftsperson.

While few would deny that the competent craftsperson and the reflective practitioner discourses may offer some help and support to teachers and student teachers in improving classroom relations and practice, experience suggests that they are just as likely to cause concern, confusion and misguided behaviour through their over-personalisation and indeed over-simplification of teaching *activity* (Mitchell and Weber 1996). As McLaughlin and Talbert observed a few years ago – though of educational systems other than our own – good teaching, if considered at all, needs to be considered both in terms of effective learning and as a collaborative, *collective* enterprise:

> As ideas about the task of teaching have changed from the relatively mechanistic notions that spawned an industry of teacher-proof curricula to recognition of teaching as a professional enterprise requiring individual judgement, we have also come to understand that effective

teaching depends on more than just teachers' subject-matter knowledge and general pedagogical skills or even pedagogical content knowledge. Effective teaching depends significantly on the contexts within which teachers work – department and school organization and culture, professional associations and networks, community educational values and norms, secondary and higher education policies.

(1990, p. 2)

Interrogating discourses: the aims and purposes of the book

In the light of all this, readers will not be surprised when I say that the purpose of this book is neither to seek to define 'the good teacher' nor to suggest the means of becoming one: indeed, the words 'good' and 'teaching' are conceptually contestable, and perhaps demand rather more contestation than they often receive, particularly when they are bracketed together in this way. All of us carry, of course, however provisionally, a notion of what we need to be doing and achieving in order to be happy with our professional actions and our corresponding relationships, and to feel that we are performing to the best of our abilities. We may also agree that, for a variety of reasons, some of which may lie largely beyond our control, it is not always possible to meet our own demands (Billig *et al.* 1998). As *teachers*, we are likely to be very concerned, both for 'personal' and for 'altruistic' reasons (more contestable terms!), to do the best for our students – though we may disagree markedly as to what that best is and how best to achieve it. Furthermore, this notion of the ideal professional self that we carry with us will have been *constructed* from a wide variety of (re)sources over time and through social experience rather than having 'appeared' somehow as the internalisation of some universal truth.

Where all this leaves us may or may not become clear during the course of the pages that follow. Immediately, however, it provides us with the rationale for the book, and the beginnings of a response to the question put by a colleague of mine when I suggested that I might write it, along the lines: 'Do we really need another book about teacher education?' My answer to this was and still is that I think we do need another book about teacher education (indeed, that we need several more books about teacher education), but a book that is of a different *kind* from the ones my colleague was thinking of. As I have already indicated, *The Good Teacher* is not in any sense a handbook or training manual for would-be teachers. Rather, it is a book that has at its heart a belief that an essential aspect of developing and improving one's teaching lies in a capacity and a willingness to learn – and that this learning relates not just to teaching skills, strategies and 'knowledge' but also to understanding and critiquing the discourses within which our formal and informal learning *about* teaching is framed. As such, it seeks to encourage and support teachers and student teachers in:

- constructively responding to and critiquing some of the advice they are given from a wide variety of sources;
- locating, understanding and critiquing some of the dominant beliefs and discourses within which that advice is often presented and made sense of;
- promoting some 'alternative', currently marginalised approaches to practitioner learning that
  - ➤ take account of the fragmented, material nature of the self;
  - ➤ offer constructive, strategic self-help through what I shall refer to as processes of textualisation;
  - ➤ seek to reunite the teaching experience with its idiosyncratic, contingent roots without surrendering it to an attitude of 'anything goes'.

That the dominant discourses of teaching and teacher education *need* unpacking and critiquing is precisely because they have a nasty habit, if we let them, of getting in the way of teacher development, excluding much that is important from our consideration and (a point that cannot be stressed often enough) heaping far too much responsibility for educational consequences on the individual teacher or pupil when the policy within which practice occurs is often itself manifestly faulty. In keeping with this agenda, a fundamental underpinning of my analysis and advice is a belief that we need to be particularly careful to avoid being seduced by models of good teaching – particularly when these emanate from official discourses – that constrain the parameters within which we seek to grow as professionals, and that we need to be permanently aware of what Ruddock (1985, p. 284) calls 'a hegemony of habit': that is to say, the 'domination of routine practice' whereby 'educational ideas and the acts that embody them become stereotyped or derelict if they are not constantly worked on'. As Ruddock warns us:

> Good teaching is essentially experimental, and habit, if it is permitted to encroach too far on practice, will erode curiosity and prevent the possibility of experiment.
>
> (ibid.)

The position I shall be taking throughout the book is, consequently, close to that suggested by Smyth *et al.* (1999), who indicate that instead of seeking to become good or better teachers by matching the requirements of some externally provided profile or template – a practice which almost inevitably serves to deprofessionalise us and to limit our horizons – we need to develop our teaching through seeking better understandings of what it means to be a teacher, of the dialogic relationship between our classroom perceptions and practices and the wider social contexts within which those perceptions and practices are situated, and of possible *alternatives*, both to our practice and to those wider social contexts. As we enter the beginning of the twenty-first century, Smyth *et al.* advise us,

> there is confusion and misunderstanding about what constitutes 'good' teaching . . . being clear about what it means to be a teacher living and working in the ambiguity, perplexity and contradiction of current times is an important starting point for the *reclamation* of teaching. Being clear about what is going on in your work and the forces operating to shape it and make it the way it is, is an important part of moving beyond the paralysis of 'being done to' and seeing instead what the alternatives might look like.
>
> (1999, p. 1, my italics)

This representation of the complexities of being a teacher chime with those of other commentators (e.g. Goodson and Walker 1991; Van Manen 1991; Hargreaves 1994), and point to an important feature of practitioner learning that is particularly difficult for many *student* teachers who, quite understandably, come on to pre-service courses wanting neatly packaged advice on how to survive and flourish in the classroom situation: that is, in order to move on we need to abandon easy answers, and in particular those which claim universality. Such a view may not (Boler 1999) hold out much hope for a pedagogy of 'comfort' (an issue I shall return to in Chapters 6 and 7), and may initially leave us feeling somewhat ambivalent and confused. What is harder, however, is to maintain faith with the easy answers and to feel continually disappointed, guilty or responsible when they let us down.

Structure and content of the book

In seeking to address these matters, I have divided the book into three main parts. The first part, comprising the current chapter and Chapter 2, unpacks further some of the issues I shall go on to consider in more detail in the later chapters. It also provides a context for the argument (including, in this present chapter, the empirical evidence on which the argument is based), indicates what – and, by implication, who – the book is for, and explains more fully, in Chapter 2, what I mean by that other contested expression, 'discourse'. I shall also attempt, in these two chapters, to 'position' myself. I want to assert, for instance, in contradiction to some of the more essentialist discourses of teaching and teacher education, that teaching, and learning to teach, *are* complex, often messy matters, that to pursue the Holy Grail of the (universal) 'good teacher' is neither the only nor always the best way to promote positive, constructive, classroom-based learning (indeed, for many people it may prove to be one of the worst ways), and that while we can (and indeed have a duty to) render our teaching more successful and productive, in order to do so we must resist allowing certain dominant discourses of teaching to narrow our ambitions and horizons. From the point of view of *teacher education and training*, there is a particular imperative that we do not allow *ourselves* to become constrained in this way (an increasingly difficult act of resistance in the light of current highly detailed, highly prescriptive and highly monitored curricula for pre-service courses), or our practice to become defined too narrowly *within* specific discourses with the result that when our students do hit difficulties we are left with nothing useful to offer them.

In Chapters 3–5, I am concerned to explore, in greater detail and with reference to the research data on which the book is based, each of the three dominant discourses I have identified – those of the charismatic subject, the competent craftsperson and the reflective practitioner – highlighting some of the 'pros and cons' of each of these discourses and relating these to what I see as a common root in Cartesian, 'old Enlightenment' thinking.

In Chapters 6 and 7, and in the Afterword, I shall consider two 'turns' that might be taken in relation to these dominant discourses when negotiating a pathway through them becomes difficult for the practitioner. The first of these, the 'pragmatic' turn, may involve occupation of an additional discourse – that of pragmat-*ism*. Professional pragmatism, I shall argue, not only plugs into current 'Third Wayist' ideological and political trends in the wider society, but provides a socio-practical space of 'middle ground' both between the competent craftsperson and reflective practitioner discourses and between classical traditionalist and progressive pedagogic 'positionings'. In Chapter 7 and in the Afterword, I shall introduce discussion of a more reflective response to discursive difficulties – that of *reflexivity* – raising issues concerning the possibility of teacher and student-teacher positionings 'outside' – or in the spaces and overlaps between – the dominant discourses identified in the earlier chapters. Emphasis will be given here to considerations of the strengths, dangers and limitations of the reflexive turn, as well as of the importance of critical 'self-removal' from the dominant discourses if one is genuinely to progress in one's own terms both as a professional and as a social being. Chapter 7 in particular will introduce theory drawn from psycho-analysis to report on some of the ways in which student teachers have made better sense of their classroom experience through reflecting critically not just on 'what happened' in their classrooms but on how – and why – they responded as they did and were affected as they were.

The evidence base

These arguments will be supported by – and indeed have emanated from – a variety of research studies that I have been involved in during the last twelve years, each of which has sought to prioritise the views and voices of practising or student teachers. In particular, I have drawn on three studies which I shall refer to throughout as the *Autobiography Project* (carried out between 1990 and 1998), the *Professional Identities Project* (1998–2001) and the *Reflective Practice Project* (2001–2003).

The first of these, the *Autobiography Project*, was, in fact, a series of overlapping, unfunded studies in which student teachers on one-year pre-service (Postgraduate Certificate in Education or 'PGCE') courses were invited to keep diaries and journals in which they recorded their reflections and feelings about classroom life and to identify and discuss with their tutors issues arising from these written reflections. Over a period of time these studies, reported at greater length in Moore (1992, 1998a) and Moore and Atkinson (1998), evolved to encourage students to think about and discuss an increasingly wide-ranging set of topics in an increasingly wide variety of ways, to include not just 'reflection-in-action' (Schon 1987) leading to the development of more appropriate – or simply more – teaching and classroom management strategies, but also the ways in which the students' previous life experiences – including those of home and school – had impacted on the ways in which they were responding to and experiencing current classroom events. This development, which we felt might, to quote Thomas (1995, p. 5), 'help make more clear to the individual the way in which a personal life can be penetrated by the social and the practical', became particularly helpful in supporting students who were experiencing serious classroom difficulties and, in particular, students who were adopting what seemed to be inappropriate strategies and behaviours in response to such difficulties – often through what we came to refer to, after Freud (1991), as *repetition*, whereby the classroom appears to become a site for the playing out or re-enactment of previously unresolved social/emotional conflicts. (This was a situation that was not helped in the case of some students who were clearly receiving contradictory messages about what constituted 'good teaching' from their school and HEI-based tutors on the one hand and from family, friends and, occasionally, pupils on the other.)

The second study, the *Professional Identities Project* (Halpin, Moore, Edwards, George and Jones 1998–2001), involved not student teachers but already qualified classroom teachers and headteachers. The purpose of this study, which was funded, under the title *Educational Identities and the Consumption of Tradition*, by the Economic and Social Research Council of Great Britain, was to investigate the various resources – including traditions, ideologies and philosophies of pedagogy and education – that teachers draw upon in constructing and reconstructing their professional 'selves'. The study entailed semi-structured interviews with seventy classroom teachers and eight headteachers at nine London (England) schools, three of which were in the primary (4–11) sector and six of which were in the secondary (11–18) sector. Something of particular interest to emerge from this study – which will be drawn upon and elaborated in Chapter 6 – was the way in which rapid, externally driven educational reforms were responded to by teachers, especially when the substance of those reforms did not always sit comfortably with individual teachers' and headteachers' views as to what education should be principally about or as to what they should be prioritising in the classroom (see also Troman and Woods 2000).

Just as one of the key issues to have arisen from the earlier *Autobiography Project* had related to the tensions experienced by student teachers faced with mixed messages about what good teaching was, so we found that these more experienced teachers very often found themselves having to negotiate a professional identity that expressed what Britzman (1991, p. 223) calls 'a cacophony of calls'. (See also Ball's reference (1999, p. 14) to the 'complex of overlapping, agonistic and antagonistic discourses' which 'swarm and seethe around the teacher' in the current reform scenario.) For many of these teachers and headteachers, a new hegemony which located good teaching within discourses of technicism, performativity and curriculum 'delivery' was plainly at odds with existing personal preferences that favoured whole-child, whole-class and lifelong-learning approaches to teaching, learning and curriculum. This had effected what McLaughlin (1991) calls a 'reorientation' change of practice in some, whereby (Ball 1997, p. 261) the 'language of reform' is absorbed, 'but not its substance', but a more hardened, durable, 'colonization change' in others whereby the dominant discourses become internalised, validated and perpetuated. Of particular interest in the *Professional Identities Project* was the emergence of what I shall call a 'discourse of pragmatism', whereby teachers adopted pragmatic, compromise positions in order to cope with the competing 'calls' to which they were subjected, while at the same time investing pragmatism itself with a self-referential *value*: that is to say, perceiving pragmatism as desirable in itself, both as a response and as a position.

It was this concern about the ways in which both novice teachers and more experienced teachers negotiated a range of demands, 'calls' and discourses that initially provided the rationale for the last of the three studies on which I have drawn, the University of London-funded *Reflective Practice Project*. If qualified teachers were often – as seemed to be suggested in the *Professional Identities Project* – adopting professional identities and pedagogic practices that depended less on informed reflection on classroom interactions than on strategic responses to influences that were often 'externally imposed', what might be happening to student teachers as they entered the profession at a time of very rapid and quite far-reaching educational reform in which, in addition to the advent of increased standardised testing of pupils, league tables of test and examination scores and marked increases in record-keeping and other forms of bureaucracy, old-fashioned forms of pedagogy were being promoted, based on what for many teachers and teacher educators had become outmoded views of learning? In particular, was it still possible and reasonable to expect student teachers to participate in the kinds of informed, critical reflection on practice that had marked the *Autobiography Project* some years previously?

The *Reflective Practice Project* itself (Moore and Ash 2002; Ash and Moore 2002) was a one-year, interview-based study following ten student teachers through their pre-service (PGCE) year, supported by evidence from written accounts of 'What Makes a Good Teacher?' produced by these and twenty other student teachers during their first two weeks on the same programme. The study aimed to build on the findings of the two earlier projects, by way of exploring the influences affecting student teachers' development and learning in general but particularly the development of reflective practice at this early stage of a teacher's career. It was additionally informed and prompted by a considerable volume of other writing and research suggesting that student teachers often learn very little on their pre-service courses that may actually challenge or change pre-existing views of teaching and learning and that they are more likely to remain influenced by previous experiences of school, by memorable teachers of their own, by media representations of teachers and teaching, and by the opinions of family and friends. Afonso and others have argued, in this regard, that the power of the beginning teacher's prior beliefs and perceptions can be so strong that they act as 'filters', affecting the ways in which pre-service programmes are experienced and approached (Afonso 2001; see also Hollingsworth 1989; Weinstein 1989; Amiguinho 1998; Wideen *et al.* 1998; Britzman 1991) – a view which chimes with Mezirow's wider analysis of adult learning, in which acquired 'meaning schemes' and perspectives effectively 'protect' the individual from challenging existing assumptions and beliefs, acting as a mechanism through which new information, advice and experience are accommodated within an essentially unchanging philosophy. Such schemes and perspectives, Mezirow argues,

> constitute our 'boundary structure' for perceiving and comprehending new data [, allowing] our meaning system to diminish our awareness of how things really are in order to avoid anxiety, creating a zone of blocked action and self-deception.
>
> (1991, p. 49; see also Rose 2001)

Given these concerns, the specific aims of the *Reflective Practice Project* were:

- to identify – and consider the possible roots of – personal pedagogical preferences, orientations and (Bourdieu 1977) 'dispositions' that student teachers on a one-year pre-service course might bring with them into their pedagogical understandings and classroom practice;
- to assess the extent to which the perceived realities of classroom life, including the behaviours of colleagues and pupils but also the curricular and pedagogical constraints experienced by the teacher, impacted on and entered into 'dialogue' with those pre-existing positions;

- to explore the possibilities for authentic reflection on practice in the light of these possible dispositions and dialogues.

Findings from this project, which are explored in greater detail elsewhere (e.g. Moore and Ash 2002), have been particularly drawn upon in Chapters 5 and 7, in discussions of professional reflection and reflexivity. One particularly significant suggestion to arise from our interviews with these ten student teachers (and indeed from the larger sample of written testimonies of thirty student teachers from the same cohort) was that they appeared very willing (as Brookfield 1990 puts it) to 'challenge their assumptions', and were very conscious of the need to negotiate professional identities within dialogic spaces. (The dialogic spaces, that is, between pre-existing views and ideologies; the advice and teaching of others; practical circumstances and practice-based learning; and wider local and government policies.) We were led to conclude that while such negotiations might indeed lead some student teachers to be resistant to new learning or to modifications of practice – a resistance we had noted in several of the struggling students during the course of the *Autobiography Project* – other students showed a willingness and even an enthusiasm to change, as well as a preparedness to undergo the pain that is sometimes associated with change, and to seek out and make effective use of whatever support was available to help them achieve it.

Themes and complexities: locating the professional self

The three studies raised a number of common themes and issues. One of the principal of these was that participants tended, regardless of their historical positionings, to exemplify Coldron and Smith's hypothesis that teacher identities are 'partly given and partly achieved' by 'active location in social space' (Coldron and Smith 1999, p. 711) – 'social space' here being conceived as 'an array of possible relations that one person can have to others' (ibid.). Some of these relations, Coldron and Smith suggest, are conferred by 'inherited social structures and categorizations', while others are 'chosen or created by the individual' (ibid.).

Most of the teachers we interviewed on the *Professional Identities Project* tended to adopt an essentially pragmatic orientation to pedagogical practice (Moore, Edwards, Halpin and George 2002), occupying – albeit with varying degrees of comfort – social and ideological spaces within which they drew eclectically on a range of practices and philosophies, some of which appeared to have been somewhat forced upon them from 'outside' (often in the shape of National Curriculum, National Strategy or national testing requirements), while others represented beliefs and dispositions that had been strongly held prior to their entering the teaching profession or elaborated 'independently' during their teaching careers. So it was with the student teachers in the *Autobiography* and *Reflective Practice* projects:

while these novice teachers – precisely because they had no existing 'history' as teachers – were not having to make the same adjustments as many of their more experienced colleagues in the light of externally mandated curriculum or pedagogical reform, they were nevertheless enagaged in struggles to accommodate general principles with local demands, 'personal' with 'public' values, and often competing representations of good practice.

Coldron and Smith's suggestion that external policies which 'impose greater degrees of uniformity and conformity' threaten to '*impoverish* the notion of active location, restricting the number of potential positions the teacher might assume' (1999, p. 711, my italics) was certainly borne out by our interviews with classroom teachers on the *Professional Identities* study. While all the teachers appeared to be active rather than passive in constructing their professional identities and pedagogical orientations and preferences, some clearly felt that they had less choice in these matters than others, in some cases complaining that external pressures – both in the form of public educational policy and in relation to perceived cultural changes that had rendered young people more likely to be 'confrontational' and 'disobedient' – had restricted their choices and compromised personal preferences to such an extent that teaching was no longer the satisfying profession they had once found it. To quote one respondent among the many who *regretted* changes that had occurred to their professional identities:

> I have become less progressive: I have become reactionary, I find . . . I have become less liberal . . . in my thoughts about education. As a teacher, I have become more abrasive.
>
> (Graeme: secondary-school English teacher,
> *Professional Identities Project*)

This project also reminded us how elusive and open to interpretation and change the notion of the 'good teacher' is: how it can vary from site to site, from person to person, from time to time; how 'culturally embedded' it is (Calderhead and Shorrock 1997). Even in terms of the individual practitioner, the concept is clearly subject to development and change, and that change is itself linked to the historical, social and political situation within which the teacher positions themselves at any given point in time and space. For every teacher such as the one quoted above, who regretted repositionings and reidentifications that appeared to have been imposed upon them, we could find another who was able to embrace or justify such repositioning, even when, as in some cases, it entailed moving away from a more 'progressive', student-centred approach to a more 'traditional', teacher- or curriculum-led one. One much younger teacher (Edward), for example, at the same school as the teacher quoted above, told us how he had begun his teaching career organising his classes into small groups and encouraging discussion, but in his quest to become a better, more effective teacher had come to 'realise' that this had been 'idealistic' and now organised his classes in rows with far more teacher input.

Not surprisingly, these positionings and repositionings took place, as Coldron and Smith imply, within the contexts of overlapping and sometimes competing discourses and models of what good teaching represents. The young teacher Edward, for example, described in interview what he saw as a passage from one model of good teaching – inscribed within discourses of reflective practice, nurturing, and charismatic classroom presence – towards another, inscribed within a more technicist discourse of the competent craftsperson, but overlaid itself with a modified version of the charismatic subject in which the 'popular', empathetic version of that discourse had been replaced with a more disciplinarian, managerial one. The difficulty for Edward's colleague, Graeme, appeared to have resided in his reluctance to subscribe to the same competent craftsperson discourse, which he felt he was being pushed into by government policies and by the unruly behaviour of his students. (For fuller details of these and other stories arising from the *Professional Identities Project*, see Moore, George and Halpin 2002 and Moore and Edwards 2002.)

Themes and complexities: repetition and the gaze of the other

All the teachers in our studies were deeply concerned not only that they should feel that they were doing as good a job as possible, but that they should be seen to be doing a good job by those around them: by teachers, by pupils, by fellow students – and indeed, in many cases, by family and friends; a situation in which, regardless of other professional positionings, they were forever positioned, self-consciously, within a bright circle of light produced at the intersecting spotlights of a variety of gazes.

For the student teachers taking part in the *Autobiography* and *Reflective Practice* projects, who had no substantial history of professional success and failure behind them and who entered the profession as (to quote one student) 'unknown quantities', this issue of how one is perceived by others was especially important and often extremely disconcerting. As one student teacher observed in interview:

> With teaching, it's not just how you see yourself, it's about how you see how other people see you: how you see yourself being seen. . . . What you inevitably end up doing is looking at the pupils and judging yourself through them. The children are in your head all the time.
>
> (Mizzi: student teacher, *Reflective Practice Project*)

The gazes to which these novice teachers felt themselves exposed were, not unlike Britzman's competing 'calls', many in number and various in nature. Some were, no doubt, objectively critical: opinions on performance, or articulations of expectation, passed on verbally from tutors, colleagues or pupils. At other times, though (as, perhaps, in the example quoted above), they were equally likely merely to be *perceived* by the practitioner as critical – through the projection on to others of personal dissatisfaction with performance (a point I shall return to when we look at 'reflexivity' with reference to Zizek (1989) and Lacan (1977, 1979) in Chapter 7). In all cases, however, the balancing act between one's own preferred method of doing things and the preferred – often imposed and often antagonistic – methods and preferences of others appeared to be at the heart of the practitioner's self-worth, self-belief, professional satisfaction and consequent effectiveness in the classroom.

It is not surprising, perhaps, that in each of the two studies involving student teachers – and indeed in the study involving practising teachers and headteachers – it was those who found the required accommodations particularly great who also experienced their professional identities as under the greatest threat. Even for those teachers and student teachers who were able to make the necessary accommodations in a relatively untroubled way, however (as with each of the students involved in the third of the studies, the *Reflective Practice Project*), there remained inevitable and important areas of conflict and uncertainty that clearly required a very subtle understanding on the part of the practitioners and their advisers. In this regard, one particularly interesting issue highlighted in both the *Autobiography* and the *Reflective Practice* projects concerned the Freudian concept – described by Freud as 'new editions of old conflicts' (Freud 1968, p. 454) – of *repression*.

I do not want to suggest that any of the student teachers taking part in these projects were in any need of psycho-analysis! However, we came to accept that an acknowledgement and understanding of the concept of repression – of its role in behaviours and in our experiencing and understanding of behaviours, and of the related notion of 'transference' – can offer considerable help both to (student) teachers and to the teachers of (student) teachers in making constructive, ultimately productive sense of classroom events, particularly during times of stress. We also came to understand how readily the classroom can become a *site* for the playing out of 'new editions of old conflicts' (ibid.) and how easily, because of this, emotional experience and response can impact negatively as well as positively on pedagogy and classroom management. As Britzman and Pitt have argued:

> The classroom *invites* transferential relations because, for teachers, it is such a familiar place, one that seems to welcome re-enactments of childhood memories. Indeed, recent writing about pedagogy suggests that transference shapes how teachers respond and listen to students, and how students respond and listen to teachers. . . . [T]eachers' encounters

with students may return them involuntarily and still unconsciously to
scenes from their individual biographies.

(1996, pp. 117, 118, my italics; see also Felman 1987; Gallop 1995;
Penley 1989)

This idea that we may assume roles and adopt discursive positionings in
one setting – perhaps that of the workplace – which unconsciously repeat
patterns of interaction, infused with power relations, previously experienced
in another (our own schooling, perhaps, or our home life during the period
of our upbringing) struck us as being potentially a very powerful one, and
informs much of what I shall argue for in this book. Why, for example, do
some pupils – apparently regardless of their cultural-linguistic backgrounds,
of how relevant or dull they find their lessons, or of their personal histories
of academic success or failure – unfailingly comply with their teachers'
requests while others, almost in spite of themselves, adopt positions of
opposition or confrontation? How is it that some teachers feel able – and
prepared – to 'detach' themselves from the interpersonal aspects of classroom activity, while others are drawn all too readily into antagonisms? To
attribute such matters over-easily to aspects of 'personality' ('this class and
I simply do not get on', for example, as one of our student teachers
remarked after an observed lesson) is to surrender debate to the notion of
the charismatic subject – a surrender that, as will be argued in Chapter 3,
more often than not proves unhelpful to the student experiencing difficulties in classroom management. Nor, however, is it helpful to allow such
students to carry on using their classrooms as the analyst's couch – in particular, as a way of resisting any development *beyond* repetition (for instance,
of refusing to acknowledge *which* previous experiences may be centrally
implicated in the current problem). The view we arrived at by way of the
Autobiography Project was that student teachers can often benefit enor-
mously through 'getting in touch with' – i.e. through 'textualising' – their
own histories, and through *con*-textualising their actions within those histories: to try, in this way, to stand back a little from their own actions, and
to address those actions critically through informed reflection rather than
merely 'experiencing' them. To put it bluntly, in understanding the development of pedagogical practice, one needs to access not only what is
'immediate' and 'visible', but also what is not always immediately accessible
in the specific classroom situation – what is sometimes called 'the baggage'
teachers bring into the classroom with them – which offers a broader, typically unacknowledged context both for developing practice and for understanding and facilitating it.

The particularity of schoolteaching

Britzman and Pitt's observations regarding repression, repetition and transferential relations are also important in reminding us of the very particular

circumstances experienced by schoolteachers, including, and perhaps in particular, those studying and training to *become* schoolteachers, which set them apart from all other professionals. On the one hand, there is a very important sense in which student teachers do resemble most other students or trainees working towards a 'public-duty' career: that is to say, prior to beginning their pre-service courses they will already have formulated – both consciously and unconsciously – very clear ideas and orientations concerning the nature of the particular professional and institutional domain within which they will be working, including its virtues and its faults. As with other starting-out professionals, those ideas and dispositions may be confirmed, modified or, in some instances, seriously challenged once they are in the *practicum* situation and once their role and perspective have shifted from that of the 'participant observer' to that of 'agent in the field'. Unlike most other trainees, however (for example, trainee medics or trainee law enforcers), student teachers will already have had very extensive experience of being active agents *within* the field now providing the training context, albeit in an alternative role: they will already have spent much of their lives as *pupils* going to school. As a consequence of this, their particular circumstance is that they will, in most cases, have already undertaken some very profound experiential adjustments and positionings within the school setting, and are likely to come to the training situation with particularly well-formed ideas and dispositions as to what to expect in the classroom and as to what represents 'good teaching', appropriate 'teacherly' behaviour and indeed appropriate pupil behaviour. Though these positionings and adjustments will have occurred idiosyncratically and contingently – i.e. within the context of particular schools and classrooms and of particular responses and reactions to those schools and classrooms – such is the power of experience in the formative years that the students may well seek to apply any conclusions drawn from those experiences to other schools and to other classrooms, and to a much wider range of teaching and learning situations.

To this already complex situation needs to be added a further complication: these adjustments, carried out within one objective (but subjectively experienced) position in the educational hierarchy – that of the relatively disempowered *pupil* – may require *additional* adjustments within the alternative position now occupied within that hierarchy: that of the relatively empowered *teacher* – a relatively empowered teacher, however, who, through having the status of a *student teacher*, has relatively little power within the teaching body of the school. Evidence from our research into student teachers' experiences during their initial classroom encounters indicates that for many student teachers (who, in the case of post-graduate courses, are generally expected to make the adjustment from 'non-teacher' to 'teacher' in less than one calendar year) the readjustments themselves demand very high concentrations of energy and labour, as well as leading the student teachers into awkward and often troubling situations. These situations cannot always be anticipated and therefore prepared for in advance; however, their successful negotiation is crucial in terms of professional growth and perseverance through the training course. To quote three of the student teachers on the *Reflective Practice Project*:

> [Y]ou're constantly being tested by the children. Where are my notes? Where am I going to draw the line? When am I going to pretend that I've drawn the line, when maybe I've actually got a little bit further to go? . . . Most of us hadn't been in school for a long time, and suddenly to be in a class, you need time to assimilate these things. . . . And I think it's too quick in a way. It doesn't give you the time to reflect in that kind of structured way.
>
> (Mizzi: student teacher, *Reflective Practice Project*)

> I wanted to be liked by the children. . . . At the start, I was intimidated by them and my aim then was to fight back: if I get them to like me, they won't intimidate me, they'll like me.
>
> (Carrie: student teacher, *Reflective Practice Project*)

> It's a bit of a persona in a way and not really wanting that persona to be too far away from who I [really] am, because then it feels like you are having a role all day long and I think that's very hard work, having to actually pretend to be someone different.
>
> (Celia: student teacher, *Reflective Practice Project*)

I want to suggest that if we do not acknowledge the classroom as a site of transference in the way that Britzman and Pitt (1996) have suggested we should, we deprive ourselves – as student teachers or as the teachers of student teachers – of a vast amount of knowledge and understanding, as well as an important strategy without which our aim of promoting even relatively productive and harmonious classroom interactions and experiences is bound to fall ludicrously short, especially when classroom difficulties arise and really have to be resolved. Telling a student teacher, for example, that they may be 'over-reacting' to certain classroom incidents is unlikely to effect more than a partial resolution to the perceived problem, unless some effort is made to understand *why* they are over-reacting and the extent to which their over-reaction might be related to issues – present or past – that lie outside the immediate classroom situation.

The importance of the pre-service experience

Not surprisingly, given all this, many student teachers (Moore and Ash 2002) experience quite profound adjustment difficulties on re-entering schools no longer as pupils but as teachers and professional learners: difficulties which may confront them most uncomfortably and without hope of resolution when dispositions and messages sited within their current and previous lived experiences jar with behaviours, expectations and experiences sited within the less familiar role and context of their own teaching of young people. Such difficulties – reflected by repeated complaints from students of 'mixed messages', in which (Moore 1992) they feel they are 'being told one thing at college and another at home', or are 'being criticised for being trendy by my family and friends', or are discovering that 'what seems to be all right now just runs totally counter to everything that was allowed and encouraged then', or are simply experiencing bewilderment in the face of the wealth of exemplars of good teaching being continually thrust before them (from representations in films and television dramas, to lists of competences and standards produced by government agencies, to an ever-increasing array of books with the words 'teach', 'teaching' or 'teacher' in their titles) – can lead, at their most severe, to a crisis profound enough to cause the student to question whether or not to carry on in the teaching profession at all. And all the time, within this confused and confusing situation, the student teacher must develop their *practice*: a process, largely unseen, which must somehow be rendered visible in order that the student may consciously reflect upon it, demonstrate it for assessment purposes, and make deliberate, strategic decisions about improving, changing or consolidating it!

To refer back to the directions of 'call' to which I have already alluded, the following list of sources of demands and potential confusions (by no means intended to be exclusive) begins to emerge for the student teacher, all of which have quite profound implications for the teaching and training of student teachers on pre-service courses:

- the encounter and recontextualisation of predispositions and assumptions based on previous experiences of schools and schooling;
- the imprint and 'replay' of unresolved tensions, uncomfortable roles, interactive breakdowns and successes on classroom practice and experience;
- the often conflicting exhortations and professional mandates of others.

We might add to this potential maelstrom:

- possible conflicts between values inherent in the curriculum and values held by the teacher – referred to by Britzman (1989, p. 150) as 'the push and pull of institutional values that can trigger an uneasy compliance to the very values [the teacher] may dispute';
- the desire to be recognised, valued, liked, loved even: we might say, after Zizek (1989), the need for a 'mandate' from a range of people who may themselves be in some disagreement about what it is they want from the teacher (How does the teacher satisfy the often competing demands of pupils – who may or may not want to do things that the curriculum

insists that they should or shouldn't – and a curriculum itself that provides ever fewer opportunities for teacher flexibility? How does the teacher establish order in the classroom while still appearing to the pupils and to themselves as on the pupils' side?);

- the fact that, unlike members of some other public-service professions, teachers are continually called upon to make sophisticated acts of understanding and interpretation of situations, in response to which there may be any number of useful responses – a factor which becomes particularly significant when we consider the notion of teacher as 'reflective practitioner'. As Van Manen puts it:

> [U]nlike the medical doctor, the pedagogue seems less involved in problem-solving reflection than in reflecting on the pedagogical meaning or significance of certain experiences. Problems seek situations, 'correct' knowledge, efficient procedures, solution strategies, productive techniques or methods that get results! When I consult the doctor with a physical ailment, I have a problem that the doctor can hopefully solve and rectify.
>
> But problems of teaching are seldom 'problems' in this sense. Rather, teachers deal with situations, predicaments, possibilities, and difficulties.
>
> (1991, p. 107)

In connection with these numerous and often conflicting calls, the following points need to be made in relation to how we work with student teachers during the pre-service experience. They are intended to underpin the argument of the book, but also to suggest a major agenda-item for preservice courses for teachers and to underline the importance of such courses not merely in developing teachers' subject knowledge, classroom strategies, behaviour-management techniques and so on, but in promoting authentic, constructive understandings of the classroom encounter – including what it means to be a teacher and a learner.

- First, these calls and the resulting external and internal conversations and arguments they engender do not take place in isolation from one another but are inextricably interwoven: to give a straightforward example, the sense that the teacher or student teacher makes of the exhortations and mandates of others will inevitably depend in no small part on both the pedagogic predispositions *and* the tensions, personality traits and coping strategies which accompanied them into the teaching profession.
- Second, the end result of the teacher's engagement with these agonistic, sometimes antagonistic, voices is not one of 'resolution' into a unified, complete 'good teacher' or of a positioning in which the voices can all, at any given point in time, be received and answered with satisfaction

on all sides; it is, rather, another kind of resolution, in which, tacitly or explicitly, a recognition emerges that the teaching identity is indeed multi-faceted, fluid and even contradictory.

- Third, the teacher's struggle with and through competing voices, discourses and mandates is not to be seen as inherently a 'bad' or even, necessarily, a problematic thing; nor is the (student) teacher to be cast in these encounters as a passive victim whose only activity can lie in arriving at some kind of put-upon compromise with which they can feel relatively (if not ever entirely) comfortable. To quote Britzman (1989, pp. 146–7), we need to replace 'the myth that teacher socialization is largely a passive process of adapting to the expectations and directives of others, routinely accomplished through imitation, reinforcement and assimilation' with a view of socialisation as 'an active construction of meaning that is lived as a process of becoming'. From such a perspective, student teachers are best understood as 'complex beings struggling to make sense of the work of teaching', key to which understanding will be an acknowledgement of:

> the moral and existential dilemmas that are so much a part of the work of teachers and the rich complexities of social interaction, subjective experience, and dependency and struggle that characterize life in and outside the classroom.
>
> (Britzman 1989, p. 150)

- Fourth, any search for a single model of 'good teaching' is ultimately doomed to failure. Each teacher must, ultimately, discover their own 'best way(s)' of doing things. They may, indeed, be supported – as well as hindered – in achieving this through the 'cacophony of calls' which are experienced both outwardly and inwardly and by any of these in isolation at different points and stages in their career development; however, no single one will (or should) hold exclusive sway, and the individual's relationship with each one will need to be an informed and knowledgeable one if unhelpful confusions or discomfort are to be avoided.
- Fifth, the learning of teaching cannot be accomplished effectively by reducing it wholly or in great part to the development of 'technique'. As Van Manen reminds us: 'The essence of an educator does not lie in technical expertise, but in a complex of pedagogical qualities' – a view endorsed by Cummins, who advises us:

> Fortunately, good teaching does not require us to internalize an endless list of instructional techniques. Much more fundamental is the recognition that human relationships are central to effective instruction.
>
> (1996, p. 73)

- Finally, teaching – and teaching to teach – should never be reduced to holding the teacher wholly or overly accountable for social difficulties over which they may have little or no control. Teachers and schools can, of course – and very often do – 'make a difference' (one would hope, a very substantial difference), and few would deny that some teaching is better than other teaching or that schools often have an important function to play in promoting human values that may not be as strongly promoted elsewhere in society. The point is that in thinking about their practice, teachers do need to think about who they are and what they want to achieve. They need to do this, however, in such a way that they *situate* themselves. It is this situatedness that enables practitioners to hold themselves accountable for their actions but to understand (Wacquant 1989, p. 45) that those actions are both historically/socially produced and historically/socially contextualised.

It is to this 'situatedness', and specifically to the nature and role of 'discourses' in promoting, restricting or compelling it, that I shall turn in the next chapter.

2 Identifying the good teacher – a shifting concept

[The teacher] must exhibit the authority of law, and this is never arbitrary, but always calm, equitable, just. Rigid as maintainer of law, his judgements, and still more his penalties, must yet lean to mercy's side. . . . His manner must be direct, candid, sincere, and friendly, yet, withal, suggestive of high purpose and unbending law. He must dominate his school as its presiding genius, its spiritual standard, its type of culture; and yet he must be a child among children, a boy among boys, a youth among youths.

(Laurie 1882, pp. 63–4)

A good teacher . . . is kind, is generous, listens to you, encourages you, has faith in you, keeps confidences, likes teaching children, likes teaching their subject, takes time to explain things, helps you when you're stuck, tells you how you are doing, allows you to have your say, doesn't give up on you, cares for your opinion, makes you feel clever, treats people equally, stands up for you, makes allowances, tells the truth, is forgiving.

(Descriptions by 8-year-old pupils – selected and cited in the DfEE-commissioned Hay McBer Report (2000))

Formal education has a dual ideological importance. It is often claimed to be the process by which ideology is transmitted, but it is also something that people have ideologies *of*.

(Billig *et al.* 1988, p. 43)

A word about discourses

So much has been written about the notion of discourse (e.g. Harré and Gillett 1994; Belsey 1980; Macdonell 1986; Fairclough 1992) that it is in danger of losing its usefulness as a conceptual framework for social analysis under a welter of debate about what it actually means. I certainly do not want to add to this difficulty, mainly because I take the view that linguistic terms are often – perhaps always – open to interpretation, that this does not generally represent a communication problem, and that readers will be able to work out for themselves from my contexts and usages what I intend the term 'discourse' to connote. I don't think we should be too precious about these terms, either. Meanings do evolve, proliferate and expand over time, and I am all in favour of using and reading language creatively. Because many readers will already have definitions of discourse in mind, however, because the sub-title of this book includes the word 'discourses', and in order to avoid a debate about the meaning of 'discourse' obscuring the issues I really want us to think about, it seems useful to say something about how I am using the term before I proceed *to* use it.

For the purposes of this book, then, I have adopted a more or less Foucauldian view of discourse, wherein the term is used to denote the constructed parameters within which our perception(s) of the social world and our actions within it are framed – parameters essentially produced and sustained by language and 'knowledge' and (at least in the case of what I am calling 'dominant discourses') controlled and patrolled by ideologies that generally serve the interests of the already powerful at the expense of the already disempowered. Describing the way in which all social practice can be perceived in terms of the establishment of and participation in a *range* of discourses, Foucault has argued that discourses are not *about* objects (that is to say, the 'object', however concrete or abstract, does not 'pre-exist' the discourse or give birth to the discourse), but construct or constitute them and, furthermore, in the process of doing so 'conceal their own invention' (Foucault 1992, p. 49; see also Eagleton 1983; Parker 1992; Burr 1995).

In Foucault's definition can be found four key characteristics of discourse which are particularly relevant to what I shall be arguing in this book. First, there is the concept of *'naturalisation' and concealment*: that is to say, discourses may be constructed by (certain groups of) human beings and may serve particular interests; however, their general intention is to be perceived, experienced and made use of as though they had not been constructed at all but had rather 'arisen' as some kind of natural process, representing and incorporating shared, common-sense wisdom that might be prefaced by the thought 'Of course no one would seriously disagree that . . .' This naturalisation has the corresponding effect of rendering *opposition* to any dominant discourse as *un*-natural and pathological. As Kress puts this:

> If the domination of a particular area by a discourse is successful it provides an integrated and plausible account of that area, which allows no room for thought; the social will have been turned into the natural. At that stage it is impossible to conceive of alternative modes of thought, or else alternative modes of thought will seem bizarre, outlandish, unnatural.
>
> (1989, p. 10)

It is this emphasis on the notion of discourses as *socially constructed* that is the second feature of Foucauldian discourse that I want to highlight, while the third concerns the ways in which *authority and legitimacy* are both embedded in and bestowed by discourse. To quote Boler on this aspect of discursive power:

> Rather than assuming that utterances and language are transparent or self-explanatory, 'discourse' refers to the culturally and historically specific status of a particular form of speech, and to the variable authority and legitimacy of different kinds of languages or utterances.
>
> (1999, p. 5)

Boler's suggestion – after Foucault and in accord with Britzman's view of the operations of cultural myths – is that in providing structures through which to make sense of and to experience the social world, discourses also limit our conceptual, experiential and perspectival horizons, constraining us to understand things in certain 'legitimised' ways rather than in other (pathologised or unacknowledged) ones – a suggestion taken a step further by Kress, who suggests that discourses also limit what we perceive as *possible*, that they constrain not only what we do, but what – and how – we think:

> Discourses are systematically-organised sets of statements which give expression to the meanings and values of an institution. Beyond that, they define, describe and delimit what it is possible to say and not possible to say (and by extension – what it is possible to do or not do) with respect to the area of concern of that institution, whether marginally or centrally. A discourse provides a set of possible statements about a given area, and organises and gives structure to the manner in which a particular topic, object, process is to be talked about. In that it provides descriptions, rules, permissions and prohibitions of social and individual actions.
>
> (1989, p. 7)

Such an *inhibiting, delimiting effect* – which represents the last of the four characteristics of Foucauldian discourse that I want to highlight – may be supported socially, including in the world of work, by what Foucault (1971) refers to as 'societies of discourse' comprising groups of individuals held together by 'structured knowledge in their field' (for example, groups of individuals working within the field of education). It is also supported by the power of discourse to 'internalise' itself: that is, for us to absorb the discourse into our conscious, subconscious, even unconscious minds in the manner of Bourdieu's 'habitus' (1971, 1977, 1990), from where it guides our thinking and actions for us, partly through an act of 'self-policing'. Certainly, as we shall see later on, a number of the student teachers taking part in our *Reflective Practice Project* were very aware of teachers' capacity for this kind of self-policing, as well as having internalised themselves a delimiting sense of their actions being watched and judged.

Discursive constraints and discursive spaces

By way of illustrating the nature and impact of discourses on teachers' perceptions and practice, we might consider, briefly, the notion of 'leadership' in the educational domain. Leadership begins as a signifier that can have many different signifieds. Once it evolves into a *discourse* of leadership, however, the term becomes unproblematic, its differing interpretations and understandings relegated to the status of the marginal, the irrelevant or the non-existent. What leadership might *mean* is replaced as the principal topic of discussion by subjects like 'the importance of leadership' or 'leadership training'. Leadership subsequently becomes both a good and an essential characteristic of the 'effective' (a similarly evolved concept) school. A certain (positively presented) conceptualisation of leadership, that is, becomes legitimised and dominant: leadership moves beyond the descriptive to becoming a framed lens through which we see and understand the world – or at least those aspects of the world which the discourse sets out to describe. The 'floating', contested nature of the signifier is superseded by a form (however temporary) – an illusion, perhaps – of fixity.

A further, perhaps more immediately relevant example of this evolution of signifier to discourse can be found in the lists of competences (or 'standards', as they are now known in England and Wales by dint of another concealing sleight of hand) with which teachers these days tend to be bombarded and to which I shall return in Chapter 4. As has already been indicated, for Foucault discourses do not represent the crystallisations and expressions of pre-existing 'realities' which are, so to speak, there to be excavated or 'discovered'; nor do they merely 'conceal their modes of production' (Eagleton 1983). Rather, discursive practices are themselves 'producers', actually *creating* 'common sense', 'reality', 'truth'. Furthermore, it is the very function of discourses to make it appear as if the reverse were true – as if common sense, reality and truth really *did* have an existence external and prior to the discourses within which they are elaborated. In terms of lists of teaching standards or competences – especially when they are presented *as* competences and standards (rather than, say, as assessment criteria) – we may say that, unless deliberately contextualised alternatively, such lists will be apt to be read by students and teachers as attempted articulations of eternal truths rather than as selections that create truths and mask their presuppositions. As such, rather than inviting discussion, debate and reflection about practice, they offer the student merely a sense of 'closure' – or, as one student taking part in the *Autobiography Project* put it, a feeling that 'there just isn't anything left to be said'. Through lists of competences and standards, not only are the parameters of practice and discussion firmly set in what Barthes (1975) would (with a negative inflection) call a 'readerly' or particularly 'hardened' text; additionally, the very form of their presentation seeks to disguise their socially constructed nature, rendering them – along with the carefully chosen, apparently value-free expressions themselves ('competences'; 'standards') – universal and some-how supra-human: the possessors and elaborators of a set of intrinsic, unquestionable rightnesses or 'truths'.

The point of all of this is that if we allow them to, discourses will con-strain our actions, limit our understandings, force us into subservience to the agendas of dominant social groups, and lead us, as teachers, to blame ourselves for things which are not our fault rather than offering us the capa-city and strength to make fairer, more balanced assessments of our practice or to analyse the feelings we have which underpin that practice. (Feelings, interestingly, have no place in lists of competences or standards, or indeed, typically, in the discourse of training as a whole.)

Fortunately, however, discourses, for all their objective power and domi-nance, and for all their capacity to infiltrate the consciousness, are neither immutable nor impenetrable. Indeed, I want to suggest that both their con-stantly evolving nature and our ability at least to be aware of (and be wary of) them inevitably render them contestable and challengeable. Further-more, and in any event, our practice is likely, as was indicated at the end of Chapter 1, to be embedded in a number of different discourses (Kress 1989), and indeed to be situated at the sometimes turbulent intersections and 'overlappings' of discourses. Such a location was certainly evident in the initial 'What Makes a Good Teacher?' assignments written by thirty student teachers on our *Reflective Practice Project*, most of whom were happy to describe good teaching in relation to a complex of skills and activ-ities even when concretising their idealisations of good teaching with reference to teachers who had previously taught *them*. While some of these student teachers were undeniably vague in their representations of such role-model teachers, referring to charismatic qualities rather than (for example) thoroughness of preparation, and often remembering the teacher rather more clearly than what they had actually learned, the vast majority of them – more, indeed, than we had imagined would be the case given our readings of other researchers in the field – were inclined to ascribe a range of qualities to these teachers rather than categorising them as a parti-cular 'type':

> Ms K was a firm but fair teacher – she didn't tolerate misbehaviour, commanding respect. She seemed to genuinely care about us, when we were in her classroom and how we were as people. She had a good grasp of her subject and communicated it well to us with just the right amount of enthusiasm. . . . Her presentation skills were polished and used different teaching methods . . . using different media, encouraging self-learning, research and experiential learning in groups. . . . [W]e were treated more like equals than pupils . . . we were taught in the sixth form suite and expected to behave like adults. She knew how to question us and draw us out.
>
> (Sarah: student teacher, *Reflective Practice Project*)

Rote learning, parrot learning, talking at pupils, teaching and learning straight from textbooks, working in strict silence, stifling individuality and creativity, lack of subject knowledge, no passion or empathy for the subject – these are some of the main negatives I recall from my 'worst' teachers and lecturers.

Group work, role playing, project work, encouraging external experience of the subject, interesting and interactive lessons and lectures, broad subject knowledge, passion and love of the subject, encouraging individual thinking, analysis and creativity, inspiring people to learn – these are some of the main positives I recall from my 'best' teachers and lecturers.

(Celia: student teacher, *Reflective Practice Project*)

If, as I have suggested, we consider our personal and professional 'selves' in terms of constructed, situated *texts*, it becomes possible to take such accounts a significant step further, adapting understandings of how discourses operate in terms of, say, written texts (books, periodicals, prospectuses, journal articles and so forth) to our understandings of what we are doing, how we are experiencing, how we are positioned professionally, and indeed how our 'personal' and our 'public' selves relate to one another. As Kress (1989) suggests, discourse finds its *expression* in texts; however, this is never a straightforward relation, and any one text may be the expression or realisation of a number of sometimes competing and contradictory discourses.

Valerie Walkerdine (1990, p. 199), in a passage in *Schoolgirl Fictions* that bears immediately on our considerations of the 'good' in 'good teaching', takes this suggestion a little further. Arguing that it is precisely the overlapping of discourses that enables us to challenge them – to struggle against and to contest the ways in which we are encouraged to 'identify' ourselves and others and to make sense of the social world – she suggests:

Modern apparatuses of social regulation, along with other social and cultural practices, produce knowledges which claim to 'identify' individuals. These knowledges create the possibility of multiple practices, multiple positions. To be a 'clever child' or a 'good mother', for example, makes sense only in the terms given by pedagogic, welfare, medical, legal and other discourses and practices. These observe, sanction and correct how we act; they attempt to define who and what we are. They are, however, crisscrossed by other discourses and practices – including those of popular entertainment, for example. This multiplicity means that the practices which position us may often be mutually contradictory. They are also sites of contestation and struggle. We never quite fit the 'position' provided for us by these regulatory practices.

Walkerdine concludes, boldly:

What I am proposing . . . is a model of how subjectification is produced: how we struggle to become subjects and how we *resist* provided subjectivities in relation to the regulative power of modern social apparatuses.

(1990, p. 199, my italics)

Discourse and location: the 'good teacher' as a variable and shifting concept

While concepts both of teaching and of 'good teaching' are located or embedded within and between different discourses and (Kress 1989; Oliver with Gershman 1989; Gergen 1990; Ricoeur 1994; Tunstall 2003) expressed in terms of different metaphors and myths, so such concepts and the discourses which support and inform them may, as the quotations with which this chapter opened suggest, vary from time to time, from society to society, from culture to culture and (to use current parlance) from 'stakeholder' to 'stakeholder'. As was indicated in the previous chapter, one of the more interesting findings to emerge from the *Professional Identities Project* related to the way in which *individual teachers'* conceptualisations of good teaching themselves changed and developed during the course of a professional life and the manner in which – as with the student teachers in the *Autobiography* and *Reflective Practice* projects – teachers drew on a range of resources in positioning themselves professionally, so that they were never positioned solely within any one of the educational discourses I have identified in this book. Indeed, it is clear that those discourses themselves do not exist in isolation from one another. As Billig *et al.* (1988, p. 44) have argued with reference to *ideology*, teachers' positionings and ways of experiencing and responding to professional life are seldom internally consistent discursively: not only are teachers likely to occupy positions at the overlapping margins of various discourses, shifting their ground constantly and pragmatically in relation to what is possible in an ever-changing wider world, but they should not inscribe such movement in terms of failure, and may even find in it a source of strength. As Billig *et al.* put this:

> Teachers do not have the luxury of being able to formulate and adhere to some theory or position on education, with only another theorist's arguments to question its validity. They have to accomplish the practical task of teaching, which requires getting the job done through whatever conceptions and methods work best, under practical constraints that include physical resources, numbers of pupils, nature of pupils, time constraints, set syllabuses and so on. But these practical considerations inevitably have ideological bases, which define what 'the job' actually is, how to do it, how to assess its outcomes, how to react to its successes and failures, how to talk and interact with pupils, how many can be taught or talked to at once. For example, in the traditional chalk-and-talk lecturing method, a large class size is not so great a

practical or ideological problem as it is for a teacher who upholds the value of individual, child-centred learning.

> (1998, p. 46; see also Cole and Knowles' description of teaching *practice* in terms of its 'multiple roles and contexts' (1995, p. 131))

Certainly, many of the teachers interviewed in the *Professional Identities Project* appeared to confirm the view that teachers are frequently aware of ideological contradictions in their work, and often 'feel themselves involved in difficult choices [involving] having to make compromises' (Billig *et al.* 1998, p. 46). When problems arose, it was often when teachers became uncomfortable with or confused by these competing ideologies – perhaps because of the specific circumstances in which they found themselves. For such teachers, it was Britzman's (1991) account of professional identities in relation to ideology rather than Billig *et al.*'s that came more strongly to mind, and in particular her suggestion that 'there are always antagonistic discourses that urge particular dispositions *at the cost of others*' (Britzman 1991, p. 223, my italics).

Both the suggestion that some ideologies have dominance over others (in the case of some teachers in our study, it was evidently those ideologies embedded in official public policy, reinforced by the force of law and by financial and promotional penalties and rewards, that held dominance over 'personally held' ideologies embedded in individual histories) and the suggestion that competing 'calls' can create discomfort and confusion for teachers provide very useful support in understanding the difficulties encountered by teachers – even very experienced ones, like Graeme (cited in Chapter 1 above) – in reflecting constructively upon their practice when the underlying causes of the discomfort and confusion may manifest themselves 'emotionally' rather than 'rationally'. It is, as others have suggested (e.g. Boler 1999; Moore and Atkinson 1998), precisely an overlooking of the emotional in classroom practice, in favour of an elusive and illusory rational, that often renders classroom experiences and interactions so hard to understand or explain, and that can leave the practitioner in an impasse in which resolution seems impossible.

An additional issue for practitioners and policy makers, however, is that discourses may also be seen to shift societally over time as well as *within* any given society or culture – partly because they are, typically, tied to equally fluid notions of what should be taught and what education is for (see also Calderhead and Shorrock 1997, p. 1). If, for example, we consider that a central purpose – perhaps *the* central purpose – of education is to produce a more competitive, efficient workforce aimed at enhancing the wealth and prosperity of a nation state and of all or some of the citizens within that nation state, official discourses are likely to construct that 'good teacher' according to how effective the teacher is in promoting and contributing to that particular end, and may use easily produced statistical evidence (numbers of students achieving qualifications, numbers entering the workforce, etc.) against which to measure the extent of the teacher's (or of teachers') 'goodness'. We might consequently expect to find pedagogies driven to a considerable degree *by* those external measures. (We may then, of course, consider a number of sub-discourses that seek to unpack 'effective' and that provide various perspectives on how each of those subversions of effectiveness translates into practice.) If, on the other hand, we adopt the view that a – perhaps the – prime purpose of education is to teach people that there is a lot more to life than the world of work, that education is more about helping the individual to develop creatively, collaboratively, spiritually, morally and 'personally', as a means of facilitating their own and others' enjoyment of life, then we may look for a teacher who is effective in contributing to alternative goals, whose pedagogical approaches may be linked more closely to those particular goals, and whose success may be assessed by different means (for example, if we remain within a metrics orientation, against student evaluations, levels of bullying, truancy rates and so forth).

As was implied in the passage from Valerie Walkerdine's *Schoolgirl Fictions* quoted in the previous section, there are, also, as many different views of what makes a good school as of what makes a good teacher. For some people – teachers, parents and pupils – the good school may, for example, be one where there is an appearance or perception of 'good discipline' linked to high levels of academic success. Such a school might also have a fairly strict dress code for staff and students, set regular homework and so forth. Without necessarily disapproving or distancing themselves from the above, for others the central characteristics of the good school might concern the extent to which the school encourages creativity, independent thinking and self-expression (which might include, for instance, a firm *rejection* of strict dress codes). For others, the good school might be characterised less in terms of its curriculum, pedagogy or 'ethos', more in terms of factors such as the ethnic make-up of the school. Some, again, might be more impressed by the levels of equipment and facility offered by the school – the computers, drama spaces, general décor of the building and so on – or by certain characteristics of the headteacher.

By and large, the notion of what represents good teaching is inevitably linked to notions of what represents a good school and a good education (and even, in some cases, to how a specific subject area should be taught), and equally inevitably these are all variable concepts. Sir Richard Livingston, for example (1941, cited in Abbott 1999 and Broadfoot 2000), incorporated the notion of the good teacher within a notion of appropriate education that appears some way distant from the current emphasis – in England and Wales at least – on the teaching of a fixed, identified body of skills and knowledge and on the regular (we might say over-) assessment of these through 'outcomes' and 'productivity':

the test of a successful education is not the amount of knowledge that a pupil takes away from a school but his [*sic*] appetite to know and his capacity to learn. If the school sends out children with the *desire* for knowledge and some idea of how to acquire and use it, it will have done its work. Too many leave school with the appetite killed and the mind loaded with undigested lumps of information. The good schoolmaster [*sic*] is known by the number of valuable subjects that he *declines* to teach.

(Broadfoot 2000, p. 8; italics in the original)

This is not, it has to be said, a clear-cut issue: education may be seen to have many different, not necessarily contradictory purposes (it may, for example, be perceived as contributing to *both* of the ends outlined above), and teachers may need to be effective in their contribution to this *range* of purposes. It may also be the case that some of these different purposes are closely linked to one another in some aspects (for example, one way to be happier is, arguably, to have a wide choice of interesting and reasonably well-paid work), and that different purposes may be achieved by similar pedagogies. The point is, however, that from a discursive perspective the concept of the good teacher cannot sit 'outside' or untouched by the larger social conversations, situations, ideologies and purposes within which it is situated: it cannot easily, therefore, make claims to 'universality', despite what documents such as lists of required 'standards', from which temporal and ecological issues and concerns are deliberately omitted, seem to suggest to the contrary.

If we return to the first of the quotations with which this chapter opened, we can see a very close and deliberate connection between the classroom and the legal system, between the teacher and the policeman or lawyer, and, by implication, between the child and the (potential) law-breaker. There is also, however, in Laurie's account a Godlike quality attributed to the good teacher: he (*sic*) is both just and merciful. It is not difficult to locate this emphasis within one of the prime rationales for introducing universal education in the first place: that is to say (Moore 2000, pp. 54–5), to tame an increasingly lawless 'lower class' at a time in which organised religion was losing much of its power to manipulate and control the populace. More, however, is required of the good teacher in Laurie's account: the teacher is not only a law-enforcer; he (*sic*) is the school's 'presiding genius, its spiritual standard, its type of culture', and, as if that were not enough, 'a child among children, a boy among boys, a youth among youths'.

In this nineteenth-century description of Laurie's we can trace one source of what I have called the 'charismatic subject' discourse of good teaching. There is no reference here to careful planning or subject knowledge or classroom management or understanding learning: the teacher here is presented as an authoritative role model and exemplar, who requires no justification for standing before groups of young people to pass on wisdom, morality and behavioural norms, and who succeeds by the sheer force of personality. The whole point of being a law bearer and law enforcer, after all, is that the law that one is bearing and enforcing is beyond question – certainly, beyond the questioning of those it seeks to normalise and control. The emphasis here is on 'standard' behaviour and on learning the basic requirements for effective contribution to the national economy.

Lest we are too quick to dismiss such a view of teaching as passé, the following testimony of a student teacher (George), on our *Reflective Practice Project*, produced in his first written assignment, offers a sharp reminder that it is still a commonly held conception:

> Academically I was a lazy child in my early years, especially when it came to my French lessons, as I was never a natural linguist. . . . I attended a public school . . . where I was generally considered a lost cause, apart from my outstanding sporting achievements. My French teacher was the only one who saw my innate intelligence, having spent time, resource, and plenty of patience on me, whilst all my other teachers generally ignored me.
>
> [This teacher] more importantly understood how to lay down the law and always knew what the class was up to. . . . I believe to this very day that he must have had eyes at the back of his head, ears as sharp as an owl and a stern look that would melt ice! He was the only teacher that threatened me with suspension and thereafter scared me into learning my French and buckle down. The end result was I started to achieve 18 out of 20 as compared to my previous 3 or 4 out of 20. More importantly he praised/motivated me and kept up the pressure so I would not fall back into my old ways. I learnt from that moment that I was not a loser or a dim-witted child; this knowledge built up my confidence which stood me in good stead when I later sat my GCSE and A-level examinations.
>
> (George went on to identify the following 'key attributes' of a good teacher: *time; resource; patience; lay down the law; a stern look; praise; preparation*.)

One of the interesting features of this student teacher's initial conceptualisation of good teaching (which changed quite dramatically during the course of his pre-service year) is the manner in which it neither takes account of variations in pupils' aptitudes, motivation, learning styles and so on nor affords the pupil anything other than a subordinate role in the teacher–learner relationship: that is, it is the teacher's job to 'work on' the pupil and it is the pupil's responsibility to be sufficiently compliant and pliable to be worked upon. To quote from another Victorian text:

It is thus seen that the educator stamps his own impress on the edu-
cated. In this respect he might be compared to the sculptor whose
genius has transformed a shapeless block into a living beautiful statue.

(Cited by Gill 1883, p. 118)

In the accounts of what makes a good teacher made by 8-year-olds over a
hundred years later and quoted – presumably with its seal of approval – in
the Hay McBer Report (2000), the notion of the charismatic teacher is still
clearly alive and well; however, it appears to have evolved somewhat as it
has shifted into the intersections of other discourses – in line, perhaps,
with a revised function of teaching to include the heightened importance of
producing citizens who can perceive themselves as customers and con-
sumers and who might additionally be required to join the ranks of an ever-
expanding customer-relations job market. Here, the good teacher continues
to be judged according to personality traits, but the ideal teacher–pupil relationship has shifted from one of authoritative exemplar to one engaged in
collective enterprise (a shift that is also apparent in the illustrative photographic material included in the Plowden Report of 1967, in which teachers
are either conspicuous by their absence or engaged in co-operative work
with their pupils). This teacher is more kindly, more responsive to pupils'
problems, needs and learning styles; allows and encourages questions; is
helpful and caring: we might say, a post-Plowden primary-school teacher
in whom, despite the influence and impact of a powerful competences discourse that prioritises subject knowledge and forward planning, what is
most highly valued is simple humanity. This is, furthermore, representative
of the kind of teacher many of the students in our *Reflective Practice Project*
said they wanted to be. To quote one student teacher, Carrie, whose testimony, like many of the other students', conceptualised the good teacher in
terms of both firmness and respect for one's pupils within a broader 'role
model' context:

A good teacher needs self-discipline. They must be responsible. The
adult is the authority and the role model in the room. They must be
patient and possess strong leadership qualities to help earn the pupils
respect. In return the teacher must respect the children and value their
right to education.

(Carrie: student teacher, *Reflective Practice Project*)

Discourse and teacher education

That notions of good teaching and the dominant discourses within which
they are situated have this provisional quality is reflected both in what
passes for teacher education at different times and in different geographical
locations, and in research and theorising *about* what good teaching might

represent. As McLaughlin and Talbert have observed in relation to research on teacher effectiveness in the USA:

> Early research on teacher effectiveness focused primarily on teachers' personal traits. . . . By the late 1970s, research on teacher effectiveness centered on general methodology . . . and the role of the curriculum. . . . Further research considered teachers' effectiveness in terms of their skills as professional decision makers who use a repertoire of competencies to meet instructional goals and student needs. . . . Finally, the focus on methodology and curriculum was meshed with a consideration of teachers' repertoires of competencies, yielding the understanding that a secondary school teacher's pedagogical skills are subject specific and context particular.
>
> (1990, pp. 1–2 – indicating, incidentally, a somewhat different take on competenc[i]es than that implicit in the official lists of teacher competences and standards currently in use in England and Wales)

Elsewhere, Alexander has observed that the changing nature of education – its changing *purposes*, indeed – in countries like England has inevitably led to changing requirements *of* schoolteachers, and therefore how good teaching is configured and understood – again linking the notion of good teaching to the wider social and economic contexts within which school practice takes place. Most notably, Alexander suggests, this has concerned a movement away from the teacher as responsible for covering a whole curriculum towards the notion of the teacher as expert in a particular curriculum area or areas:

> The class-teacher system came first; it required no justification in a system of mass education at public expense other than economic and administrative: it was the cheapest and most straightforward means of educating children to the minimum levels required. But the twentieth century has witnessed the increased professionalisation of teachers: the professional claim had to be backed up by a convincing corpus of expert knowledge which could stand comparison with the self-evident subject knowledge base of specialist teachers in secondary, further and higher education.
>
> (1984, p. 14)

If Alexander's account does not entirely match the notion of good teaching contained within the pupils' statements in the Hay McBer Report (2000), the Report goes on to bridge this gap, never losing sight of the teacher as carer and nurturer but identifying nine discrete 'teaching skills' required of an effective teacher:

- high expectations;
- planning;
- methods and strategies;
- pupil management;
- time and resource management;
- time on task;
- lesson flow;
- assessment;
- setting appropriate and challenging homework.

It is also borne out by recent changes in Britain in initial and continuing teacher education. Recent government concerns to prioritise literacy, numeracy and Science, for example, have led to a requirement for primary-school teachers to possess relatively high levels of knowledge and expertise in each of these areas, and to devote a considerable proportion of their in-service courses (often only one year in length) to developing that knowledge and expertise. However, they have also led to broader, discursive shifts of emphasis in teacher education. Figure 2.1 suggests a provisional account of these discursive relocations in initial teacher-education programmes in Britain (elaborated in Chapters 3–7 below), based largely on my own experience of working closely with student teachers, first as a schoolteacher during the 1980s, then as course tutor on a one-year pre-service course (PGCE) for teachers at a British university during the 1990s.

I do not wish to suggest that these discursive shifts – relatively modest, it might be argued, since all could be located within overarching discourses

1980s: the 'charismatic' or 'ready-made' discourse

↓

the saviour teacher; the inspirational/inspired teacher;
the carer/guardian; the sorcerer's apprentice.

early 1990s: 'the 'educational' discourse

↓

the reflective practitioner; the teacher as learner and theorist

late 1990s: the 'training' discourse

↓

the skilled or competent craftsperson; the organised organiser;
the apprentice technician

Post-2000: the 'pragmatic' discourse

↓

the 'effective' teacher; the eclectic teacher; the teacher as 'non-political'

Figure 2.1 Key discourses in teacher education and training

of idealism and modernism – have entailed the replacement of one discursive positioning with another (indeed, the 'educational' discourse has a much longer history, and was certainly of key importance in teacher education in the 1960s, 1970s and 1980s and before), but rather to indicate a shift of *emphasis* or *dominance* of the kind identified elsewhere by Calderhead and Shorrock (1997, p. 1) and by Zeichner (1983) and Feiman-Menser (1990), who link teacher classifications such as the 'academic orientation', the 'practical orientation', the 'technical orientation', the 'personal orientation' and the 'critical inquiry orientation' to reform movements in the USA. (As our *Professional Identities Project* showed, teacher identities are complex, provisional things, and the pursuit of good teaching is likely to involve the practitioner in being charismatic and caring in the classroom, in reflecting and theorising, in meeting 'standards' of competence, and, it goes without saying, in being pragmatic and eclectic.) Nor are the timings to be taken too literally. What I *am* suggesting, however, is that a dominant discourse of teaching in which the teacher is principally understood in terms of carer, saviour or inspirer of young people has gradually given ground during the last ten years or so in England and Wales to an emphasis first on the teacher as reflective practitioner, then on the teacher as competent craftsperson and technician, and, more latterly, on the teacher as pragmatic and eclectic – 'beyond left and right' and indeed beyond 'progressive' and 'traditional'.

It is also important to recognise that the discourses upon which teachers and student teachers draw may be stronger or weaker depending on which social domain we observe them in. The charismatic subject discourse, for example, in which teachers are 'born rather than made' and succeed by the sheer force of their personality, may generally be stronger in the 'commonsense' social world which teachers and student teachers occupy during the time they are outside the school classroom. The competences discourse, on the other hand, might be stronger in the political arena, including in formal policy requirements and on courses of initial teacher education. Indeed, for many of the student teachers we interviewed and spoke to during the course of the *Autobiography Project*, it was precisely their endless movement back and forth between these discourses that contributed critically to the confusions and anxieties they were feeling. As one student, who continued to live with her parents and siblings during the course of her pre-service year, said:

> Every time I go home I'm getting told why streaming is better than mixed ability, and why silent working is better than group work, and why everyone should wear school uniform; and I just can't answer it. Every time I start telling them something else, I feel I just can't argue the case. I don't even sound convincing to myself. They just keep telling me I'm following the party line and I shouldn't listen to what I'm told at [the university] because it's all full of do-gooders and lefties, and

quoting all these good and rubbish teachers I had when I was at school, and how I got good results in the subjects where the teachers were most strict. . . . And then I come back here [to the university] and I'm listening to totally the opposite. And when I'm here this all makes sense again, but . . . I'm just totally confused.

(Sharon: student teacher, *Autobiography Project*)

Performativity Victorian-style

While there is no room here to examine these different conceptualisations in any depth, the following 'déjà-vu' example of the historically shifting nature of the good teacher discourse serves as a particularly poignant and illuminating illustration both of the fragility of discourses and of their uncanny, Terminator-like habit of returning.

During the years immediately preceding and immediately following the formal introduction of universal State education in 1870, teachers and young people in Britain were subjected to the same sort of ultimately pointless and immediately damaging pressures that many of us feel they are being subjected to today. In response to a view, gathering momentum in parliament, that grants should not be made to schools automatically and that State control of funding would contribute to a raising as well as a standardisation of the quality of education across State schools, a revision to the Code of Regulations then governing grants to elementary schools was approved in 1862, whereupon grants – and the sizes of grants – would henceforth be determined by 'quality' of provision. This itself would be 'measured' against children's results in standardised assessments linked to what we might now recognise as level descriptors (Figure 2.2). The notion of what 'quality of provision' might entail appears to have been viewed rather unproblematically, and linked, for no better reason than the reliability of the assessments themselves (rather than, say, a notion of the value of what was being taught and learned), to the measured performance of children's abilities in basic reading, writing and arithmetic. To quote Robert Lowe's explanation of the thinking behind this assessment choice following the Newcastle Commission's (1858) argument in favour of payment by results:

As I understand the case, you and I viewed the three R's not only or primarily as the exact amount of instruction which ought to be given, but as an amount of knowledge which could be ascertained thoroughly by examination, and upon which we could safely base the parliamentary grant. . . . It was more a financial than a literary preference. Had there been any other branch of useful knowledge, the possession of which could have been ascertained with equal precision, there was nothing to prevent its admission. But there was not.

(Cited in Selleck 1968, p. 17)

	Standard I	Standard II	Standard III
Reading	Narrative in monosyllables.	One of the Narratives next in order after monosyllables in an elementary reading book used in the school.	A short paragraph from an elementary reading book used in the school.
Writing	Form on blackboard or slate, from dictation, letters, capital and small manuscript.	Copy in manuscript character a line of print.	A sentence from the same paragraph, slowly read once and then dictated in single words.
Arithmetic	Form on blackboard or slate, from dictation, figures up to 20; name at sight figures up to 20; add and subtract figures up to 10, orally, from examples on blackboard.	A sum in simple addition or subtraction, and the multiplication table.	A sum in any simple rule as far as short division (inclusive).

	Standard IV	Standard V	Standard VI
Reading	A short paragraph from a more advanced reading book used in the school.	A few lines of poetry from a reading book used in the first class of the school.	A short ordinary paragraph in a newspaper, or other modern narrative.
Writing	A sentence slowly dictated once by a few words at a time, from the same book, but not from the paragraph read.	A sentence slowly dictated once by a few words at a time, from a reading book used in the first class of the school.	Another short ordinary paragraph in a newspaper, or other modern narrative, slowly dictated once by a few words at a time.
Arithmetic	A sum of compound rules (money).	A sum of compound rules (common weights and measures).	A sum in practice or bills of parcels.

Figure 2.2 The revised Code of Regulations (1862) governing State grants to elementary schools.

Source: Maclure (1990)

The 'good teacher' implicit in this policy reform is likely to be conceived in strictly functional terms: the teacher's primary role is not to enthuse or excite young people, not to fill them with a passion for learning and a thirst for knowledge, not even to shape their moral development, but primarily to ensure that they reach appropriate standards in a small number of 'basic' subject areas (or rather, to ensure that they do sufficiently well in tests to 'indicate' that they have reached these standards) – a conceptualisation reinforced by its attachment to State *inspection* leading to State *funding*.

When the then inspector of schools, Matthew Arnold, wrote his General Report of 1867 (by which time new grant-bearing tests had been introduced for Language, Geography and History), he was not, however, pleased with the quality of teaching and learning in elementary-school classrooms, regardless of what the 'evidence' of test results might appear to be telling him. As Arnold put it:

> The mode of teaching in the primary schools has certainly fallen off in intelligence, spirit, and inventiveness during the four or five years which have elapsed since my last report. It could not well be otherwise. In a country where everyone is prone to rely too much on mechanical processes and too little on intelligence, a change in the Education Department's regulations, which, by making two-thirds of the Government grant depend on a mechanical examination, inevitably gives a mechanical turn to the school teaching, a mechanical turn to the inspection, is and must be trying to the intellectual life of a school. . . . More free play for the inspector, and more free play, in consequence, for the teacher is what is wanted. . . . In the game of mechanical contrivances the teacher will in the end beat us; and as it is now found possible, by ingenious preparation, to get children through the Revised Code examination in reading, writing and ciphering, so it will with practice no doubt be found possible to get the three-fourths of the one-fifth of the children over six through the examination in grammar, geography and history, without their really knowing any one of these three matters.
>
> (1867, cited in Maclure 1986, p. 81)

Continuing to rue the impact of performativity and mechanistic teaching methods on teacher creativity and pupil pleasure, Arnold added to this, two years later:

> [The teacher] limits his subject as much as he can, and within these limits tries to cram his pupils with details enough to enable him to say, when they produce them, that they have fulfilled the Departmental requirements, and fairly earned their grant. . . . The circle of the

children's reading has . . . been narrowed and impoverished all the year for the sake of a result at the end of it, and the result is an illusion.

(Cited in Selleck 1968, pp. 40, 43)

It was not until the Bousfield Sub-Committee's findings nearly twenty years after this that mechanistic teaching and the ubiquitous pressures of tests were having a detrimental effect on young people's experiences of learning, schooling and life, with concerns being expressed that numbers of children were being driven to mental breakdowns, that the London School Board adopted twenty-nine new recommendations, including:

[t]hat the teaching of Reading should be especially directed to give children an interest in books, and to encourage them to read for their own pleasure;

[t]hat in order to allow for experimental teaching and manual work, the time now given to spelling, parsing and grammar generally be reduced;

[t]hat teachers be informed that the Board do not pay so much attention to the percentage of passes obtained at the Government Inspection as to the general tone and character of the school work.

(1888, cited in Maclure 1990, pp. 48–9)

If in the 1860s good teaching had been situated (at any rate, within official education policy) within discourses of the transmission of knowledge and skills, of performativity and control, and of national competition and the changing requirements of the labour market (the need, for example, for more and more modestly paid and limitedly literate and numerate *clerks*), by the end of the 1880s, at least in some areas of the country, it had been officially relocated to re-include what we would now refer to as child-centredness, the development of lifelong learning and the therapeutic dimensions of education aimed at personal enrichment and fulfilment.

Not only does this particular historical episode provide an illustration of how, in education, what goes around comes around, and of a curious inability (most surprisingly, perhaps, on the part of those who are forever telling us how lessons need to be learned from history) to pay any attention to past failures, but it provides another example of the tensions that often face headteachers and classroom teachers when there is a conflict between government diktats and personal philosophies and ideologies. With reference to our thinking about the 'good teacher', diktats such as that eventually deplored by Arnold but currently resurrected by Britain's 'New Labour' government may run counter to teachers' views about what education is for and how best it is carried out: through, for example, encouraging 'teaching to the test' and all the attendant ills, long since noted by swathes of teachers, of rote learning, memorisation and uncritical regurgitation.

Good teaching and the curriculum

As I have already suggested, it is not only across time that notions of good teaching change (and change back, and change again), but also across cultures and nations. In Britain, we are currently in a situation in which good teaching is inevitably linked to and configured within a particular model of school *curriculum* with a strong emphasis on an identified body of knowledge and skills and the formal, standardised testing of the teaching and learning of that knowledge and those skills: that is to say, an essentially content-based rather than an essentially process-based curriculum. It is also, some would argue, a curriculum that is in many respects backward-looking or 'retrospective', in that (a) the selections of knowledge draw upon what is already, in Arnold's famous phrase, 'the best that is known and thought in the world' (Arnold 1909, pp. 10–11), and (b) the *selections* of skills tend to marginalise the social and expressive/creative skills in favour of the mechanical or technical ones (Moore and Klenowski *et al.* 2003).

In such a situation, as in Arnold's time – given that once again pupil performance in standardised tests has become linked to funding – a degree of 'teaching to the test' is inevitable, and the quality of teaching is most strongly associated with the test and examination scores of one's students. Not surprisingly, perhaps, subject knowledge, as Alexander (1984) has suggested, has become prioritised – not least in initial teacher education – over other qualities such as communication skills or even *knowledge about learning*, within a competences discourse that is itself located within wider discourses of performativity and skilled craftspersonship. (The teacher 'works on' the raw material of the pupils in order to turn out products whose quality can be reliably measured, enabling judgements to be made in turn about the cratfsperson's technical skills – a model which does raise questions as to whether such a development can be truly linked to the 'increased professionalisation' of teachers, or whether it might rather be an indication of their de-professionalisation.)

This is not to say, of course, that teachers are not 'good' in other ways, or that there are not other, equally pressing 'good teacher' agendas and demands, including, in the case of student teachers, those promoted by their college and school tutors. It is merely to point out that within official policy discourses teachers are *judged and rewarded* (or penalised) not so much on whether their pupils find them – say – inspirational, fair, hardworking or many of those other things cited by the children in the Hay McBer Report, but on the basis of their students' results in SATs and public examinations, neither of which tend to assess lifelong learning skills, creativity or reflection, but rather the demonstration and regurgitation of acquired skills and items of 'knowledge'.

The worst we can do, however, is to assume that there are no perfectly workable – and possibly more desirable – alternatives to the models of good teaching we are currently encouraged towards by officialdom, or to fear that those good qualities we may continue to cherish 'unofficially' (or that were cherished in the past) have gone for good. Indeed, it is particularly heartening – if paradoxically depressing – for some teachers working in English schools to learn not only that in many countries around the world new and revised national curricula are being produced that are very different in content, style and rationale from our own, but that the models of good or effective teaching consequently embedded – sometimes explicitly, sometimes implicitly – in these curricula are also very different and much closer to the personal, 'therapeutic' agendas that many British teachers continue to hold dear and that certainly emerged very strongly indeed in interviews with teachers and student teachers involved in the three projects to which I alluded in the previous chapter. Not only are these curricula far less detailed and prescriptive than that of England and Wales, consequently providing for far higher levels of school-based curriculum development and teacher autonomy (Skilbeck 1984a, 1984b; Marsh 1990), but they are also patently more future-oriented than ours, far more process- and skills-based, and adopt a different view of education for citizenship and democracy which suggests that young people are far more likely to participate in democratic practices when they are older if they have genuine democratic experiences while they are at school.

Part II
Dominant discourses

3 'Made in heaven' – charismatic subjects

I hoped that I could be like my economics teacher, who kind of stood up for me and said 'This girl's worth it' and allowed me to get into a course at college which I shouldn't have been in, really.

My English teacher at GCSE level managed to stimulate my passion to learn by being impassioned himself about the characters in 'Wuthering Heights'. Somehow I related to this, respected him and listened to his future advice. Then he advised I start reading more than just teenage girl fiction stories at home and gradually I began to be much more motivated in other subjects too.

There are some teachers whose enthusiasm for their subject is infectious. That is the type of teacher I want to be. Some teachers somehow just seem to command respect; they never shout or threaten, but just their presence is enough to produce calm and order in the classroom.

My favourite teacher never did anything by the book. She just got us involved through the sheer force of her personality.

(Student teachers' written testimonies, *Reflective Practice Project*)

Introduction

Having established what I mean by discourse and how dominant discourses construct and affect classroom practice and teacher education, it is to the three educational discourses that I have labelled 'dominant' in terms of identifying and describing good teaching that I want to turn in this and the next two chapters. The first of these 'dominant discourses' – the one that has more of a foothold in the worlds of folk pedagogy and cultural mythology than in the more 'official' fields of government policy and teacher-education programmes – is that of the charismatic subject.

The charismatic subject

The point has already been made that even before student teachers come on to pre-service courses they have very clear ideas about what classroom life is and should be like, and about what it means to be a successful teacher. I have also indicated that for some commentators this represents a major problem both for student teachers and for teacher educators. Afonso, for example, reminds us that student teachers are, from the outset, 'strongly marked by positive or negative *images* of teachers [and] by banalized and partial images of the teacher's work' (Afonso 2001, p. 197, my italics; see also Calderhead 1991; Calderhead and Robson 1991; Johnson 1994). As Afonso goes on to suggest, these images can, ultimately, be reduced to stereotypes (see also Weber and Mitchell 1996) or, as Britzman puts it, to 'well worn and commonsensical images [which serve as] the frame of reference for prospective teachers' self-images' (Britzman 1986, p. 443). Once formed, Afonso fears, these images are often very hard to modify, acting as 'intuitive screens through which information is filtered' (Goodman 1988, p. 130) and through which behaviour is shaped (see also Clandinin 1985; Connelly and Clandinin 1985, 1986; Pajares 1992; Clift *et al*. 1994).

My own involvement with student teachers – both in my teaching and via research – suggests that in many instances these images and stereotypes come from experiences students have had themselves as pupils of teachers whom they have found particularly memorable. Certainly, when student teachers are asked such questions as 'What good teachers do you remember from your own school days? What was it about those teachers that made them good?', they generally experience very little difficulty in nominating exemplary teachers, tending to highlight, in their elaborations of what made such teachers exemplary, often sketchily defined 'personal qualities' including those of being 'inspirational' and of having an 'infectious enthusiasm' (see also Wragg 1974; Moore and Atkinson 1998). To quote students on our *Reflective Practice Project*, interviewed shortly after having been awarded a place on their pre-service course:

> Lessons should be exciting and stimulating to encourage and motivate pupils. . . . Lessons should be delivered with enthusiasm. . . . A good teacher promotes a calm and positive atmosphere . . . is decisive, assertive and understanding. . . . A good teacher is remembered, he or she is able to influence, give guidance and set up strong foundations for their pupils' future.
>
> (Carrie: student teacher, *Reflective Practice Project*)

> A good teacher must be patient, enthusiastic, motivating and above all interested, both in their subject and in the students they teach. In my opinion it is this interest and passion that obtains the best results in students. . . . When I think back to my school days and to the subjects

that I liked or disliked, what stands out the most is those teachers who were enthusiastic and interested. As a result these were the subjects that I enjoyed the most. I therefore think that a teacher has two primary roles. Firstly, to be regarded as an enthusiastic and patient person so that students will want to study their given subject. Secondly, to carry this forward and have the know-how and interest to give their best to students, thus resulting in the best possible results for those students.

(Alexandra: student teacher, *Reflective Practice Project*)

For many of these teachers-to-be, the image of the ideal teacher they carried with them into their pre-service course was of one who did not simply 'teach' in the sense of 'passing on' or quickening skills, knowledge and facts, but one who would 'make a difference', 'touch lives': one for whom pupils' cognitive and affective development was paramount, but for whom such development needed to take place within what might be called a fundamentally pastoral mode of pedagogy. For these novice teachers, the teacher they envision eventually becoming is a carer, nurturer and role model as much as an 'educator' in the narrower sense of the word, one whose *modus operandi* is characterised by personal 'performance' and student admiration along the lines described by Harris and Jarvis (2000, p. 3) in their finding from their own research with student teachers that 'the cultural images dominating the minds of intending teachers are those of charismatic individuals who have *changed the lives* of those with whom they work' (my italics).

There is nothing wrong, of course, about teachers being remembered or about new teachers wanting to emulate the ways and styles of teachers whom they have previously experienced as successful themselves. Nor, on the evidence of the testimonies of the teachers and student teachers involved in the projects on which this book is based, would many prioritise the charismatic, enthusiastic, caring, inspirational conceptualisation of the good teacher to the extent of ignoring or refuting other, less obvious qualities and skills that a successful teacher might require. We might also agree that at a time when technicist models of teaching appear (certainly, to the *student* teachers we spoke to) to be holding centre stage, the more intuitive, spontaneous, collaborative aspects of teaching need celebrating more than ever. As Hartley poignantly asks: '[W]here is the pleasure for the teacher in this emerging and empowered charisma-free zone called the 'competent' classroom? . . . What now is the pedagogical relationship when contract replaces trust?' (Hartley 1997, p. 79) – reminding us of Woods' timely reminder that teaching is, very often, 'expressive and emergent, intuitive and flexible, spontaneous and emotional' (Woods 1996, p. 6).

There are, however, difficulties with the notion of the charismatic subject, one of which I have already alluded to and which emerges when student teachers are asked to elaborate on their recollections of good teaching. While it is not uncommon for them to recite qualities such as a sense of humour, a commitment to fairness, good communication skills or infectious enthusiasm for the subject area, these are often expressed in the very vaguest of terms, suggestive of an over-reliance on notions of 'personality' and a corresponding under-reliance on matters of technique – something which can prove both very dangerous and very unhelpful to practitioners setting out on their teaching careers. There is, certainly, seldom reference in these accounts (explained partly, perhaps, by their 'invisibility' as far as the school-student may be concerned) to such things as planning, preparation, classroom management skills or assessment of students' work and progress. As Rousmaniere *et al.* have observed in this connection:

> Often the stories that we remember and tell about our own schooling are not so much about what we learned, but how we learned and with whom. There are stories about teachers we loved, teachers we hated and those we feared.
>
> (1997, p. 4; see also Mitchell and Weber 1996)

Always, in such stories, the emphasis is on the teacher as personality, and always the implication is that good teachers are 'born' rather than 'made', that their qualities are somehow inherent and perhaps even inheri*ted*.

An additional difficulty is immediately apparent: if the identified qualities of good teaching are inherent, what hope does the student teacher who self-perceives as charismatically deficient have of acquiring them, or of even knowing *how* to acquire them? And how might the student teacher's own teachers contribute to the achievement of such a difficult goal? As Dalton (1999) observes, the spectre of the charismatic teacher often has the unfortunate effect of making life very difficult for student teachers when, in the classroom situation, they discover that they *cannot* emulate, or be instantly respected in the manner of, the only truly effective teacher they can remember from their own school days. One reason for this, I would suggest, is that the attempted emulation of such role models is typically based on a simple misunderstanding: a misunderstanding that although a teacher's 'charisma' may appear to be embodied in and to 'emanate from' the teacher, it is in essence an attribute that is conferred *upon* the teacher *by* their students. (This is what Zizek and others, after the psycho-analyst Jacques Lacan, have referred to as the 'transferential illusion', whereby a quality that one invests in another object *appears* to reside, intrinsically, *in* the object itself. See, for instance, Zizek 1989, p. 146.)

This particular misunderstanding explains, at least in part, why student teachers so often discover to their cost that while it may be possible to draw lessons from their own previous teachers on how to handle difficult students, how to make work interesting and accessible, or how to promote self-esteem and motivation through sensitive, constructive assessment, it is usually a futile and ultimately destructive task to seek to copy their manner of self-presentation. A far more useful project for student teachers, consequently, rather than trying to work out and emulate the 'charisma' of a particular teacher or teachers, is to try to analyse *why* it is that a teacher's students invest in the teacher in the way they do – a project which might involve, centrally, an identification of the particular personal and professional qualities and techniques that the students appeared to be responding to most positively in the teacher.

Such an approach may certainly help to avert another danger inherent in the charismatic subject discourse, which is that, in any event, it may not be desirable or acceptable to emulate the perceived charismatic qualities of a model teacher, given that charisma, as I shall argue in relation to filmic representations of teachers, has the capacity to mask a number of pedagogic deficiencies and indeed much that we might be inclined to perceive, in other circumstances, as bad practice. A common feature of the charismatic teacher – certainly as featured in the movies – is that the teacher is presented as achieving success in often highly unconventional ways, including, very often, ways that have very little to do with such mundane matters as planning and preparing for lessons. On the contrary, the charismatic teacher is often presented as coming into the classroom deliberately *un*prepared – solely reliant on their subject knowledge (though not even, always, that), inherent popularity, and intangible ability to enthuse and inspire the students. Not uncommonly, this teacher is configured as something of an institutional rebel, not merely taking up an oppositional stance to some of the pettier school rules, but identifying much more closely with the student population than with other members of staff in ways that one might want to discourage as a teacher educator in the interests of achieving successful pedagogic activity.

Charismatic teachers in popular culture: carers, saviours and connectors

As I have indicated, it is not only actual teachers who provide new teachers with models and prototypes. The notion of the charismatic teacher has long been commonplace in popular culture (see Farber and Holm 1994), not least, in recent years, in feature films about schools and teaching, and if the student teachers we spoke to rarely referred directly to such representations in terms of role models, they often did so by way of illustrating or reinforcing accounts of charismatic teachers recalled from their own school days. Thus, one of the young teachers taking part in the *Reflective Practice Project*, Peter, having listed the personal qualities he felt he should possess and exhibit as a teacher (being 'inspirational', 'wanting and being able to make a real difference to people's lives', 'leading through my own commitment and enthusiasm'), mentioned, in his written assignment, the teacher portrayed in the film *Stand and Deliver*:

The film 'Stand and Deliver' is based on the true story of a teacher in California who, through much hard work and a heart attack, got all of his pupils, who were essentially street kids from Puerto Rico going nowhere in life, to pass their calculus exam. . . . If I achieve something along those lines with pupils who think it is impossible to succeed in anything and that nothing will change the status quo in their lives, that would be wonderful.

(Peter: student teacher, *Reflective Practice Project*)

Peter's conceptualisation of the good teacher is closely linked to two popular versions of good teaching, each of which I would include within the charismatic subject discourse: that of *the teacher as carer/nurturer* and that of *the teacher as saviour*. The former, which is particularly popular in Hollywood films about teachers and their students, focuses on what I have called the 'pastoral' rather than the strictly academic aspects of teaching, suggesting that most young people – particularly those identified as troubled or troublesome – will sooner or later respond to what is sometimes called a 'pedagogy of love' (Boler 1999), divesting themselves of notions that everyone in the larger System (including, often, their own family members) is working against them, and becoming better students – both behaviourally and academically – through identification with a caring adult. As Boler puts this, with a nod to Foucault, such pedagogies are about '[t]eaching children to internalize self-control through a pedagogy of maternal love' (Boler 1999, p. 42) – their roots lying in conceptualisations of the 'virtuous mother/schoolteacher' that were popular in the earliest days of formal State education in America and elsewhere, when education itself was seen as having as much to do with social control as with cognitive/academic development, and when the majority of schoolteachers were women.

The notion of the *saviour teacher* is also popular in filmic representations of classroom life, particularly when such films concern themselves very specifically with social issues related to class and race. (For a fuller analysis of the representation of teachers in feature film, see Dalton's book *The Hollywood Curriculum* (1999).) Here, the teacher is represented as one who enters the imperfect, put-upon world of constrained, symbolically abused young people, first winning their confidence, then showing them an alternative world and then, if they are really successful, taking some of them into that alternative world (as in the case of the teacher in *Stand and Deliver*, referred to above). The characteristics of the saviour teacher – though they prefer the term 'teacher hero' – are outlined by Claudia Mitchell and Sandra Weber in their book *Reinventing Ourselves as Teachers* (1996, p. 183). These authors, who are also teacher educators, argue that portrayals of successful, 'popular', 'hero' teachers in fictive texts are typically characterised by romanticism, and they offer the following conventions within which such teachers tend to be inscribed:

- Teacher heroes are usually *outsiders* who are teaching through circumstances rather than through choice.
- Teaching is represented as 'natural'; i.e. you do not need training if you've got 'the right stuff'.
- Teacher heroes are rare, and stand out in contrast to anti-hero teachers.
- Teacher heroes liberate students by defying the official school rules and curriculum.
- Real learning occurs outside school.
- Teachers become heroic through a turning point of sudden enlightenment, divine intervention or the 'a-ha' experience.
- Teaching is a heroic and solitary act: teachers do not work collectively for reform.
- Teacher heroes are devoted to their students and are rewarded with their undying love and gratitude in a dramatic scene.

By way of illustrating how the teacher hero or teacher saviour is represented in practice, we might consider, briefly, two relatively well-known films about teachers who 'infiltrate' the system as resistance workers seeking to effect rescue missions in relation to their benighted students: *Dangerous Minds*, starring Michelle Pfeiffer as Ms Johnson; and *To Sir, With Love*, starring Sidney Poitier as Mr Thackeray. Each of these fictional teachers conforms to Mitchell and Weber's requirements of teacher heroes as outsiders who are teaching through circumstances rather than through choice; as gifted, 'natural' teachers who require no training; and of liberating – or seeking to liberate – their students by defying the official school rules and curriculum. Ms Johnson, in *Dangerous Minds*, is a young ex-marine turning her hand to teaching and initially finding combat in the urban American classroom every bit as hard as life in the army, while the pre-Ofsted, pre-compulsory-teacher-training Mr Thackeray is an engineer finding it difficult to gain employment, taking on teaching – again in an urban school full of students with acute social problems and learning difficulties, though this time in London – very much as a stop-gap, and finding that life as a teacher is made even harder by the fact that he is black and that his students are largely white.

Each of these 'outsiders' or 'incomers' is initially appalled by what they encounter in the classroom. For Ms Johnson, it is the students' lack of motivation and prior knowledge that leads her into the kind of despair in which she must fall back on the resources of her own native wit, quickly abandoning the formal, traditional, textbook-led lessons with which her predecessors have tried and failed, and making 'connections' with her students by introducing her version of pop culture into the classroom, by sharing with them some of her army skills and training, and then, when their attention has been won, by instilling in them a sense of worth and self-belief by telling them, via her own version of the pedagogy of love, what no other adult has apparently told them before: that they are capable, talented,

valuable people. For Mr Thackeray in *To Sir, With Love*, it is likewise the
lack of student motivation and knowledge, manifested – as in the early
scenes of *Dangerous Minds* – by classroom unruliness and disrespect, that
leads him to abandon the textbooks, in his case replacing them with his
own brand of morality and manners through whose replication his rag-tag
students also, ultimately, find respect for themselves, for one another, and
of course for the teacher who has led them to the Promised Land – reminding us that the pedagogy of love is not only about reproducing conformity
through example and 'care': it is also about achieving the love of those
whose interests we seek to further.

If there is nothing reprehensible – and indeed everything laudable – in
wanting to help underprivileged, underperforming students to do well,
then it might not matter that these ends are achieved in unconventional,
contingent ways, or that they are partly carried out for the benefit of the
teacher (in both Ms Johnson's and Mr Thackeray's case, the desire not
simply to be loved but, more importantly, perhaps, the desire to be *vindi-
cated* – to have one's practice and position in some way validated, mandated, authorised). The problem with Ms Johnson and Mr Thackeray,
however, is that although they are presented as mavericks they are essentially very *conservative* characters, each of whom may be said to be operating with and within versions of an Enlightenment project aimed not so
much at attacking the social conditions that *generate* inequalities in educational achievement as at producing 'better' (i.e. happier and, in the case of
Ms Johnson and Mr Thackeray, more law-abiding) citizens through exposure to 'high' (that is, middle-class) culture and 'respectable' (i.e. middle-
class) manners and cultural preferences. In either case, the point at which
the students' 'awakening' is marked is through the replacement of a classroom culture of vocal cacophony, characterised by competition for the
floor and the trading of insults, with a new culture of classroom *discussion*
characterised by listening and turn-taking in the spirit of collaborative,
co-operative enterprise.

The conservative nature of these teachers, which, in spite of their being
represented as saviours and nonconformists, may be read as contributing
to and confirming social and culture biases inherent within educational
systems, is indicated both in the curriculum 'rejections' that they make and
in the classroom practices that they adopt. Ms Johnson's success in producing orderliness in her classroom, for example, is partly attributable to
her rejection of (as the school principal puts it) 'the curriculum dictated by
the Board', partly in her introduction into the classroom of popular culture
in response to her colleague's advice that 'All you gotta do is catch their
attention', and partly through her rejection of the standard behaviour-
management manual *Assertive Discipline* (obviously, we are, presumably,
to think, written by some do-gooding educator at a university who lives at
too great a distance from the 'real world'), in favour of a more direct

approach to classroom discipline that speaks to the students in their own language. Each of these approaches, however, is problematic. To begin with, Ms Johnson's rejection of the curriculum 'dictated by the Board' is a contingent rejection rather than a principled one. It is not that she challenges the value of the set curriculum – or, significantly, its *values* – but that she finds it inappropriate for *her* students in the particular set of circumstances in which she finds them. Her lamentation that 'Most of my students don't even know what a verb is' (and therefore will not be in a position to *conjugate* a verb as required by the curriculum) may be raised by her as a part-justification for departing from the set curriculum; however, it also reveals a somewhat outdated and naïve understanding of learning and language development (what, when all's said and done, does it *matter* whether or not her students do or do not know 'what a verb is'?), both on the teacher's part and, we might assume, on the part of the film-makers (who may, in turn, feel that many in their audience will be equally shocked by this revelation).

Ms Johnson's pedagogy of love, with which she replaces 'assertive discipline', is the kind of 'tough love' her students may have been used to at home, laced with overtones of American foreign policy and the role of the US marine. 'OK, you little bastards', she says to herself, prior to writing in bold letters on the chalkboard: 'I AM A US MARINE' and asking her new charges: 'Does anyone know karate?' – while her introduction of pop culture into the classroom consists of what may be seen as the rather odd choice (given the social and cultural backgrounds of her students) of the songs of Bob Dylan – a performer whose work has always enjoyed far greater popularity with the conscience-stricken white middle classes than with the de-privileged black, Hispanic and working-class communities represented in Ms Johnson's class.

It is interesting to consider what is going on in *Dangerous Minds* from the point of view of the film's ideological positioning and the way in which the apparently idiosyncratic, revolutionary model of teaching is reclaimed by a very conservative notion of what schooling is about: not least, the notion that one of its prime functions – perhaps its most important function – is to reproduce 'model' citizens who reject violence- or apathy-inducing cultures in favour of 'civilising' middle-class ones. It is no coincidence that (in contrast to the real teacher on whom the film is based) Ms Johnson does not introduce into her lessons rap-based songs like 'Gangsta's Paradise' with which the film opens against a background of images of anarchy and alienation. Clearly, there is pop culture and there is pop culture – and urban rap, even when it offers clear possibilities for promoting the discussion of ethical issues in both the private and the public domain, is precisely the kind of pop culture through which *not* to 'catch the students' attention'. We might say that the very selection of the white, middle-class, 'message'-laden and highly moralistic songs of Bob Dylan in preference to those

that would be preferred by the students (despite their unconvincing enthusiasm for 'Mr Tambourine Man') itself serves to undermine what *really*
catches the students' attention when they are not having to sit in school
classrooms because they are legally obliged to do so. Regardless of all this,
Ms Johnson's project is, despite the odd stumble here and there (a parent
who chooses to withdraw her son from school because of Ms Johnson's
idealistic methods, another student who is killed on the streets), ultimately
successful in relative terms, and her reward is not merely the academic
success of her students but their love: 'You're our tambourine man', one of
them tells her; and, reminding us again of the roots of Ms Johnson's
methods and philosophy: 'We see you as being our light.'

Like Ms Johnson, Mr Thackeray in *To Sir, With Love* is quick to reject
the official curriculum – mainly consisting of basic numeracy ('weights and
measures', 'tables') and literacy (assessed by reading out loud) – on the
grounds that it is irrelevant to his charges: a rejection symbolically reinforced
by a rejection of the books to which his students have had to become
accustomed: 'Those are out. . . . They're useless to you.' In place of these,
Mr Thackeray introduces not poetry (as in the case of Ms Johnson) but
manners: we might say, his own version of the 'finishing school'. Again
this task is accomplished via tough love – so tough, in fact, as at times to
be downright insulting: 'I've seen garbage collectors who are cleaner [than
you]', Mr Thackeray tells the young men in his class with a bluntness
bordering on slander; and to the young women, after a particularly distaste-
ful 'prank' involving setting fire to a 'disgusting object' (*sic*) in the classroom: 'Only a filthy slut would have done this. . . . No man likes a slut for
long.' Like Ms Johnson, Mr Thackeray's achievement in 'civilising' his
class is illustrated and measured by the replacement of rudeness (partly,
ironically, via his own rudeness), competition and chaos in the classroom
with 'conversation': 'We are just going to talk . . . without interruption.'
To begin with, this 'conversation' is very teacher-centred: 'You are going
to listen to what I say. . . . I teach you truths: my truths . . . [about] life, survival, love, death, sex, marriage, rebellion.' And while he adds to this list
'anything you want', Mr Thackeray has already made very clear to the class
that 'anything they want' has to coincide with anything *he* wants. (A debate
about marriage, for instance, is quickly curtailed by Mr Thackeray's per-
emptory observation: 'To my mind marriage is no way of life for the weak,
the selfish or the insecure.') Gradually, however, the class are inducted into
Mr Thackeray's conversational *modus vivendi* until lessons are able to
begin and proceed in an atmosphere of calm and mutual respect:

Mr T.: Good morning.

Class: Good morning, Mr Thackeray.

Mr T.: What would you like to talk about today?

By the end of the film, Mr Thackeray's hero status has been confirmed. His pupils are able to tell him: 'We'd like to thank you very much for everything you've done for us', while one of his colleagues, reminding us that Mr Thackeray embodies that model of teaching in which good teachers are perceived as 'born' rather than 'made', tells him, admiringly: 'I wish I had your *gift*.'

Charisma and conservatism: the explicit, implicit and null curriculum

In judging the 'success' of fictive teachers such as Mr Thackeray and Ms Johnson, we might think it not unreasonable to ask: *What, exactly, have they 'done' for their students?* Eisner and others (Eisner 1985; Flinders *et al.* 1986; Britzman 1989) have written of three aspects of the school curriculum: the *explicit* curriculum, which refers to what has to be covered academically and creatively; the *implicit* curriculum, which comprises such matters as what is or is not acceptable behaviour, who is allowed to do what, what are acceptable models of learning; and the *null* curriculum, which comprises all those things which are deliberately excluded from the curriculum, many of which may feature large in the students' lives outside the school buildings – we might say, in their domestic or private curricula.

A closer look at Ms Johnson's and Mr Thackeray's approaches suggests that while they are happy and (as is not the case with, for example, British teachers these days, who are legally obliged to follow a set national curriculum) prepared to abandon the explicit curriculum, they do so merely in order to make visible, to strengthen and to give a higher priority to an equally oppressive and inappropriate *implicit* curriculum – that is to say, the 'hidden' curriculum of middle-class manners and mores. The 'null' curriculum of the pupils' own out-of-school lives and cultures, meanwhile, is left as marginalised as ever, and arguably more so; for these hero teachers have not merely come to 'save', but have also come to restore 'order'. That is to say, these teachers are not really subversives so much as missionaries (Moore 1999c). Furthermore, their very definition as 'heroes' is located within another dominant discourse of education – that it is fundamentally (though we might not always like to admit it) about reproducing compliant rather than critical citizens, and that appropriate pedagogies, even when classroom conversation is being prioritised, are – as is indicated in the title of the film *Stand and Deliver* referred to by the student above – essentially transmissive and teacher-centred.

One implication of all this is that the good teacher represented via these charismatic subjects, these hero or saviour teachers, is not judged according to their ability to help their students become critical, independent thinkers and activists, nor are they given this desire via the words that are put into their mouths. When Mr Thackeray talks of his students changing the world, he is very specific that they must achieve this 'as individuals' rather than in what he refers to as 'a mob', introducing a recurrent theme of such films in which learning and the fruits of learning are very much individual, privatised affairs aimed at helping the individual to 'do well' within a social system that may be seen and presented as unfair (as in *Dangerous Minds*) or that may simply be accepted with an air of inevitability (as in *To Sir, With Love*) but that remains essentially unchallenged and unchanged. Neither Mr Thackeray's nor Ms Johnson's students, despite the development of their collaborative, conversational skills, have been better enabled to act collectively to critique and change the *conditions* of their situations and circumstances; rather, they are encouraged to attend to their own immediate interests – to achieve as much as they can within an essentially unfair system.

It is for this reason that the project of the hero teachers portrayed in films may be seen, as I have suggested, as a fundamentally conservative one. Not only is the hero teacher, as Mitchell and Weber (1996) and Harris and Jarvis (2000) have pointed out, presented as working alone – that is, as opting out of any attempt to change the social conditions within which teachers as a body of professionals work – but the solutions they offer their students to social problems are at the level of individual experience and are dependent on the interrelations of a very small group of people (often, one teacher and one pupil). That is to say, they suggest a route out of the problem as experienced rather than an attack on the problem itself: we might say, a conservatively *symptomatic* rather than socialistically *causal* reading of and response to the issues. (Indeed, as Harris and Jarvis (2000, p. 2) suggest, the systemic problems themselves are effectively denied through another characteristic of the filmic hero or saviour teacher, which is that – in contrast with the lived world, where we are obliged to be accommodatingly responsive to the demands of test and examination syllabuses, to operate within the constraints of class size and lesson duration, and to balance and juggle our professional lives with our often very full and complex social lives – 'the good teacher has an infinite amount of time to spend on individual students'.) Correspondingly, the charismatic, individualistic *teacher* can, often, only succeed in relation to motivating individual *learners* (or local groups of learners) to 'do their own thing', just as, pedagogically, they can only succeed at all if the conditions for them to exercise and display their 'charismatic qualities' are (re)produced in the classroom – essentially (since it is difficult to preside charismatically over, for example, small-group work) conditions in which the acceptable pedagogies are teacher-centred and in which, for all their allegiance to empowerment or power-sharing, the control over classroom content is predominantly the teacher's, and the teacher's is the dominant (perhaps domina*ting*) classroom voice.

Charisma, curriculum and fetishisation: Mr Keating

Fortunately, most student teachers tend to take filmic representations of good teaching with a large pinch of salt, quickly realising that the contexts within which Hollywood teachers operate bear little or no relation to the contexts within which they are working themselves (Dalton 1999). They are in most cases very aware, for example, that teachers like Ms Johnson and Mr Thackeray, despite the horrendous chaos and disrespect that greet them on their arrival in the classroom, rely for their success on the remarkable compliance of their students, who very quickly adopt the conversational mode and find some motivation to learn – even those students who at first are particularly opposed to authority. (Indeed, a key feature of such films is that the class's troublemaking 'ringleader' eventually comes round to the teacher's side, making life much easier for the teacher by acting as a kind of pedagogical lieutenant.) As one student teacher in the *Autobiography Project* was to observe, just as the extreme behaviour of the students in these films is a gross exaggeration of what student teachers would normally expect to find even in challenging inner-city classrooms, so the subsequent levels of student compliance and transformation are also greatly exaggerated. It is worth reminding ourselves, too, that filmic and other media representations of teachers can be – and often are – used on pre-service courses such as the PGCE as part of the teaching material, in ways that Greene describes as 'informed confrontation' (Greene 1988; see also Harris and Jarvis 2000): that is, images such as those presented in films like *To Sir, With Love* and *Dangerous Minds* may be criticised and deconstructed in the PGCE seminar room, and consideration given, perhaps, to other models of good teaching that may be conspicuously absent from such media representations.

Discussions with student teachers reveal, however, that some filmic representations of charismatic teachers are taken considerably more seriously than others. This is indicated in the testimony of the student already quoted, for whom the teacher in *Stand and Deliver* proved inspirational, and it is also true, for many teachers, of the more widely known film starring Robin Williams, *Dead Poets Society*.

Dead Poets Society presents us with another hero teacher, the character played by Robin Williams: Mr Keating. Mr Keating is different in some key respects from representations in other films, and does not conform quite so neatly to the set of characteristics identified by Mitchell and Weber. Though new to the school at which he is teaching, for example, he is not new to teaching and there is no sense that he has entered the profession accidentally. He is also working not at a tough, inner-city State school, but at an exclusive boys' public school in which the students' school and (during term-time, at least) after-school lives are, broadly speaking, lived out under the same roof. He is, furthermore, saving his students not so much from their apathy, hostility and underachievement as from a straitjacketing curriculum which, although it will no doubt prepare them more than adequately for the privileged social positions already lying in wait for them, will do so at the intolerable cost of their creativity, their individuality and their *joie de vivre*.

Despite these differences, Mr Keating shares many characteristics with Ms Johnson and Mr Thackeray. He is represented, for example, as *something* of an outsider, in that he is a new teacher at the school in which the action of the film is located. His methods, too, are unconventional, particularly when measured against the very conventional curriculum of the school and the traditional pedagogies of the other teachers. He also seeks to liberate his students by defying – and effectively encouraging them to defy – the official school rules and curriculum, and by encouraging them to carry their learning outside the school gates as well as outside the academic-cognitive (into the affective) domain, through the resurrection of the 'Dead Poets Society'. ('Membership' of this society involves the students escaping the confines of the school walls to enjoy symbolic freedom – in the company of some local young women – through the pleasure of reading and sharing poetry for pleasure's rather than academic necessity's sake at an undisclosed outdoor site in the surrounding countryside.) As in other movies involving hero teachers, Mr Keating's encouragement of such activities leads to the odd catastrophe along the way – most notably the suicide of a boy whose parents are adamantly opposed to his desire to initiate an acting career through performing in the school play. Despite this, Mr Keating secures the undying love of his students, illustrated in a dramatic scene at the end of the film, in which, improbably, his charges stage a symbolic demonstration of solidarity and resistance in front of the head-teacher by standing on their desks, Spartacus-like, one after the other and calling out 'Captain, my captain!' when Mr Keating, sacked from the school as a result of his subversive behaviour, returns to the classroom to collect his books.

On the face of it, *Dead Poets Society* may be seen to stand in opposition to fixed, backward-looking curricula, inviting us to favour one that is more relevant, student-centred, creative and empowering – as is suggested in the following exchange between the sympathetically portrayed Mr Keating and a fellow teacher:

Nolan: But John, the curriculum here is set. It's proven. It works. If you question it, what's to prevent [the boys] from doing the same?

Keating: I always thought the idea of education was to learn to think for yourself.

Nolan: At these boys' age? Not on your life. Tradition, John. Discipline. Prepare them for college, and the rest will take care of itself.

Closer inspection, however, reveals that the alternative curriculum we are being invited to support is not very much of an alternative at all. Just as Ms Johnson continues to ram ennobling song lyrics down her students' throats, Mr Keating's answer to his students' bombardment with Latin, maths and science is to bombard them with the canon of English-speaking poets. Furthermore, his emphasis on the development of the *individual* is embedded within a school culture that, for all its piousness about traditional values and teamwork, is fundamentally about the business of producing individual operators who will be fit to compete with one another in the domestic marketplace and with competitors in other countries in the global marketplace. While we may have sympathy for Mr Keating's rejection of a mechanical, fetishistic approach to the analysis and 'grading' of poetry during the course of his first lesson with the boys whose progress the film charts, we may be less inclined to support his own fetishisation of poetry within the discourse of 'soul-food' and imagination, or his own support of individualism in favour of, say, collective action or the development of a social conscience. When Mr Keating exhorts his class to 'seize the day', it is, as with Mr Thackeray's (somewhat less extravagant) exhortation, an invitation to get out of life what they can *for themselves* rather than envisioning and pursuing a wider political agenda:

> I stand upon my desk to remind myself that we must constantly look at things in a different way. See, the world looks very different from up here. You don't believe me? Come: see for yourselves. Come on. Come on. Just when you think you know something you have to look at it another way. Even though it might seem silly or wrong, you must try. Now, when you read don't just consider what the author thinks. Consider what you think. Boys, you must strive to find your own voice because the longer you wait to begin the less likely you are to find it at all. Thoreau said: 'Most men lead lives of quiet desperation.' Don't be resigned to that.

We might say that Mr Keating's highly individualistic teaching style, which repeatedly draws attention to his classroom persona as much as – perhaps more than – to the substance of his lessons (indeed, in the film Mr Keating is presented almost *as* the substance of his own lessons), supports a pedagogic agenda aimed essentially at the fulfilment of the individual student. Similarly, his treatment of the inherited curriculum confines its critical edge to the manner in which the curriculum is 'covered' rather than to the curriculum itself. In this regard, his vitriolic – and, of course, wholly appropriate – rejection of an old-fashioned literary criticism that removes the 'soul' from poetry, reducing its study to a pseudo-scientific enterprise, is replaced by an essentialist, aesthetic approach to literature that totally accepts the curricular *selections* of poets and poetry (essentially, the work of white, dead males), that makes no attempt to extend the boundaries within which literature is recognised and inscribed (by, for example, encouraging the boys to study modern or black literature), and that appears to adopt a 'Leavisite' approach to the study of literature in which 'greatness' is perceived to lie within the text under study, in which the wider social and cultural contexts within which the work was produced are ignored as irrelevant, and which renders the central task of literature study that of 'discovering' the elements of a text that give it its 'greatness'/worthiness to be an object of study and then describing these elements, and how they work, in writing to an academic audience.

Those of us who believe that the 'greatness' or indeed the 'value' of a text does not lie within the text itself but is, rather, invested *in* the text by people who engage with it (that is to say, as I have suggested elsewhere, it is 'fetishised' (Moore 1998a)) may see a pattern emerging in Mr Keating's teaching, in which essentialism, individualism, romanticism and fetishisation are core elements: in other words, a 'charismatic', 'rebellious', 'outsider' teacher encourages the individual's development *of* their 'individuality' through the appreciation of a selection of poetry deemed to possess intrinsic, 'therapeutic' and emancipatory qualities and through special emphasis on the 'rebellious' qualities of the writers who produced it (see Mr Keating's reference to Thoreau, above). The teacher, just like the object of study, is judged according to 'internal' personal 'qualities' – according to what he 'is' rather than what he does. In terms of what he 'achieves' – for his students – his own strong sense of self is mirrored by his students' self-centred achievement of attaining (in this case) some measure of personal freedom in a world in which individual freedom (the watchword of conservative politics) is configured as both laudable and marginalised.

The charismatic teacher: issues of empowerment

Given its nature, it is not difficult to see how, paradoxically, the charismatic subject both prioritises the idiosyncratic and negates it: prioritises it by emphasising the personal attributes of the good teacher; negates it by telling teachers that those attributes exist 'within' some practitioners only and cannot be truly replicated, only 'mimicked'. Herein lies the particular form of essentialism or positivism peculiar to the charismatic subject discourse. On the one hand, the discourse argues that teachers are 'made' (i.e. by God or within the womb), not taught – that the exceptional or 'gifted' teacher owes their success to personality traits that are, as it were, within the person's 'essence'; on the other, it advises other teachers – the mere mortals – that their own essence is not up to the task and, presumably, never can be, precisely because the essence is that which we are born with – that 'untouchable', immutable core that *is* 'us'. Faced with such a scenario, the would-be teacher is faced with two choices: either give up all hope of trying to be a charismatic (i.e. exceptional) teacher, or try to emulate a charismatic teacher – even a composite of charismatic teachers – from one's experience in the hope of becoming not them but as *like them* as possible – a course which, our experience suggests, is as likely to lead to failure, professional self-loathing and despair as it is to improved practice.

The charismatic discourse has parallel difficulties, however, for the *learner*, whose initial sense of 'empowerment' at the hands of the charismatic teacher may also prove to be mere illusion. While it is the purpose of this book to consider pedagogic and educational discourses rather than to explore different teaching 'styles' and how they work in practice, the following observations of one PGCE student illustrate both the positive and the negative capabilities of the charismatic subject discourse when it does manifest itself in classroom practice, as well as offering a way into understanding and critiquing the discourse more fully:

> We had a history teacher – Mr Harland. He was almost like a god to us: you know, from the minute he came through the door . . . he just had this 'presence'. He was SO enthusiastic. He just somehow seemed to make the subject come alive, like it had never done for us before. It was just his amazing enthusiasm . . . and love for his subject. And all the different stories he had, that he could tell you – really making it come alive. . . . He really got you actually WANTING to go home and read about the stuff – and go to the library and research things on your own. He was really the one that got me to apply to do history at university.
>
> *But you got an English degree . . .*
>
> Yeah, I know. It was a great shame, really. I went right off the subject during my first year, and I ended up re-applying to do English. It [history] just wasn't the same subject. And the style of teaching just didn't suit me.
>
> *What sort of style was that, then?*
>
> Lectures . . . Mainly . . . And very issues-based, when I suppose what I was really interested in was the stories – which is probably why I ended up doing English!
>   (John: PGCE English student, *Autobiography Project*, in interview)

It is by no means a rarity for university students to switch courses, or to discover huge and unpalatable gaps between a subject as it looks and is taught pre- and post-university entrance. Two particularly interesting points to emerge from John's testimony, however, are (1) that his 'enthusiastic', story-telling, 'godlike' teacher was clearly able to enthuse and 'inspire' him to want to go out and study independently – something that had not happened to John before, either in this subject or (as it transpired later on in discussion) in any other school subject, including his eventual specialism,

English; (2) that there was, however, a *temporary* aspect to this independence of study – that is, it did not survive the split between John and his teacher once John had left school. John's subsequent observations rather underscored this difficulty, highlighting an unfortunate symbiosis between teacher and learner rather than a genuine teacher-assisted *empowerment* of the learner.

This issue of the teacher–student relationship itself raises another concern related to the charismatic mode of teaching, linked to the questions: Was the historical research John carried out independently *useful* to him as well as being diversionary? And to what extent had he been cast in the role of the child wanting to please a *parent*, providing the required response for a teacher who perhaps required, in turn, the 'love' of a surrogate child? This particular characteristic of the charismatic subject mode, touched upon by Boler (1999) and by Harris and Jarvis (2000), will be returned to when we consider reflexivity and notions of 'identification' in Chapter 7. For now, the following sentiments, expressed by John a little later on in the same interview, are offered merely as food for thought:

> In a way, I think we really wanted to do the study for *him* [Mr Harland] – which is kind of the motivation I'd like to instil in my pupils in English.
>
> *Not to want to do it for themselves, then?*
>
> Oh, yeah, of course, that too. But maybe that comes later?

Pros and cons of the charismatic subject discourse

If the notion of the charismatic subject, with its over-reliance on 'personality' and its frequent under-reliance on technique, is potentially a very dangerous one for the student teacher, this is not to say that it should be rejected totally or in all its parts. Indeed, the notion of the charismatic teacher has much to recommend it. For one thing, it offers, as was suggested at the start of this chapter, important checks and balances to other dominant discourses related to technicism, mechanism and performativity that currently threaten to colonise teaching philosophy and practice, as well as to the universalising tendencies and perspectives associated with these discourses. With reference to this latter point, it specifically maintains the presence of idiosyncratic and contingent issues and perspectives (Maguire 1995; Moore 1999b) in considerations of classroom practice, emphasising such matters (somewhat marginalised in these other discourses as currently configured in Britain) as teacher flexibility, creativity, adaptability and sensitivity; pupil difference; and the variable contexts of educational experience, including inconsistencies in local needs and situations which may be related to socio-economic and cultural circumstances.

On the other hand, there are clearly difficulties with the notion of the charismatic subject, especially when it is given discursive status (cf. Chapter 2 above): that is to say, when it is allowed to become the single or dominant lens through which practice and circumstances are understood and responded to. These difficulties include:

- a capacity – perhaps a tendency – of the approach to mystify teaching, putting it beyond the reach of the collective skills, strategies and competences that the teacher might be expected to learn or to develop;
- an over-concern with one's own performance and 'high-profile' personal attributes rather than with the progress and development of one's students;
- a devaluing or marginalisation of such key pedagogical concerns as careful planning, constructive feedback and differentiation;
- a coercion to *emulation*, often leading practitioners to place unreasonable demands on themselves and to embed such demands within an unrealistic and unrealisable pedagogical project;
- an over-emphasis on the 'unified', morally responsible individual which serves to deflect attention away from the wider socio-cultural circumstances, including the socio-economic inequalities, within which schooling is located and which may support a certain 'de-politicisation' of the teacher;
- an unhelpful separation of what are sometimes called (misleadingly, perhaps) the 'practicalities' of teaching (the preparation, the selection of appropriate materials, the provision of constructive and relevant feedback and so on) from the 'practice' (the ways in which prepared lessons are operationalised, the manner in which feedback is presented and responded to and so on);
- a reluctance or inability (on the part of more experienced teachers wedded to the discourse) to provide teachers newer to the profession with constructive, practical advice on how to develop their own practice.

The following two extracts from case studies conducted as part of the *Autobiography Project* illustrate the impact of some of these difficulties on student teachers. Both are related to student teachers who had first identified and then begun to struggle with problems of classroom 'discipline'. As we all know, classroom discipline – or 'the problem of control' (Goodman 1988, p. 124) – is one of the most difficult aspects of teaching practice for any student teacher, that which is probably most feared prior to the event and most worried about during it: 'Will my pupils do what I want them to do?', the student asks. 'Or will they, regardless of everything I have learned about classroom management, attempt to operationalise their own agendas?' Observations and interviews from the *Autobiography Project* indicated that for many students in difficulty it was precisely the fact that their pupils were not doing what was being asked or demanded of them that was at the heart of their difficulties – *and*, it is important to add, whose misinterpretation lay at the heart of their inability to deal with the problem.

It often appeared to such students that, despite all their efforts, all their perceived personal qualities, all their references to lists of competences and other course documentation, all their lecture and seminar notes, all the advice of their school- and college-based tutors, their pupils simply refused to do what they asked of them. The student teacher was, to use Lacan's terminology (1979), reduced to the role of the 'impotent master' (*sic*): possessing all the sanctions at their disposal, they were still unable to use them to the required effect.

For most student teachers in this situation, as was borne out during the course of our subsequent *Reflective Practice Project*, the reaction to this difficulty is constructive and the problem is resolved, further advice being sought out and responded to wherever and whenever it is available. For the 'student in danger of failing', however, this may just be the beginning of the story. Not unusually, such students experience a far more negative reaction to the communicative breakdown, often leading to an apparent impasse and very deeply felt anxiety. In this situation, the student teacher may initially seek to apportion *blame* as a way of making sense of what is happening, in so doing pathologising their pupils, their teaching-practice school, their course, their tutors and eventually, almost certainly, themselves: a situation which may lead them to a belief – sometimes retrievable, sometimes terminal – that they will never make a satisfactory teacher, let alone a good one, no matter how hard they strive. While they may be aware of and hold partially responsible the impact of external social conditions on what takes place in the classroom, this recognition is often perceived fatalistically rather than as something which must be met as a challenge, along the lines (to quote one student teacher on the *Autobiography Project* who found herself in just such a situation):

> The problems are just too great for *me* to deal with. . . . *I'm* just not up to it. I admire people who are – good luck to them, they're saints – but *I just don't feel I've got what it takes.*
>
> (Ted: student teacher, *Autobiography Project*, my italics)

The first of the two specific examples I want to refer to by way of illustration and elementary analysis of this difficulty concerns a young student who had manoeuvred himself into a bizarre situation in which he had locked horns with a particularly difficult class of 12-year-olds with whom he saw himself engaged in a battle of wills. Unprepared to lose this battle, or to agree to any kind of compromise settlement, he attempted to solve the class's refusing to listen to his instructions, drifting off task, walking around the room and generally disrespecting what he referred to as his 'authority' by telling both the class and his tutors:

> I am not even going to attempt to teach this class until I have everyone's absolute attention.

Lesson after lesson had subsequently degenerated into his standing at the front of the class loudly and aggressively chastising individual pupils every time they showed signs of being inattentive: an activity quickly colonised as a game by the students themselves, who took it in turns to be mildly disruptive in ways that did not merit their being ejected from the room or placed on report but that would succeed in their own aim of making the teacher ever more angry and of indefinitely postponing any possibility of engaging in serious work. The student teacher, meanwhile, appeared unable or unwilling to accept his tutors' advice to seek to attract the pupils' attention *through* the substance of the lessons (or that this might be a gradual process which would not yield instant results of the kind he required), simply because '*discipline*' – essentially, the triumph of one will over others – had, for him, replaced *learning* as the most important element of classroom interaction. This prospective teacher had – for reasons, we suspected, partly to do with his own personal circumstances and emotional needs at the time – configured his classroom task not, initially, as a pedagogic one but rather as a social or cultural one, in which a certain code or order that had apparently broken down needed to be restored: a 'normality' had to be resurrected before meaningful classroom (inter)action was *possible*. This entailed a refusal to adopt pedagogic strategies in preference to an ultimately doomed attempt to impose a version of the parent–child relationship, replete with respect, obedience and affection (in the direction *from* child *to* adult) in his classroom, linked to an inevitable sense of despair and personal worthlessness that grew deeper – yet simultaneously rendered the faulty approach ever more firmly entrenched – with each failed attempt.

The second illustrative example concerns a young student teacher already referred to, who, even before embarking on her extended teaching practice, had been experiencing difficulties and confusions related to the 'cacophony of calls' referred to in the previous two chapters. This student, who came from a white, financially secure working-class family and who was the first member of that family to attend university and to seek to enter the teaching profession, had chosen, chiefly for financial reasons, to live at her parents' home during the course of her pre-service (PGCE) course specialising in the teaching of high-school English. The course itself espoused what might be called liberal attitudes and approaches to teaching and schooling, advocating, for example, the benefits of pupil–pupil interaction and negotiated codes and rules for classroom conduct. The student teacher's family, however, had very different views as to what constituted appropriate classroom behaviour and pedagogy, and the young woman had complained of the stress caused at the end of each day when she was effectively interrogated and cajoled by family members who told her not to listen to the 'soft left-wing nonsense' that was being 'crammed into her head at college' and that children needed to have basic information and skills crammed into *their* heads through silent, individualised activity within a classroom context of zero tolerance.

During her teaching practice, the student became a cause for concern, and the following assessment was written by the tutor working with her on the *Autobiography Project* at the end of the teaching practice after the student had, to a satisfactory degree, resolved her difficulties:

> There came a point when the student's [college- and school-based] tutors came into the classroom to observe some lessons. In contradiction to the student's view that she had tried everything and that nothing worked, the tutors' impression was that the student had left many avenues unexplored, and many strategies untested. In contradiction of the student's assessment that the pupils were inherently unpleasant and hostile, the tutors both went on to witness the same pupils responding positively to other teachers, including student teachers and newly-qualified teachers. Furthermore, the student's own behaviour seemed oddly and inappropriately confrontational, and her expectations of her classes' [non-academic] behaviour unreasonable. After much discussion with the student, the tutors concurred that this student had reached an impasse, in which she was personalising the communicative break-downs in her classes while simultaneously remaining impervious to advice. The student expressed a feeling of being caught up in a 'battle of wills' or personalities, in which she had convinced herself both of her own irremediable inadequacy and of a fundamental impossibility in the situation she was in – this congruence of negative feelings being expressed in her mantra-like repetitions 'I just can't teach these kids' and 'These kids are unteachable.'
>
> (See also Moore and Atkinson 1998, pp. 172–3)

This kind of response underlines a particular difficulty of the charismatic subject approach, in that the student's response is one in which, to quote Jenkins (1992, p. 8) '[r]ather than blaming the "objective order" for their disadvantage, [subjects] fall back on their own inadequacies as the explanation of their distress'. Such an analysis, invoked by Bourdieu (1979) as a way of explaining why and how it is that suppressed subjects do not rise up more readily to challenge unequal socio-economic arrangements (see also Moore 2000), is relevant in looking at relatively successful teachers for whom charisma is the dominating principle as well as those for whom it has contributed to failure. Just as the failing student may recognise external factors as contributory elements to classroom difficulties but may respond to them negatively in terms of personal inadequacy, so the more successful 'charismatically inclined' teacher (successful, that is, in terms of capturing and sustaining the interest and enthusiasm of their classes) may be aware of such circumstances but may, through configuring themselves as the saviour or hero teacher, believe that they can *overcome* such difficulties *on behalf of their particular pupils* without needing to challenge the causal circumstances more directly. This is precisely the orientation of Ms Johnson in *Dangerous Minds*, and of a small number of students in our *Reflective Practice* project who spoke, in different ways, of wanting to 'rescue' young people from the impoverished backgrounds from which they came but were less sure about working, through the education system, to combat the existence of those backgrounds or the conditions in which they flourish.

The communicative teacher

As suggested at the start of this chapter, the difficulties inherent in the charismatic subject discourse are partly overcome if we focus on charisma less as some mysterious, innate 'quality' and more on why it is that subjects are perceived *as* charismatic (why, for example, some pupils think that some teachers are more worth listening to and more deserving of their respect than others); that is to say, on 'charisma' as an *effect* rather than an essence, and therefore something that can be achieved through the pursuit or development of something or some things other.

In this regard, and inasmuch as the charismatic subject foregrounds one essential ingredient of successful teaching – the ability to communicate clearly, purposefully, sensitively, responsively and interestingly with groups of individuals with very different psychological make-ups and from many different cultural backgrounds – a more useful concept than that of the 'charismatic' teacher might be that of the *communicative* teacher.

The communicative teacher relies not so much on some difficult-to-define 'personality' as on more easily recognised and more readily acquired communication and presentational *skills* which themselves can be referenced to a particular set of *understandings* as to how learning takes place and what the pedagogic enterprise should consequently entail. To quote Broadfoot (2000) on this matter, the communicative teacher might continue to perceive education, despite the universalising efforts of recent government policy in England and Wales, as 'as much emotional as intellectual' (2000, p. 7) and as:

> an emancipatory activity, an activity which, if it is to be worthy of the name, is experienced by learners as something personal and profound; something that meshes with their personal ambitions and interests; something that equips them to engage critically and productively with the world.
>
> (ibid., p. 2)

The communicative teacher, bent on pursuing such an educational career, will not only be able to decentre sufficiently to be understood by the range of students in any class, but be sensitive to the range of needs in the classroom and will work at and plan effective communication strategies

both before lessons (in the planning stage) and after lessons (in the evaluative stage). Additionally, the teacher will think carefully about how they
'self-present' – an aspect of their work which might include such issues as:

- how to position oneself physically, linguistically and relationally in the
  classroom;
- how to develop and display a genuine interest in what one's students
  have to say;
- knowing when to talk, when to listen and when to interrupt;
- being appropriately approachable, courteous and firm;
- self-presenting as engaged in a joint learning experience rather than as
  the font of all wisdom.

If this sounds like an easy task, it is not meant to. To adopt a passage of
Medgyes' – out of context, perhaps, but equally relevant here –

> the communicative classroom requires a teacher of extraordinary abil-
> ities: a multi-dimensional, high-tech, Wizard-of-Oz-like superperson –
> yet of flesh and blood. He or she must be confident without being con-
> ceited, judicious without being judgmental, ingenious without being
> unbridled, technically skilled without being pedantic, far-sighted with-
> out being far-fetched, down-to-earth without being earth-bound, inquir-
> ing without being inquisitive.
>
> (1990, p. 104)

If developing as a communicative teacher requires a considerable degree
of art and craft, improvement – often, very rapid and considerable improvement – is at least attainable. Seeking to 'achieve charisma' as a direct goal
may, on the other hand, not be.

4 The training discourse – competent craftspersons

A well considered and carefully arranged scheme of work is invaluable in school . . . it confines the attention to one thing at once, prevents undue digressions, and settles the limits within which the teacher has to accomplish each section of his instruction; it has a moral value from the encouragement it gives to habits of order, steadiness, and attention to duty at fixed periods.

(Landon 1886, p. 232)

I hadn't realised how much planning went into things – how organised you had to be. . . . My assumption [as a pupil] was that the teachers were just really clever. I had no understanding of the hours and hours of preparation and marking in evenings and weekends that had gone into it.

(Felicia: student teacher, *Reflective Practice Project*)

Children soon accommodate themselves to a regular discipline, just as they do to a law of nature. They may kick at it at first, but, if it be not unreasonable in its demands, and if it be regularly maintained, they will fall in with it as an inevitable condition of things which it is useless to resist.

(National Society 1879, p. 174)

The competent craftsperson: a word on contexts

I have already made the point that the charismatic subject discourse is much stronger in the 'popular domain' than it is as a presence on courses of initial and continuing teacher education. Such courses have, rather, tended to emphasise either the theoretical aspects of teaching and their relation to practice (what might be called the notion of the teacher as expert) or – more recently – the discrete *skills* of teaching, in what has come to be known as the *competences* discourse (Moore 1999b).

As Wolf (1995, p. 1) points out, '"competence" and "competencies" are vexed terms, over whose definitions acres of print continue to be expended'. Wolf offers her own definition of competence-based *assessment*, in terms of its focus on outcomes and demonstrable achievement in a context of clarity and transparency. I will not attempt to add either to this definition or to the acreage of print to which Wolf refers. It is sufficient to say that when I refer to competences, which, within the terms of the discourse I am writing about, is conflated with competenc*ies*, I refer to the skills that student teachers are expected to acquire, to develop to a particular standard and to display (partly for assessment purposes), and that are to be found in lists and elaborations of competences and standards currently produced in Britain and elsewhere for use on (in this case) courses of initial teacher education and training. As I shall argue, these lists of competences and standards have the capacity to offer a more open and honest account to student teachers of the measures against which they will be judged to have succeeded or failed: that is to say, they have an assessment function linked to transparency. They also, however, have a curricular function, establishing parameters for what should – and consequently can be – 'covered' during the course of a one-year programme of study.

I have already suggested that the notion of the 'competent teacher' or 'competent craftsperson' has its roots in books of practical advice for teachers on such matters as controlling awkward classes and individuals, making sure that lessons are interesting, accessible and well thought out, planning for and assessing students' work, and working constructively with colleagues (see, for instance, Marland 1975; Cohen and Manion 1977; Stephens and Crawley 1994) – books whose proliferation may itself be linked to what Alexander (1984) has described as changes in the profession in which primary-school teachers in particular are no longer expected to be generalists responsible for providing a challenging curriculum that draws principally on their existing strengths, knowledge and expertise, but are required to be specialists in a number of specified subject areas, most recently to enable the operationalisation of a national curriculum.

The competent craftsperson has also, however, been linked – often, rather less positively – to wider models of teaching and learning, as well as to past and present models and vogues in educational assessment. Smyth, for example, has located the competenc(i)es discourse in teacher education within a wider scenario in which:

> teaching is often being delimited and deskilled by overly-stringent impositions of standardized testing and accountability procedures, and by reductions in the tasks of teaching in many places to instilling basic competencies in young people.
>
> (1995, p. viii)

In their critique of the competences discourse in relation to further education, Jones and Moore (1995) have also traced the impact of competence-related changes in student education and assessment on the pedagogic practices – and indeed the working conditions – of the teachers of such students, situating the competences discourse unequivocally in opposition to less prescriptive, more trusting models of teaching and learning:

> The impact of competency [*sic*] upon the Further Education sector (where the influence is most pronounced) has involved a major restructuring of the professional culture, working practices, college management styles and conditions of service that has overturned the liberal educational, technical and craft traditions in that sector.
>
> (1995, p. 86)

Ball (1999) has been equally critical of the impact of the competences discourse on compulsory education, relating this to companion discourses of managerialism and anti-intellectualism and to 'exercises in performativity' such as school inspections and 'league tables' of test and examination scores:

> Teachers are inscribed in these exercises in performativity through the diligence with which they attempt to fulfil the new (and sometimes irreconcilable) imperatives of competition and target-achievement. . . . The humanistic commitments of the substantive professional – the service ethic – are replaced by the teleological promiscuity of the technical professional – the manager. This shift in teacher consciousness and identity is underpinned and ramified by the introduction in teacher preparation of new forms of de-intellectualised, competence-based training.
>
> (p. 13)

Such a view of the competenc(i)es discourse tends to locate the *competent craftsperson* within latter-day Enlightenment discourses in which the influence of science as the great, dispassionate answerer and measurer has spread from the physical to the social world – including, centrally, the world of formal education – where it promotes 'rank ordering according to normative criteria' (Hartley 1997, p. 75) and finds a ready companion in 'discourses of explicit obedience' (Boler 1999, p. 45).

Regardless of whether we perceive the growth of the competences discourse in this negative way or adopt a more positive view – one based, for example, on the notion that listing competences offers practical help to practitioners, makes explicit to them the criteria by which they will be assessed, and introduces a new layer of accountability into teacher education and training – there is no doubt that, despite a persistent recognition that teaching 'in many of its aspects . . . is expressive and emergent, intuitive and flexible, spontaneous and emotional' (Woods 1996, p. 6), the competences model of teaching has become a – perhaps the – dominant discourse in initial teacher education, first in the USA and more recently, in a slightly but significantly altered guise, in England and Wales since the 1990s.

In the case of England and Wales, this domination has coincided with a shift away from an approach to teacher education in which teacher educators enjoyed a considerable degree of autonomy in designing and teaching their courses (Bernstein 1996, p. 70) to one of increasing direction and surveillance on the part of central government. Arguably, a defining moment in this shift occurred in 1992, when the discourse had *legitimation* bestowed upon it with the full force of the British law through a circular dispatched by the Council for the Accreditation of Teacher Education (CATE) in the September of that year to all higher education institutions in England and Wales providing courses of initial teacher education. This circular laid out the basic requirements for all such courses clearly and unambiguously in the terms of the competences discourse, as the following extract indicates:

> The main objective of all courses of initial training is to enable students to become competent teachers who can establish effective working relationships with pupils. To do so, they will need to be knowledgeable in their subjects, to understand how pupils learn, and to acquire teaching skills. . . . It is recognised that . . . the acquisition of competences is not the totality of training [and] each competence is not a discrete unit but one of many whose sum makes for a confident start in teaching.
>
> (1992, p. 9)

Emphasis in this circular was placed on key areas of competence that were to become teaching priorities on pre-service courses for the next six years: 'subject knowledge', 'class management' and 'assessment and recording of pupils' progress'. Since the publication of '9/92', the Council for the Accreditation of Teacher Education in England and Wales (CATE) has been replaced by the Teacher Training Agency (TTA), and the word 'competences' has in turn been superseded by the more politically appealing 'standards'. I want to suggest that these changes, however, have represented not a break from the later pronouncements of CATE, but rather a natural progression and development of them which continues to identify and prioritise discrete, universal skills (TTA 1998: see, too, DfEE 1997b). In this light we may discern in the competences discourse a shift of emphasis away from the notion of teacher *education* traditionally favoured by universities and teachers (NUT 1976; Institute of Education 1972; Alexander *et al.* 1984; Popkewitz 1987) towards one of '*training*' (Ball 1999), which had always been more popular in the official documentation (see, for instance, DES 1981; Allen 1994). This shift of emphasis may be seen to place less importance on – and to allow for more limited coverage of – matters of teaching and learning *theory* and – arguably – considered *reflection* on developing practice, and a correspondingly greater emphasis on the 'practicalities' of life in the classroom and the school.

Positives of the competent craftsperson discourse: criteria-sharing and transparency

Much of what is contained within the competent craftsperson discourse may be seen to make relatively uncontentious good sense, and it is important to note that the development of profiles of competence as a way of structuring pre-service courses for teachers and assessments of student teachers' capabilities were widespread in education departments at institutions of higher education long before they were formally and universally imposed by central government. The following account of the development of such a profile at one such institution indicates that although lists of competences may have subsequently attached themselves to more technicist, mechanistic and performance-related educational discourses, other sources included a desire on the part of many teacher educators for greater transparency in terms of accounting for and sharing the criteria by which student teachers would be assessed; for moving towards more structured curricula in order for student teachers to have a better understanding of how the elements of their course fitted together; and for providing greater opportunities for students to 'own' their courses through self-monitoring their development against the competence criteria:

> In common with most such systems, our own Profile had, from the outset, two separate but related functions, that we associated with perceived needs within the institution rather than with explicit diktats from without. The first of these arose from a desire to give students a set of common strategies, broad approaches and areas of knowledge and understanding that would be of use to them in their various teaching activities when a more experienced colleague was not immediately available to help them: that is to say, a curricular function that was simultaneously instructional and advisory. The second function arose from a belief that, on the grounds of fairness, of equality of opportunity, and of enabling our students to do their best, it was necessary formally and unambiguously to share with them the criteria by which they were being assessed: that is to say, an essentially informative function.
>
> (Cited in Moore 1996, p. 202)

Underpinning the development of these profiles was a belief that teachers do need to have sufficient subject knowledge to teach their students effectively, that they do need to be effective planners and classroom managers, and that a high level of personal organisation and preparedness is one of the principal requirements of good classroom teaching – elements arguably missing from the charismatic subject discourse, where priority tends to be given to the practitioner's confidence, enthusiasm and 'star quality'. An additional rationale, however, often cited by teacher educators at the institution referred to in the above example, was that the development of a notion of the teacher as the competent possessor and practiser of learnable skills helped to 'demystify' the teaching process in a way that other discourses, like the charismatic subject discourse, do not (Woods 1996, p. 19). Experience suggests that such a demystification does, indeed, often provide for more confident and more effective teachers, as in the case of the student quoted at the start of this chapter, for whom the realisation that teaching involved the acquisition and development of learnable skills gave both increased clarity and increased optimism in terms of her pedagogic project.

The following is an example of how this kind of approach sometimes looks in the official documentation. It also offers a further illustration of the difference between the competences discourse and that of the charismatic subject: the former offers clear, if yet to be developed, guidelines and strategies while the latter relies more on the development of the force and strength of an equally vaguely defined 'personality':

> For all courses, those to be awarded Qualified Teacher Status must, when assessed, demonstrate that they . . . use teaching methods which sustain the momentum of pupils' work and keep all pupils engaged through . . . matching the approaches used to the subject matter and the pupils being taught; . . . structuring information well, including outlining content and aims, signalling transitions and summarising key points as the lesson progresses; . . . clear presentation of content around a set of key issues, using appropriate subject-specific vocabulary and well chosen illustrations and examples; . . . clear instruction and demonstration, and accurate well-paced explanation.
>
> (DfEE 1998, p. 13)

When perceived and approached in this way, the lists of competences, more recently redefined as 'standards', provided by the Office for Standards in Education (Ofsted) and the Teacher Training Agency (TTA) for student teachers via their course tutors, may be seen as helpful descriptors of the qualities that all good teachers need to have, as well as providing a detailed set of criteria by which teachers know that they will be assessed. This latter function, which is perhaps less discussed in debates about competences, replaces often very vague and woolly assessment criteria that provided little external support for student teachers who were doing badly but who could not fully understand why. The provision of lists of competences may thus be viewed as an advance in the areas of teacher entitlement, teacher access and equality of opportunity. In the case of national lists of competences, it may also be seen as a way of ensuring that student teachers are likely to cover the same ground and be assessed against the same criteria regardless of where they undertake their studentship.

To summarise some of the more positive characteristics and anticipated outcomes of a competence-based approach to initial teacher education when it is operated effectively, sensitively and with some degree of subtlety, we might suggest that it offers:

- encouragement and support for teacher educators and student teachers in more effective monitoring and assessment of their own and their students' work;
- the development of better understandings, leading to more effective practice, of the circular relationship between planning, outcomes and evaluation, whereby the success or failure of previous planning feeds constructively and critically into future planning;
- a greater emphasis on the teacher's need to keep up to date with developments in subject knowledge and not to over-rely on knowledge gleaned during their own previous educational experience;
- a sharper focus on the purposes of individual lessons and sequences of lessons, in terms of both whole-class and individual students' development, including a more thoughtful approach to target-setting;
- an insistence on teachers' adopting a wide range of teaching strategies and materials in order to achieve stated aims, rather than being over-reliant (as can more readily happen within the charismatic discourse) on a narrow range of strategies and materials including the teacher's own front-of-class performance.

There are, however, serious difficulties with the competences approach to teacher education, particularly (and perhaps *when*) the approach becomes a dominant discourse, as it certainly has in England and Wales at the time of writing. Sadly, these disadvantages far outweigh and to a considerable degree negate the potential advantages – a particularly notable feature of the approach since it has been taken over and mandated by a central government that, like others before it, appears to have little understanding of how teaching, learning and educational policy development work, and even less inclination to seek out and respond to the advice of those who do. The attempt to 'universalise' educational curricula and assessment criteria, though arguably a worthwhile project ethically, is, in the end, an unrealistic and unreasonable one *unless the parameters between what is common and what is not are drawn sensibly, clearly and with due regard to difference.* In this respect, the various difficulties of the competent craftsperson, outlined under the five sub-headings of the next section, mirror a wider trend in recent British educational policy that has also witnessed the birth of – and widespread resistance to – an overly prescriptive, maximally detailed National Curriculum and the proliferation of standardised tests for school students in both the secondary and the primary phases of education.

Difficulties with the competences model

The problem of universality

Perhaps the most immediately obvious difficulty with the competences discourse is that, once universalised, it almost inevitably (as with other universalisations such as those in National Curriculum 'level of attainment descriptors') lends itself to misinterpretation. As we have already seen, CATE 9/92 very specifically stated that

> the acquisition of competences is not the totality of training. The criteria do not provide the entire syllabus of initial professional training

and

> each competence is not a discrete unit but one of many whose sum makes for a confident start in teaching.
>
> (CATE 1992, p. 9)

However, the typically list-like nature of competences – *particularly* those emanating from 'official' sources in which a high degree of universality is implicit – along with the perceived need to 'leave nothing out' for fear of implying that some areas of competence are more or less important than others, gives teachers and teacher educators a very clear impression that identified competences do, indeed, provide 'the entire syllabus', that the skills listed are indeed 'discrete', and that the lists are, indeed, intended as finite representations of essential truths (Moore 1996).

It could be argued that this impression, which has been reinforced by subsequent documentation (for example, DfEE 1997a, 1997b), sustains a view – consistently rejected by many teachers and teacher educators – that the ingredients of 'good teaching' can be itemised and that, subject to their being appropriately acquired, anyone can make an effective teacher: a 'teachers-are-made' perspective which may, in the end, prove just as unhelpful – and be as inherently misleading – as the 'teachers-are-born' one in discourses such as that of the charismatic subject. One particular problem with this is that many student teachers do appear – to themselves and to others – to acquire, in a satisfactory manner and to a satisfactory degree, the various requisite competences, but still, as has been described in the previous chapter, have huge difficulties in the classroom and cannot begin to understand why this should be so (Moore and Atkinson 1998; see also Van Manen's observation (1991, p. xi) that 'A person may have learned all curriculum methods and all the techniques of instruction and yet be a poor teacher').

The latter difficulty arises partly because the universalisation of competences through their identification, itemisation and 'legalisation' makes them particularly resistant to considerations of the personal and responsive aspects of teaching, as well as of the impact of the variability of locations in which formal education takes place. That is, the discourse is essentially flawed in that it attempts to isolate and define inevitably generalised skills and kinds of knowledge that all teachers will need *regardless of the kind of person they are or the circumstances in which they operate* (Maguire 1995; Woods 1996).

As many – perhaps most – teachers will agree (see, for example, Moore and Edwards 2002), there is no one model of good teaching, any more than there is any one model of the good student or the good school. It is also clear that attempts to identify the universal good teacher, student or school through measurable 'outcomes' are themselves misleading, precisely *because of* the contingent and idiosyncratic aspects of schooling itself – a weakness recognised elsewhere in official policy, in the notion of 'value added' whereby raw examination results of school students are translated into more meaningful data by taking account of such matters as the social and initial academic backgrounds of schools' students in the construction of 'league tables'.

Goudie (1999) has taken this particular issue a stage further, relating the absence of contingency and idiosyncrasy from the competences discourse to questions of *dis*-empowerment and the *suppression of creativity* in teaching activity – effectively configuring the competences discourse as the Foucauldian discourse *par excellence* in its power to constrain potentially 'dangerous', individual approaches and perspectives via the enforced internalisation of an ideal, universally and totally rule-bound practitioner. As Goudie argues:

> Deference to any prescriptive theory is out of pace with time and context and suppresses consciousness of the self as a social being; it results in conformity, and disempowers social actors from acting authentically in response to the particular situation. It also turns practice into a technical performance, debilitating the creative imagination as it interacts with external reality.
>
> (1999, p. 60)

Goudie suggests that teachers need to be encouraged to *expose* 'the ideology of technocratic control' implicit in the competences discourse, in order to 'have a chance to struggle over the inequity of social forces of domination and subordination' upon which formal State education systems are partly structured (ibid., p. 93).

The problem of language

A second problem with the competences discourse is that language – however precise and 'scientific' it may be – seldom, if ever, says exactly what we want it to say or, indeed, *everything* that we might want it to say

(Moore 1996). It is, consequently, highly resistant to the kind of inventorising that characterises the competences discourse, so that however many hours may go into their construction, lists of competences and standards will never, finally, be able to answer the question they set themselves: 'What makes a good teacher?' The 'sum' of the advice, that is to say, will never entirely match its parts.

One result of this linguistic problem is that statements of competence may themselves be reduced to the vague forms of language that often characterise the charismatic subject discourse. The insistence that (DfEE 1998, p. 13) student teachers should demonstrate their teaching skills through 'stimulating intellectual curiosity, communicating enthusiasm for the subject being taught, fostering pupils' enthusiasm and maintaining pupils' motivation' is, for example, arguably much less helpful than other, more easily assessable competences, in that it gives rise to a number of unanswered questions and tends to reduce both teaching and learning to much less complex and sophisticated activities than they actually are. 'Communicating enthusiasm' in particular seems to suggest some kind of invisible, infectious, esoteric and almost spiritual quality reminiscent of the charismatic subject discourse, while the call to 'foster enthusiasm' comes with no indication as to how best to achieve this or how the student teacher's success in this area might be assessed. (How, for instance, does one reliably measure 'enthusiasm' during the course of one lesson, let alone across a longer period of time, when enthusiasm may come and go according to a wide range of circumstances and events, many of them totally beyond the teacher's reach or control?)

The 'macro'–'micro' problem

The capacity of the competences discourse to de-skill the classroom teacher or undermine their professionalism is directly related to another difficulty with the competences/standards discourse, recently identified by Basil Bernstein: that is, its capacity to contribute to misdiagnoses of perceived educational failure, and to deflect solutions of educational difficulties away from analysis and reform of social conditions (i.e. 'macro' considerations) towards the blaming of individual students, teachers and schools (i.e. 'micro' considerations) (Bernstein 1996). Another way of putting this is to say that the competences discourse can lead to an unhelpful, misleading and conservative *localisation* of educational issues – including educational problems – not in terms of recognising and validating local differences as described under 'the problem of universality' (p. 82), but as part of a divide-and-rule policy that deliberately hides the wider social inequalities and inconsistencies at whose door so much educational failure can and should be laid. It does this in large measure by prioritising skills and knowledge which may be perceived as residing 'within' the *individual* over more complex issues of educational *process*es that may be seen as residing in larger educational and social *systems* – and in so doing by (re)constructing both teacher and pupil as (Boler 1999, p. 75) 'the autonomous organism' which 'acquires "skills"'.

From Bernstein's perspective, the power and importance of the competences discourse for central governments is plain to see: it is both far easier and more economical to treat perceived social difficulties *symptomatically* – for example, to concentrate blame on schools and teachers for educational failure – than it is to take a *causal* approach which might imply a drastic readjustment in the social distribution of power and wealth: what Bernstein refers to as pointing us 'away from the macro blot on the micro context' (Bernstein 1996, p. 56).

Details of this process of shifting blame and responsibility for educational failure from the wider society – and of course from politicians and policy makers – to individuals working within that larger society are developed by Smyth in his account of the interrelationship between the development of competences in teacher education and dominant conceptualisations of teaching and learning generally:

> Much of the implicit argument behind these [competence-based] approaches is that if standards of teaching can be determined and set (usually arbitrarily by people at a distance from schools), then surveillance and quality control procedures can be put in place to ensure adherence to what are claimed to be community expectations. The unfounded and unproven claim is that the current batch of economic problems can be blamed on teachers who have been less than diligent in the discharge of their duties, who act in self-interested ways and are incapable of pursuing the wider national agenda, and who are therefore in need of careful control, auditing and monitoring to ensure the production of acceptable educational outcomes.
>
> (1995, p. 2)

Linking the competences discourse, supported by stringent and regular inspection mechanisms, to a wider educational discourse whereby 'teaching is increasingly construed as a technical activity' (ibid., p. 6), Smyth suggests that teacher education and therefore school teaching are becoming effectively impoverished in terms of the marginalisation of creativity and innovation, with both schools and institutions involved in the education and training of teachers in danger of becoming compliant, fearful locations engaged in the pedagogical equivalent of painting by numbers:

> Teacher development against this kind of backdrop, far from being a process of enlivening teachers and turning schools into critical and inquiring communities, becomes a process of ensuring cost cutting and

of putting in place procedures to ensure compliance, docility and the creation of schools as institutions whose main concern is meeting the requirements of centrally devised diktats.

(ibid., p. 3)

The problem of closure

Research undertaken during the later stages of the *Autobiography Project* indicated that from the student teacher's point of view one of the major difficulties of the competences discourse relates to the fact that competences statements themselves tend to take up a very large proportion of the overall profiling documentation (in the case of the DfEE *Requirements for Courses of Initial Teacher Training* (DfEE 1998), virtually *all* the documentation), and that these statements are themselves presented, as I have already indicated, in what looks very much like an inventory or list (in the DfEE document, there is copious use of headings and sub-headings, colour-coding, numbering and lettering, boxing and bulleting, and the bulk of the text is in non-continuous prose). Evidence of objections and fears from students when confronted with such a document was found in abundance in their end-of-year evaluations of their courses, during which sets of competences and standards were described as 'daunting', 'scary' and 'off-putting', with 'far too much to take in'. For many students the system was described in terms of 'a counsel of perfection', while it made others 'wonder if it's even worth trying [to achieve all the competences]'.

Fortunately for student teachers, most providers of initial teacher education and training seem to adopt a more laid-back approach to the lists of competences/standards nowadays. If our recent research involving the development of reflective practice in student teachers is anything to go by, there seems to be less pressure on students to be overly familiar themselves with the details of the lists, with tutors taking on the not insubstantial burden of familiarising themselves with these details and ensuring that the competency requirements are being met. These 'inventorial' difficulties, however, continue to cause difficulties even when the details are summarised for students and passed on in more digestible forms.

The first of these difficulties connects closely with what has already been said about the difficulties of language (above), and can be identified in terms of what, after Lacan, we might call the 'dead' (or 'deadening') letter (see, for instance, Lacan 1979, p. 207). The 'dead letter' refers to the way in which symbolic systems (essentially, 'languages') are perceived by those who experience and use them as fundamentally fixed and unchallengeable, finding their origins both prior to and 'external to' the formation of the individual subject (who is, in fact, formed *by and within* those pre-existing systems). Such systems appear, in essence, as products of the collective, disinterested wisdom of 'other people'. As far as the perceiving subject is concerned, these systems may change over time, as circumstances change, but they cannot be changed by the actions of the individual alone. The individual subject obeys and even makes creative use of them, but does not consciously contribute to their creation. In the domain of *spoken* language, where exchange is prioritised and linguistic 'products' normally remain unrecorded, there persists a feeling – an illusion, perhaps – of a certain openness. Writing, on the other hand, as Barthes pointed out in pre-electronic-mail times, is still typically a 'hardened' or 'closed' form of language, which is 'in no way an instrument for *communication*' (Barthes 1983, p. 38, my italics). Though open to subsequent interpretation and challenge, that is to say, what we have come to recognise as the 'printed word' does not present its basic premises to any immediate dialogue.

Eagleton (1983, p. 170) has further argued that some written texts – for example, legal documents – are more 'hardened' than others, presenting themselves as timeless, neutral, beyond challenge and ultimately (to return to one of the student quotations above) 'intimidating': what Barthes (1975) has referred to as 'readerly' texts, which invite the reader merely to uncover or 'understand' what the texts are 'saying'. Such texts achieve their impenetrability, Eagleton argues, through concealing, through the very language in which they are couched, their linguistic-conceptual histories, their specific 'modes of production' – a very important point, this, since it reminds us that lists of competences are, when all is said and done, selections (*and* select-*ed*) from a range of possibilities. To put this another way, we might say that within lists of standards or competences certain skills and qualities are 'fetishised' with importance while others are marginalised. (An interesting example of this is the way in which reflection on practice has effectively disappeared as an 'official' competence in England and Wales over the past ten years.) While these skills and qualities are presented as 'self-validating' or self-evidently important, the importance is, in reality, one which has been invested in them by certain groups of people.

A major concern with lists of competences or 'standards' concerns the extent to which they may be experienced by students in the same intimidatory way: that is, the extent to which, from the student's viewpoint, they may appear as externally fixed, 'given' skills, understandings and areas of knowledge to be acquired and developed – founded on presuppositions about how learning takes place, or what makes a 'good teacher' – that must themselves be adopted without question, rendering them as unhelpful as the charismatic subject discourse and weakening further the potential for emancipation or empowerment that was behind many higher education institutions voluntarily adopting and developing them in the first place. As one student teacher on the *Autobiography Project* put this in her end-of-course evaluation:

> You are told what a good teacher is: that's it. You get it handed down to you even before you start making your own discoveries in practice.
> (Zara: student teacher, *Autobiography Project*)

Whereas Lacan (1977, p. 33) has argued, with reference to his own teaching, that it is the teacher's prime function to encourage students to *interrogate* the histories of words in order to re-examine concepts 'deadened by routine use' (words like 'needs', behaviour', 'planning', even (Williams 1976) 'standards' itself, with which the current lists are replete), there is a danger that texts like profiles of competence and lists of standards may have quite the opposite effect. To use Foucault's terminology (Foucault 1980), we might say that the 'knowledge' of how to be a good teacher may be (mis)recognised by the student teacher, not just as having an independent, external existence but as being in the custodianship of a wiser group of individuals.

As we shall see, one of the dangers in student teachers' – or for that matter, their tutors' – perceiving competences and standards as inventories suggests an additional problem in relation to *reflective practice*, and particularly to what student teachers feel permitted to reflect upon. With reference to Gadamer's hermeneutics, Zizek has argued that '[t]here is more truth in the later efficacy of a text, in the series of its subsequent readings, than in its supposedly "original" meaning' (Zizek 1989, p. 214). If profiles of competences and lists of standards and their attendant documentation are to be perceived as a 'text' (that which invites 'readings' – or even 'writings'), and if we intend and believe that text to obtain 'greater efficacy' through 'subsequent readings' – that is to say, if we are to perceive the text as, finally, something which is absorbed, interrogated and elaborated through an interactive, interpretative process and not simply as 'dead letter' – it is clear that we need to find ways of encouraging in student teachers not only reflection on the areas identified in the documentation (the text), but, as Lacan (1977) recommends, *reflection upon the text itself*: in other words, not just an acceptance of the discourse and detail of competences or standards, resulting in a corresponding focus on how best to achieve, to exhibit and to assess them, but a questioning of the competences discourse itself that includes considerations of the potential usefulness of *alternative* discourses.

In promoting such an approach, it needs to be kept in mind that the readers of texts are not automatons but will inevitably bring interpretations to bear on their readings of texts dependent upon who they are, what previous experiences they have had, and what ideological positionings they have already assumed. It needs also to be borne in mind that if the competences discourse does drive the (student) teacher away on account of its daunting and apparently unyielding nature, they may turn to other discourses within which they feel on safer ground but which may prove equally unhelpful. It is precisely for these reasons that I have added a chapter on reflexivity in this book – an approach which, I believe, offers help both in terms of the critical reading of dominant discourses and in terms of offering an alternative set of approaches to professional learning and development.

'Maintaining the appearance'

The particular difficulty of the agenda-charting nature of the competences discourse leads us to the final difficulty with competences that I want to consider in this chapter, and this is the way in which texts like profiles of competences and lists of standards may serve, as Lacan puts it, to 'maintain the appearance' (Lacan 1979, p. 122). Basing his argument on a reading of Lacan, Slavoj Zizek (1989, pp. 47–9) describes how the various practices that comprise the social order contain inevitable, irresolvable antagonisms or contradictions. Typically, in order to accommodate such antagonisms (to 'maintain the appearance') we hide them by 'masking' them.

This masking takes place in a number of ways:

- through language itself, which, as has already been suggested, is never capable of symbolising experience 'accurately' or 'in total', and which has the capacity – perhaps even the function – of distorting reality in order for it to become personally and collectively acceptable;
- through a process of scapegoating, in which a person or concept provides a diversion from – or even an 'externalised', safely distanced symbolisation of – the antagonism;
- through the workings and structures of ideologies, which also offer an acceptable, provisional and essentially 'fantastic' picture of reality.

One way of approaching these antagonisms and of making use of such an approach in understanding (and consequently informing) our own and others' practice is to see them in terms of 'fissures' – not precisely in the way in which Lacan uses this term, where it accounts for the relationships between the conscious and the unconscious, between language and 'the real', but in a way that more directly concerns the relationships between the practitioner and the practising context. To begin with, there is a danger that, because lists and profiles of competences and standards do not – quite properly, we might argue – address matters of idiosyncrasy (except, in a very limited way, under headings like 'professional relationships and quali-ties'), they may serve to stand in place of or 'mask' the idiosyncratic aspects of a student teacher's practice: as Boler (1999) suggests, they may encourage and endorse a choice 'not to see' by presenting and validating 'what we ought to see'. When antagonisms manifest themselves in breakdowns of communication in classroom situations, for example, the student teacher may seek to explain or overcome them through reference to a text (the competences/standards text) that does not specifically include their con-sideration within its remit. All that may be achieved by this is (a) a masking of the real problem; (b) unhelpful recourse to a second text (for example, the common-sense view of the good teacher as charismatic subject) that masks the antagonism precisely by substituting a personal failing for an intersubjective impossibility. In this respect, it is vital that student teachers approach the competences/standards text as a 'not-all' rather than as the formalised answer to all their difficulties.

'Alternative' competences

Everything that has been argued so far underlines the importance of presenting competence profiling systems to students in ways that make it clear from the outset what those systems are – and what they are not – intended to be. It needs to be ensured, for example, that students do not perceive lists of competences in terms of an all-inclusive inventory or manual. Nor should we want them to conclude that, because certain elements are largely omitted from the lists (in particular, certain aspects of interpersonal relationships and skills, and skills related to reflective practice), *we as teacher educators* do not perceive those elements as unimportant or irrelevant. In particular, students need to understand – and to believe – that despite the high degree of specificity in some sets of competences (for example, the lists of standards for student teachers in England and Wales, from which I have already quoted), such lists can only offer general criteria and general advice; that they specifically do not take account of the idiosyncratic and contingent aspects of classroom practice and experience; and that those aspects are at least as important, not only in terms of students' practice but in terms of our own advice to and assessments of them. As Smyth argues, lists of competences or standards

> make teaching appear as if it is a complete, coherent and unified process, when in reality it is characterized by uncertainty, rupture, dissonance, tentativeness, provisionality and self-disclosure.
>
> (1995, p. 8)

It is in this that most of the potential and actual dangers of the competences discourse lie. It could be argued that there is nothing *intrinsically* wrong with profiles of competence as long as they merely add to the advice, support and assessment already provided through other discourses – if they fill an existing 'lack'. (This is, indeed, the spirit in which competences texts in England and Wales were usually framed and presented to students when they were being trialled and introduced in the early to mid 1990s.) The real difficulty emerges when the competences discourse effectively replaces or severely marginalises other discourses by becoming the dominant discourse in and through which we instantly 'anchor' (Lacan 1977) or make sense of every aspect of our professional experience and development. In such a situation, our creative energy easily becomes channelled into operating, writing about and even subverting the discourse, when it might be more profitably spent developing other discourses or developing strategies framed 'within' other discourses. Furthermore, whether we like it or not, such a fixation can only implicate teacher educators in masking those very fissures in our social and education systems of which they may most want their students to be critically aware.

We do not have to allow the competences discourse to dominate to quite the extent it currently does – though given the current teacher education inspection regime in Britain, it is very hard to find the time or space to mount an effective opposition. Nor do we need to dismiss the notion of competence too readily simply because we find problems with the construction of competence profiles by central government and the manner in which such profiles have to be managed. In their interviews, student teachers on the *Reflective Practice Project* often came up with their own lists of competences in writing their initial assignments at the start of the course ('What makes a good teacher?'). While these lists bore some similarity to the official lists and descriptors of standards in the DfES/TTA documentation, they tended to reveal quite different priorities, often including elements which were conspicuously absent from the official lists. One student, Lynn, for example, listed the following set of competences:

- enthusiasm for your subject
- a willingness to provide variety and interest in the classroom environment
- highly qualified in your subject area
- able to maintain discipline and order
- a mentor and role model
- showing respect [for pupils]
- trying to have a positive impact wherever possible through mature and well-judged actions and words
- the ability to plan, to be organised and to demonstrate attention to detail.

(Lynn: student teacher, *Reflective Practice Project*)

Students like Lynn are not alone in producing significantly different lists of competences from those in the official documentation. In his book *What Makes a Good Teacher?*, which claims to deal with 'the virtues and qualities which teachers should possess', Hare (1993, p. v) intriguingly produces a list of essential 'qualities' (not entirely unlike those of the student teacher Lynn) in place of specified skills or strategies. These are 'humility', 'courage', 'impartiality', 'open-mindedness', 'empathy', 'enthusiasm', 'judgement' and 'imagination' – a list not incompatible with the more familiar competences discourse, but with a different emphasis rooted within a different approach to understanding teaching and to developing good pedagogical practice. Starting with Socrates' question 'Who should teach our children?', Hare suggests, with reference to teacher education:

The dominant tendency has always been to reduce teaching to a set of trainable skills and measurable competencies, but this approach is objectionable in principle. Socrates put the point bluntly in emphasising the difference between human beings and horses as far as suitable upbringing is concerned. There are deep and open questions about the kind of life a human being should live which simply do not arise in the case of horses and cattle. People disagree about the good life, and the existence of controversy means that we must be sceptical about claims to expertise in this area.

(1993, pp. iii–iv)

Hare continues:

Too much attention in teacher education continues to be placed on rule and routine, on particular techniques which research is supposed to have deemed effective in promoting learning. This is partly because we are afraid to use our judgement in selecting and approving those who have desirable intellectual, moral and personal qualities and so we fall back on observable and measurable behaviours; and partly because we work with an impoverished concept of education itself which continues to be seen as nothing more than the acquisition of information and skills.

(ibid., pp. iv–v)

'Competence' and performance

In order to consider a little further where the competences discourse might have led us had it not been colonised so impressively by successive British governments, we could do worse than make a brief return to the work of Basil Bernstein. In *Pedagogy, Symbolic Control and Identity* (1996), Bernstein takes pains to remind us that 'competence' itself has proved something of a shifting concept, becoming transformed during the colonisation process from referring to essentially intrinsic, creative, flexible skills and practices to those which are essentially 'acquired' through education – or, rather, through 'training', for it is, suggests Bernstein, within the context of the victory of training over education that both the colonisation and the transformation are to be understood.

Tracing the history of the concept of competence in a variety of fields in the social sciences – including linguistics, sociology and anthropology – Bernstein (1996, pp. 55–6) seeks out common ground in the essential difference between various kinds of *competence* (for example, Chomsky's 'linguistic competence' or Saussure's 'langue') and various kinds of *performance* (Chomsky's 'linguistic performance', say, or Saussure's 'parole'), in arriving at a description of competence as 'intrinsically creative and tacitly acquired in informal interactions' (Bernstein 1996, pp. 55–6). Historically, Bernstein argues, competence has been defined in terms of 'practical accomplishments', constituted by procedures which are essentially 'social'. The *universality* of competence (an 'intrinsic' universality, rather than the one which the current competences discourse seeks to *impose*) renders it 'culture-free'. Part of its social logic is that 'the subject is active and creative in the construction of a valid world of meanings and practice' and that the development or 'expansion' of this subject is *'not advanced by formal instruction [or] subject to public regulation'* (ibid., p. 56, my italics). Competence theories thus have, historically, 'an emancipatory flavour', being founded on 'a critical, sceptical view of hierarchical relations'.

This notion of competence as socially, actively, creatively and yet unconsciously acquired skills, understandings and practices is critically different from the notion of competences (often conflated with 'competenc*ies*') embedded in the competence discourse of CATE and the TTA. Indeed, the term may be said to have been appropriated (Jones and Moore 1995) to describe something much more closely akin to competence's traditional 'other half': that is to say, 'performance' – a feature which brings it much closer to the *charismatic subject* discourse than at first might appear, since the notion of performance is also central to that discourse (albeit performance of a different kind which is to be seen and marvelled at rather than measured in terms of its effects). The competences discourse as it exists in the areas of teacher education and – increasingly – in education in general certainly maintains a somewhat limited notion of the universality and 'culture-freeness' of the 'old' competence discourse, inasmuch as what constitutes effective teaching at one time or place is deemed to constitute it at any other. However, it introduces three important new elements that change its character critically, rendering it anything but 'creative'. These elements are (a) the necessity for competences to be actively, *consciously* taught and learned; (b) the presentation of *selected lists* of competences whose focus is on the acquisition of 'skills' rather than on understandings or strategies; (c) an *over*-emphasis on universality, which deliberately marginalises the intuitive and the idiosyncratic as well as ignoring the wider contexts of schooling and education both at the national and at the local level.

The new competences discourse does more than that, however, as Bernstein has gone on to argue, in that it entails precisely the shift away from 'education' towards 'training' that is implied in the official language of the discourse (in, for example, the shift of terminology from 'the Council for the Accreditation of Teacher *Education*' to 'the Teacher *Training* Agency'). Furthermore, this is a highly problematic notion of training, inevitably implying a corresponding notion of 'trainability'. With reference to school students – although the same argument holds good for student teachers – Bernstein argues that:

> The concept of trainability places the emphasis upon 'something' the actor must possess in order for that actor to be appropriately formed

and re-formed according to technological, organizational and market contingencies.

(1996, p. 73: see also the suggestion of Jones and Moore (1995), that the

revised competences appropriate, in Bernstein's words (1996, p. 67), 'resonances of an opposing model, silence the cultural basis of skills, tasks, practices and areas of work, and give rise to a jejune concept of trainability'.)

One implication arising from this analysis is that, although appearing at first sight to stand in direct opposition to one another (the 'born' teacher *versus* the teacher as 'made'; the possession of 'mystical' qualities *versus* the learning of skills and strategies), the competences discourse and the charismatic subject discourse follow the same path in prioritising the individual actor over considerations of the contexts within which the actor operates, and have a common root in a particular version of the Enlightenment project that also prioritises the (social but 'ideal') individual or 'self' over the (collective and constituting) society. The point has already been made that a central difficulty of both discourses is that they lead too easily and too uncritically both to the celebration and to the pathologisation of the individual practitioner (or pupil or family or community) to the extent of banning or at best marginalising wider causes of educational success and failure, including those that may be related to unequal power relations and persistent financial inequalities. From the (student) teacher's point of view, when something goes wrong in the classroom it is not a matter of collective concern, responsibility and action, but because they are personally and individually 'lacking' – either in charisma or in competence or in both.

Competence and 'effectiveness'

This same difficulty applies to another currently popular discourse for the understanding and discussion of public education: that of 'effectiveness' – a discourse closely linked to the competent craftsperson discourse but also to early (and, in official discourses, abiding) incarnations of the 'Effective Schools Movement' in the UK (see, for example, Harris 1996; Blandford 1997; Bowring-Carr 1997).

The use of the word 'effective', like that of 'competent', is an interesting one, and resonates with what other commentators have said about developments in educational *evaluation*. In her essay 'Evaluation as Realpolitik', Harland, for example (1996), has suggested that from the 1990s the evaluation of schools and teachers in Great Britain has become increasingly influenced by the 'three e's' of efficiency, effectiveness and economy – bringing about a particular emphasis on evaluative aims and processes whereby the purposes and measures of success of formal education are very closely linked to matters of national economies, and where faster, more easily observable and measurable connections are demanded between policies and their effects.

Bernstein, too, has linked dominant pedagogical orientations to wider historical socio-economic conditions, identifying the 'three pedagogies' of faith-related, humanitarianism-related and secular. (While the competent craftsperson might be located in the third of these, we might expect to find others – for example, that of the teacher-carer – more comfortably situated within the first two.) The secular pedagogy in Bernstein's configuration is itself located within a meta-discourse of the fundamental rightness or inevitability of the national and global market economy, wherein one of education's principal functions is to fit people for individual and national success within those markets. Just like the broader market economy, so the educational economy concerns itself primarily with end products, performance and performativity, competitiveness and cost efficiency, in situations in which there must be winners and losers, profit and loss, and in which knowledge itself becomes commodified and teaching correspondingly technicised.

It is not my intention to offer a critique of the effective schools 'movement' – which, like most other movements, comprises different 'sub-movements' or schools, each, no doubt, with its own strengths and weaknesses when viewed from different perspectives. There are, certainly, some chasmic differences between the notions of effectiveness explored and promulgated by many of my own colleagues (e.g. Carnell and Lodge 2002; Pickering 1997), whose emphasis is on effective *learning*, and those to be found in some *government*-sponsored publications (e.g. Hay McBer 2000; Ofsted 2002) where the emphasis is far stronger, I would argue, on inputs and outputs. (Similar chasms may be found between official understandings of effectiveness and versions linked to 'school improvement' wherein emphasis is given to schools' capacity for managing change: see, for example, Hopkins *et al.* 1994; MacBeath and Mortimore 2001.) From the point of view of the current argument, I shall say no more than that the movement is, at its best, located within a 'schools and teachers can (and do) make a difference' view of education. This is a view that stands in opposition to an *over-*emphasis, in assessing student performance, on such matters as social background, but one that does not ignore the strong impact of such 'out-of-school' factors and indeed recognises other factors, residing within the overall education system, that may have positive or negative effects on student performance (see, for example, Slee and Weiner, 1998; Sammons 1999).

Of more immediate relevance here is that in the light of the contexts and analyses presented by Bernstein and Harland, the term 'effective' in the official discourses becomes significantly different from the vaguer yet more encompassing 'good', prioritising as it does the measurable outcomes of teachers and schools in relation to their students' measured 'performance' and the extent to which those students might have performed better or worse had they had different teachers or experienced their education at a different school. (See also Wolf's account of 'competence based assessment' in Wolf 1995.) In other words, in this particular, 'official' rendering of effectiveness, the concept becomes problematic precisely because it is too strongly tied to the (attempted) *measurement* of effects: a process which immediately shrinks the parameters within which effectiveness itself can be judged and perceived. Within this version of the discourse, the effect-*ive* teacher is one who is configured in terms of their capacity for effect-*ing* (for example, the improved 'performance' of their students). Inevitably, perhaps, attempts to define the particular 'effects' that are desired leads to the kind of reductive, formulaic inventorisation that has come to characterise the competences discourse more widely. It also, in its attempts at 'blueprinting', contributes to the marginalisation of the contingent and the idiosyncratic (including school-based curriculum development) that I have already described.

In a sense, too, this official reconfiguration of the good teacher as the effective teacher renders the nature of effectiveness resistant to categorisation: the effective teacher, that is, is judged according to their perceived achievements as end products rather than according to the means by which they achieve them, and those means may vary considerably from teacher to teacher and from school to school. There is, nevertheless, a very clearly understood profile for the effective teacher, as was evidenced by our own research on teacher identities (the *Professional Identities Project*), during the course of which teachers and headteachers regularly linked the notion of effectiveness to notions of professional eclecticism and (to coin a phrase) anti-ideologism. That is to say, the self-styled effective teacher did not just achieve their ends (usually measured in terms of test scores and examination results) by a variety of means; they also self-presented as deliberately seeking out the 'best' of differing and erstwhile 'competing' educational traditions, and adopting a conscious stance in which they refused (as they understood and intended it) to be dictated to pedagogically by educational ideologies. In particular, as will be explored a little further in Chapter 6, the self-styled effective teacher refused to be described in terms of 'traditional' or 'progressive' (terms which have often, as we shall see, been used to differentiate pedagogical approaches, learning theories and educational ideologies in the past), much preferring the term – imbued with purely positive meaning by significant numbers of the classroom practitioners we spoke to – 'pragmatic'.

Effectiveness, competence and innovation

Despite these connections with pragmatism, a central difficulty with the 'official' or 'colonised' effective teacher *discourse* is that too often it is configured, as with the competences discourse, so as to constitute a conservative force, aimed not so much at encouraging teachers and students to challenge received wisdom (including received wisdom about what should constitute teaching and learning and how they should take place) or to be experimental and innovative in their practice, but rather at preserving valued practice from the past and to *confine* eclecticism to selective drawings upon those tried and trusted practices. An example of this is to be found in the Hay McBer Report *Research into Teacher Effectiveness: A Model of Teacher Effectiveness* (2000) under the heading 'Assessment' (1.2.20) – where the test of a good (effective) teacher involves positive responses to the following 'key questions':

> 2. Does the teacher use tests, competitions, etc. to assess understanding?
> [. . .]
> 4. Is there evidence of pupils' written work having been marked or otherwise assessed?

In essence, this is an instance of *ideology* being disguised within discourse in a way reminiscent of Roland Barthes's conception of 'mythology' (Barthes 1972). The very asking of the questions, that is, *implies agreement with the premise* – in this instance, that tests and competitions are good ways of 'assessing understanding', and that assessment cannot be deemed to have been carried out without some kind of 'evidence' or 'proof'. The question effectively denies the possibility for *discussion* of these issues, inviting us only to say 'yes, the teacher has done this' or 'no, they haven't'. It is not impossible, of course, to imagine a situation in which competition is *not* considered a good way of assessing understanding, and indeed is not considered to be appropriate classroom practice in any situation. We might also argue, after Smith (1996) and others, that testing is certainly *not* the best way to assess understanding, on the grounds that the pressure of the test activates quite the wrong parts of the brain for this purpose. These lists of effectiveness, however, do not invite us to ask such questions: they are not intrinsically inquisitive about teaching and learning; rather, they tend to ossify wisdoms of the past.

A further, not unrelated problem with the effective teacher discourse, when, like the competences and standards discourse, it takes on this kind of list-like or inventorial form, is that, like the competences and standards discourse, it over-simplifies the complexities of classroom life. In particular, by itemising attributes, competences, skills and strategies, it fails to recognise and take account of something central to teachers' experience: that is, the extent to which the items on the list are or are not compatible *with one another*. To illustrate this, we might turn again to the Hay McBer Report (2000), and to the section in paragraph 1.4.3 on what the Report calls the 'climate dimension' of effective teaching. This is broken down into the following elements, some of which we may recognise from the charismatic subject and competent craftsperson discourses and from the notion of the communicative teacher:

1. **Clarity** around the purpose of each lesson. How each lesson relates to the broader subject, as well as clarity regarding the aims and objectives of the school.
2. **Order** within the classroom, where discipline, order and civilised behaviour are maintained.
3. A clear set of **Standards** as to how pupils should behave and what each pupil should do and try to achieve, with a clear focus on higher rather than minimum standards.
4. **Fairness**: the degree to which there is an absence of favouritism, and a consistent link between rewards in the classroom and actual performance.
5. **Participation**: the opportunity for pupils to participate actively in the class by discussion, questioning, giving out materials, and other similar activities.
6. **Support**: feeling emotionally supported in the classroom, so that pupils are willing to try new things and learn from mistakes.
7. **Safety**: the degree to which the classroom is a safe place, where pupils are not at risk from emotional or physical bullying, or other fear-arousing factors.
8. **Interest**: the feeling that the classroom is an interesting and exciting place to be, where pupils feel stimulated to learn.
9. **Environment**: the feeling that the classroom is a comfortable, well organised, clean and attractive physical environment.

Apart from the obvious fact that this represents a very limited notion of 'climate', leaving out, for example, all those 'environmental' factors whose origins lie outside the classroom and to a very considerable extent outside the teacher's or the school's control, another issue is that although these different aspects *may* be able to coexist, a number of compromises may have to be made and a number of possible contradictions may need to be resolved in effecting such a coexistence. Could there not, for example, be a tension between making the classroom 'an interesting and exciting place to be' and maintaining 'discipline, order and civilised behaviour'? Clearly, although it is the pupils who are to experience interest and excitement, the definitions of 'interesting' and 'exciting' are given over to the teacher, who must decide what is interesting and exciting *within the bounds of what the teacher deems 'acceptable'*. In the event of the interest and excitement being generated by the students themselves, it is not inconceivable that the ensuing 'environment' might not meet the requirement that it should be 'civilised' or indeed 'safe'.

Though they are presented, like lists of standards or competences, as universal or timeless, it is evident from these descriptions that effectiveness is, rather, a fluid concept that is socially, culturally and historically situated, and that it inevitably reflects how current social and power relations are constructed and distributed: that is to say, the concept is situated within a specific notion or notions of what schooling and formal education *are* (and what they should be) in a particular social place at a particular historical 'moment'. An example of this can be found in paragraph 13.10 of the same report, under the heading 'Holding people accountable'. Holding people accountable, we are told, involves teachers setting:

> clear expectations of behaviour and for performance, and contract[ing] with pupils on these, setting clear boundaries for what is acceptable. . . . In this way they provide a clear framework, routines and security in which work can take place.

Such a statement makes unproblematic existing power relations – for example, 'clear expectations': *whose* expectations?; 'what is acceptable': acceptable to whom? – situating the good/effective teacher within a particular discourse of teaching and learning in which the agenda is always, ultimately, set by authoritative adults.

5 The appeal of reason –
reflective practitioners

The call for 'critical inquiry' in the liberal tradition is easily subsumed within the hollow invocations of values of dialogue, democracy and rationality. Deeply rooted in Western conceptions of liberal individualism, this common rhetoric threatens to reduce genuine inquiry to an individualized process with no collective accountability. . . . The Socratic admonition to 'know thyself' may not lead to self-transformation. Like passive empathy, self-reflection in and of itself may result in no measurable change or good to others or oneself.

(Boler 1999, pp. 176–8)

Reflective practice

Working in parallel with the competences discourse – sometimes in apparent opposition, sometimes in a more complementary way – is the discourse of the reflective practitioner. The notion of 'reflective practice' places as much emphasis on teachers' own evaluations of their practice as on the planning and management skills into which such evaluations feed, and has spawned a considerable volume of theory and publications devoted to its elaboration and promulgation (see, for example, Schon 1983, 1987; Valli 1992; Elliott 1993a, 1993b; Loughran 1996; Loughran and Russell 1997; Mitchell and Weber 1996). It is this wealth of published material as much as anything that has elevated reflective practice to discursive status but that has also tended to set it apart from the competent craftsperson discourse whose validation and promulgation have taken place largely in official government documentation.

Unlike the competent craftsperson discourse, the reflective practitioner discourse emphasises not discrete practical skills, techniques and areas of knowledge but, rather, the particular skills needed to reflect constructively upon continuing experience as a way of improving the quality and effectiveness of one's work: it is as interested in the teacher who possesses and exercises the skills as in the skills themselves. While such reflection inevitably involves drawing on the range of strategies and techniques one has at one's disposal, or developing new ones, it does so selectively, flexibly and strategically, taking full account of the particular circumstances relating to any given problem at any given time. In particular, the discourse encourages teachers and student teachers to take into account the 'whole picture', analysing the effectiveness of a lesson or series of lessons not simply by measurable outputs such as test scores, but through an attempt to evaluate what was learned, by whom, and how more effective learning might take place in the future. It consequently involves careful evaluation on the teacher's part of their *own* classroom performance, planning and assessment, in addition to and in conjunction with evaluations of their students' behaviours and achievements. It also implies a sound understanding on the teacher's part of relevant educational theory and research – including theories of cognitive, linguistic and affective development – in order to address issues not restricted to the 'what' and the 'when' of education but embracing, also, questions of 'how' and even 'why'.

By way of illustrating this essential difference between the reflective practice and the competent craftsperson discourses (prior to considering some of their *similarities*), we might briefly turn to another conceptualisation of the teacher as *strategist* (Moore 2000). Linked, as they may easily be, to the competent craftsperson/standards discourse, teaching *strategies* readily become a list of approaches: some of them universally helpful, others selected on the basis of specific contexts. Here, the skill and judgement of the teacher lie in knowing what is 'on offer' and making appropriate selections in the context of the particular teaching–learning contexts in which they find themselves (cf. the notion of the 'eclectic' or 'pragmatic' teacher', referred to in Chapter 4 above). Linked more closely to the notion of *reflective practice*, however, the teacher-strategist is not configured as someone who merely selects or 'absorbs' strategies but rather as someone who *thinks and operates strategically*: that is to say, who acts creatively, flexibly and thoughtfully in seeking to match their actions to their own informed assessments of what is happening in their classroom. While this may involve dipping into 'known' strategies, at its centre is a need for the teacher to feel comfortable about recognising, taking account of and even taking advantage of the particularities of any given situation.

The reflective practitioner and the competent craftsperson

It appears that the reflective practitioner discourse is not well favoured within current official discourses of teacher education in England and Wales. The competence category of 'evaluation of one's own teaching', for example, which appeared in original 'official' lists of competences, is not included in the Teacher Training Agency's post-1997 documentation, being relegated in terms of position to the end of another broad area – 'Teaching and class management' – and in terms of wordage to '[students must demonstrate that they can] evaluate their own teaching critically and use this to improve effectiveness' (DfEE 1997a, p. 10; TTA 1998, p. 8). Unfortunately, one consequence of such a marginalisation is a reinforcement of the notion that the dominant discourses in teacher education (of competences and standards) are anti-intellectual and anti-theoretical, and that they promote a view of teachers as essentially 'clerks and technicians' (Giroux and McLaren 1992, p. xiii) rather than thinkers and creators. Fortunately, the reflective practitioner discourse has received much popular support in higher education institutions in Britain offering courses in initial and continuing teacher education, and continues to produce some of the most interesting and perceptive practice (Moore and Ash 2002).

If the competences discourse emphasises the teacher as technician and 'deliverer', whose 'internalised' skills can be easily monitored through measurable outcomes, the reflective practitioner discourse has always taken what I would call a subtler approach to teaching, recognising the centrality of much-harder-to-identify, codify and quantify skills to do with communication, presentation, analysis, evaluation and interaction (the 'human qualities' identified elsewhere by Delors *et al.* (1996) and, in a different way, by Handal and Lauvas (1987)). Such a difference clearly has implications not only for the way in which teacher education is conducted, but also for research in this domain. The competences discourse, for example, because of its contained, 'self-referential' nature, suggests an *evaluative* response, sited within a world of skills and capabilities that, as it were, already exists outside the individual – prompting such questions as 'Which system of competences works best?', 'Which courses teach the standards most effectively?' and so on. The reflective practitioner discourse, on the other hand, suggests a qualitative, research-based response along the lines, say, of ethnography or action research. Such approaches will focus not on measuring success by outcome ('How many students successfully completed this or that course?', 'What gradings were courses given by Ofsted inspectorates?' and so on) but on exploring the *nature* of the teaching and learning processes that are taking place, through an emphasis on 'the processes of meaning-assignation and situation-defining' and on 'how the social world is constructed by people, how they are continually striving to make sense of the world' (Woods 1979, p. 2).

Competence, reflection and the pathologisation of the individual

Peter Woods invites us to ask the question 'Is teaching a science or an art?', subsequently concluding that 'it is both a science and an art – *and more besides*' (Woods 1996, pp. 14, 31, my italics).

To use the terms of Woods' question in relation to comparing and contrasting the two dominant discourses of the competent, standards-driven craftsperson and the reflective practitioner, the competences discourse may be said to represent a quasi-scientific perception of teaching and learning that is firmly sited within a paradigm of educational thinking sometimes critiqued under the term 'modernism' (Moore 1998a). Such a paradigm assumes 'the possibility of completeness' (Standish 1995, p. 133) through viewing the world as 'an ordered place' and the 'elements of the world of knowledge as topologically invariant' (Hamilton 1993, p. 55). What is knowable – or what 'needs to be known' – is ultimately definable and susceptible to inventorisation and tidy assessment: it is underpinned by a tacit assumption that there is, under passing acknowledgement of the possibility of local variations, only one right way or set of ways of doing things (a view which, incidentally, underpins the current National Curriculum for England and Wales, for all its claims of inclusivity).

The discourse of reflection, on the other hand, recognises what Goodson and Walker have called 'the messy complexity of the classroom' and its only 'partially apprehendable practice' (Goodson and Walker 1991, p. xii). It is a discourse that gives full recognition to 'the central role that people play in the educational process and educational systems' (ibid., p. 1), that legitimises a range of approaches and behaviours, and that understands that 'much of the most expert practice in schools is based on intuitive judgement' (McIntyre *et al.* 1994, p. 57). Such a discourse is often associated, in the philosophy of education, with the use of the term 'postmodernism' as denoting a 'commitment to notions of process, experience and pleasure' (Green 1995, p. 402; see also Standish 1995; Levin 1987; Hargreaves 1993). Accordingly, it views teaching more as art (and 'more besides') than as science, lending itself to corresponding modes of research. (The charismatic subject discourse, of course, also views teaching as an art, but as a mysterious art, akin to magic.)

Though clearly separated from one another in this way, however, these two dominant discourses cannot be described as entirely 'oppositional', any more than the competent craftsperson and charismatic subject discourses can. Certainly, they are not mutually exclusive, and most student teachers these days will find themselves being encouraged and helped to be both 'competent' and 'reflective'. In some of its cruder manifestations, indeed, in which 'checklists, rankings, peer evaluations, etc.' are prioritised while 'student teachers are seldom given an opportunity to have a concrete understanding of their personalities [and therefore] find it difficult to understand why they react to people, situations, or circumstances as they do' (Johnson 1989, p. 340), the reflective practitioner discourse overlaps the competences discourse to such an extent that the two may often appear, to the student teacher, to merge into one.

Such convergences suggest that, philosophically, the two discourses may be closer to one another than at first appears. In particular, we might suggest that each of these discourses has its roots in a view of social development founded on the primacy of private and collective 'reason' and of the notion of the unitary, ideal 'self' (a point already made in connection with the competent craftsperson and charismatic subject discourses). Thus, although the competences discourse may be seen as focusing on universals and the reflective practitioner discourse on the contingent and idiosyncratic, both may seem to over-emphasise a particular form of agency (that which focuses on 'self-improvement' rather than that which looks 'outwards' towards reforming society) through implying the existence of 'detached', 'independent', unified identities: just as success rests on the student's responsibility, with the aid of tutors, to become 'competent' in the competences discourse, so it is incumbent on the individual student to use their own reflective, rational powers in the reflective practitioner discourse to a not dissimilar end. In this way, within either discourse it becomes an easy task to pathologise the individual pupil, teacher or student teacher for any breakdowns that occur in social interaction. Such pathologising does two things. First, as has already been suggested in relation to the competences discourse, it shifts debate away from issues related to broader socioeconomic and cultural relations. Second, through its appeal to ideal, universal reason, it promotes the discourse (already very familiar to teachers and pupils) of individual *blame*. The first difficulty, of course, can be addressed initially by ensuring locally that such issues are given adequate coverage as curriculum inputs on courses. The second is rather more difficult to address, since it involves a radical departure for the student not only in how they perceive their classrooms, but in how they perceive and understand 'themselves'.

Though reflective practice can, as I shall endeavour to show, go some way towards avoiding this particular pitfall (indeed, its main proponents would certainly desire and intend such an avoidance), it will always have this capacity for unhelpful over-personalisation as long as it is perceived and 'sold' as a private, individual practice rather than a public, collective responsibility. As Megan Boler (1999) argues, in promoting a 'pedagogy of discomfort' that emphasises 'collective witnessing' as opposed to individualised self-reflection, reflection carried out by the self on the self in isolation from other selves may end up achieving nothing of any value – least of all change – for anyone.

Defining reflective practice

Before proceeding, it is necessary, however, to define more precisely what is meant by reflective practice – a task I shall attempt to accomplish through reference to the suggestions made by student teachers taking part in our *Reflective Practice Project*, who identified various kinds of reflective activity along a continuum that ran from the perfunctory/ritualistic at one end (reflective activity, that is, which impacted very little on professional practice) to the constructively critical at the other end (reflective activity that offered an authentic challenge to existing presuppositions, actively sought out and paid serious attention to alternative practices and perspectives, and contributed significantly to development or change). We were aware from the start that we were by no means the first to attempt such a task, and we were guided by others' efforts – most notably, those of Schon (1983) – in our business of arriving at something approaching a taxonomy via our interview data.

In summary, we felt that four broad kinds of 'reflective activity' were being described by our interviewees, which we came to refer to as 'ritualistic reflection', 'pseudo-reflection', 'productive reflection' and 'reflexivity'. Only the last two of these, however, conformed to the requirements cited above that authentic reflection should be critical and challenging, seek out alternatives, and contribute significantly to development or change.

Alongside these four kinds of activity, the student teachers also helped us identify what we came to call five 'sites' of reflective practice. These were:

- thinking about your practice 'on your feet' – that is to say, *reflection in practice* or (Schon 1983; Van Manen 1991) *'reflection-in-action'*;
- solitary *'in-the-head' 'retrospective' reflections* on lessons or events, carried out some time after the lesson or event has occurred;
- *evaluations* (usually written, usually carried out after individual lessons, confined to individual lessons and focusing on pupil and teacher performance);
- *intra-professional verbalised reflections* carried out in the company of others in the same community of practice (for example, other teachers or beginning teachers, not necessarily working at the same school);
- *extra-professional verbalised reflections* carried out in the company of selected support networks (for example, family, or friends working in other occupations).

Ritualistic reflection

In relation to these different forms and sites of reflective practice, it was the formal evaluations that initially provoked the greatest disagreement among the student teachers in our study – in particular, formal evaluations carried out immediately after each lesson (a compulsory requirement of this and many other PGCE courses). Many of our respondents felt, at least to begin with, that these formal evaluations provided a useful focus and structure for authentic reflective practice. Others, however, clearly felt that such activity did not constitute authentic reflection at all and (in the case of some of the students) that they actually inhibited or obstructed such reflection.

For some of the students, not only were the evaluation forms given to them (providing headings under which to evaluate each lesson) very helpful, but being compelled to put things down in writing was itself perceived as a valued way of promoting reflection. While recognising that the evaluations 'did not work for everyone', one respondent (George) spoke very enthusiastically about the benefits he had gained from regular completion of these written evaluations and of the 'benefit of writing things down' – both in the writing itself and in the creation of a written record that could be returned to in the course of future reflections. Another respondent (Carrie) told us: 'I think it is helpful, very helpful, because at the start you do need a lot of structure', while another said:

> Evaluation of teaching is one of the most effective ways of learning. . . . I mean, it's funny, because I did my own evaluations and I thought 'Oh I don't think I'm getting anything from these', and I spoke to my tutor and he did this prompt sheet for us all.
>
> (Celia: student teacher, *Reflective Practice Project*)

Even this student, however, was not without her reservations concerning the limitations of formal lesson evaluations, suggesting that they tended to focus on problems and mistakes rather than on successes, and that much of her more positive, affirmatory reflection occurred in less structured ways through discussions with friends.

The limitations and difficulties of the requirement to evaluate all lessons on a regular basis were referred to many times by our student teachers, some feeling that they were too closely focused on individual lessons to have wider applicability, some feeling that they became less useful as the student teacher learned more about classroom practice and classroom dynamics and that therefore their completion quickly became a meaningless chore ('I don't see the point of writing down again and again the same things', to quote one student). Others resented the fact that they were constructed according to someone else's agenda, thereby reducing opportunities for subtle reflection that took full account of local circumstances and issues, or of the student teacher's particular dispositions, weaknesses and strengths:

> When we were talking about filling in these evaluation forms, I found them incredibly useless. The first one or two maybe were OK, but after a while I just didn't know what to write.
>
> (Mizzi: student teacher, *Reflective Practice Project*)

> What we're talking about here – about personal reflection – there's not really any formal room for that, not like a sheet for personal reflection.
>
> (Carrie: student teacher, *Reflective Practice Project*)

> It does become very repetitive, but in a way you should need to write less anyway, because you know the classes better. . . . As you go on, maybe your reflection is less on paper and more 'up here'. . . . I think being made to do evaluations isn't always helpful either, with the volume of the teaching load.
>
> (Sarah: student teacher, *Reflective Practice Project*)

Interestingly, by the end of their pre-service year even those students who had been initially positive about formal evaluations had become far less enthusiastic and far more likely to subscribe to the view that the evaluations had ceased to have a great deal of value and that they took up a considerable amount of time and effort that could have been better spent on other matters. In their various criticisms of the formal evaluations *when they had to be carried out over an extended period of time* (that is, regardless of any initial value they may have had), the students cited:

- diminishing returns;
- over-prescription and over-representativeness of someone else's (imposed) agenda;
- a tendency to lead to ritualistic, perfunctory forms of reflection.

With reference to this last point, one student, in the course of criticising what she saw as a dominant discourse of 'evidence', pointed out a difference between 'inking' and 'thinking':

> I think the danger is that as beginning teachers and as professionals we get so obsessed with what's down on the piece of paper and what the ink says that we're not making the connection between what the ink says and what's up here – what's in your head, what's in your memory. . . . I think there's a mismatch there.
>
> (Sarah: student teacher, *Reflective Practice Project*)

For this student teacher, the formal requirement to provide written evaluations of lessons had also, apparently, subverted the reflective practice discourse into discourses of competences and standards – not so much encouraging authentic reflection as limiting its possibilities and enhancing its capacity for negativity within parallel discourses of blame:

> The whole idea of reflective practice is all very well, but it's very individual, and I think we fall too often into the trap of assuming that reflective practice is x, y and z when perhaps for other people it's different. . . . It's like with teaching: teaching for everybody is different. . . . We've been given these sheets to help us do reflection, to be more reflective in our practice, and on the one hand they're helpful but on the other hand if a certain thing doesn't happen in your lesson or you didn't pick it up as happening in your lesson, how can you reflect on it? So whilst you may be meeting these dreaded standards, you can't always 'evidence' it. And I think one of the things with our society today is that we're obsessed with paperwork, and we're obsessed with assessment. But we're not just obsessed with assessment, we're obsessed with the way that the assessment happens, and the way that it's proven.

> And I think whilst it's helpful to have frameworks, it's easy to feel that
> if you haven't ticked all the boxes then in some way you're failing.
> (Sarah: student teacher, *Reflective Practice Project*)

This student's comments, and those of some of her fellow students – who
could 'understand' why the headings under which they were being invited to
reflect corresponded broadly to the lists of standards/competences they were
obliged to meet but who regretted the capacity of this pre-structuring to
force them (as one student put it) 'away from the things you *really* want
to think about' – take us back to the issues of *maintaining the appearance*
outlined in Chapter 4 above. The point was made that at the same time
as 'universalising' good teaching, the competences/standards text has a
capacity and a tendency to encourage the idiosyncrat*isation* – or *personalisation* – of the *causes and treatments* of perceived difficulties, principally
by inviting the (student) teacher to measure their 'value' and 'success'
against the universalised norms.

When the reflective practice discourse becomes colonised by the competences discourse, the danger for the practitioner lies in reflecting exclusively
or disproportionately on their own practice, within a very limited and externally fixed set of parameters and at the expense of reflecting on the systems,
histories and conditions within which they are practising: that is to say, the
contingent aspects of teaching are overlooked or marginalised within the
universalising turn of the competences discourse – or the colonised reflective
practice discourse – itself. The conceptualisation of reflective practice, meanwhile, becomes reduced to competence-like lists and strategies, embedded
in precisely the same assessment discourses of performativity and 'evidence'.

To elaborate this point, if we establish as desirable the state of reflective
practice, and then provide the would-be reflective practitioner with a list of
competences which are, simultaneously, assessment criteria, we yet again
run the risk of locating what are essentially systemic difficulties within the
individual practitioner: when things go wrong, the individual is immediately
responsible and, through following advice, it is the individual who can put
things right – a view which, it must be added, is frequently internalised by
some student teachers, including student teachers who are most openly critical of the wider education system, who are all too likely to self-pathologise
in relation to any perceived classroom breakdown (just as some other
students will only ever blame circumstances or entities *external* to themselves). In these situations, far from being useful, the reflective activity,
just like the competences list, can become a rod with which the teacher
beats their own back. To summarise the complaints of one student teacher,
who had been experiencing severe difficulties in the area of classroom
management:

> These are the things I'm told I have to do. I'm doing them, but things
> are still going wrong: therefore I can't be doing them properly.

While it should not be denied that the individual teacher often does have to make adjustments in practice or perception to overcome classroom difficulties, the antagonisms masked in this process of pathologisation are often those endemic to the educational system itself: the 'appearance that is maintained' is precisely the opposite – that the system is essentially free of major problems.

In conclusion, we might say that while formalised reflective activity located within competence/'standards' texts and discourses leads readily to ritualism whose impact on development is negligible, it can nevertheless contribute, like the competent craftsperson and charismatic subject discourses, to a negative culture of self-blame, which is the opposite of what most advocates of reflective practice would want it to do.

Pseudo-reflection

'Pseudo-reflection' was our term for the kind of reflective activity identified by the student teachers taking part in the *Reflective Practice Project* that involved a genuine intention to consider important issues identified or accepted by the student or teacher, some of which might lie outside the parameters of imposed boundaries, but which did not lead to genuine development or change: the kind of reflection, that is, which contributes to the durability of preconceptions and existing perspectives through selective if not always conscious interpretation of events, and through the partial selection of topics, issues and events to reflect *upon* (see also Chapters 1 and 2 above). It is essentially distinguished from ritual reflection (though it is, very often, 'ritualistic') by the fact that its parameters and topics are 'internally' set (by the teacher or student teacher) rather than 'externally' imposed. Our students suggested that often such reflection took the form of an avoidance of potentially troubling issues whose confrontation might entail a fairly radical reappraisal of practice, involving either downscaling or recasting such issues into more acceptable representations, or focusing on other issues altogether on the basis that there are (as one student teacher on the *Autobiographies Project* had put it) 'some things you can't do anything about'.

For the student teachers taking part in the *Reflective Practice Project*, pseudo-reflection was recognised as a potential problem but tended to be something they saw in other teachers and student teachers rather than in their own practice. While the students we spoke to understood that their reflections were often 'prioritised' by the influences of previous experiences (for example, one of the them had been bullied at school and was drawn to finding evidence of and pre-empting bullying in her own classroom), this did not appear to act in quite the blinkering way with these students that we had anticipated it might. Instead of previously held views and perspectives *hindering* their reflections, these particular students appeared very keen on the idea of productive reflection on their practice, clearly identifying themselves as lifelong learners, recognising and rejecting ritualistic and pseudo forms of reflection, and nominating other, more practical hindrances (lack of time and energy, difficulties related to support networks and so forth) to the development of the reflective practice that they clearly valued. While it could be argued that such hindrances might have been conveniently called upon to mask a less acceptable, more 'hidden' reluctance on these student teachers' part to engage in productive reflection, there was sufficient evidence from our interviews that this was not the case, not least in the numerous occasions on which the students themselves talked about the nature of experience and learning, or provided evidence of *reflexivity* (see Chapter 7, below).

Though pseudo-reflection could take different forms and be located in different sites, the student teachers we spoke to tended to identify it with a particular kind of solitary, in-the-head, unstructured reflection (just as they had associated ritualistic reflection mainly with the more formal, 'evaluative' forms and sites of reflection) – often linking it not just with 'avoidance strategies' but also with unhelpful feelings of negativity. Although several students were able to see a potential value in 'in-the-head' reflection (as likely to be carried out in such sites and situations as in the bus or on the walk home, in bed before sleep, or when pushing a shopping trolley around the supermarket as in a quiet corner of the staffroom), they all recognised the capacity for this kind of reflection to become counter-productive, to focus too much on negative experiences and feelings, to feed anxieties and obsessions, and to lead not so much to improved practice as to despair (at one end of the spectrum) or denial (at the other). To quote one student teacher:

> You sort of go over these things that have happened, over and over again. You know, the children are in your head all the time, so you go to sleep and you dream about what so and so said in your classroom, and you wake up thinking about them.
>
> (Mizzi: student teacher, *Reflective Practice Project*)

Another student was more specific about the potential dangers of such reflection:

> To do it on your own, in your head, on the one hand is good because it means you can be reflective without having to rely on other people, and be self-critical. But I think sometimes you become so self-critical that you don't focus on the things that went well; you tend to focus on the things that didn't go well. And I think that's the problem: it becomes a negative cycle if you're not careful, and also a self-fulfilling prophecy.
>
> (Sarah: student teacher, *Reflective Practice Project*)

It was painfully evident that for some of these students – all considered very successful by their tutors – such reflective activity was serving a purpose far removed from working towards improved practice.

'Productive', 'constructive' or 'authentic' reflection

We came to use the term 'productive reflection' (which we have referred to elsewhere (Moore and Ash 2002; Ash and Moore 2002) as 'constructive' or 'authentic' reflection) to describe reflective activity which actively seeks to problematise situations and to challenge existing views, perspectives and beliefs – promoting or leading to development or change in terms of work-related understandings and/or outlooks. In that sense, productive reflection is closely allied to *action research* (Corey 1953; Elliott 1993a, 1993b; Kemmis 1985; McNiff 1988; McKernan 1991), where the reflection tends to takes on a more fundamentally collaborative, if perhaps more narrowly focused nature, involving the application of theory and systematic analysis in moving towards better understandings of – and possible solutions to – identified issues and difficulties. As we shall see in considering one particular form of reflection – *reflexivity* – such projects, situated in the currently marginalised discourses of the teacher as theorist and the teacher as researcher (sometimes conflated with the teacher as *learner*), can, productively, place self-analysis at the heart of the research endeavour, or indeed become the locus of the research itself. As Mitchell and Weber have observed:

> Studying ourselves is a form of research, and our own accounts of 'how we got here' can contribute to a body of knowledge about teaching, learning, and adult identity. Studying ourselves might be regarded as research-in-action.
>
> (1996, p. 9)

We had anticipated that the development of productive reflection in our sample of student teachers might be hindered by the current dominance of discourses of 'competence', 'standards' and performativity in initial and continuing teacher education (leading, we had feared, to an emphasis on ritualistic reflection bounded by the parameters of the published 'teaching standards' (DfEE 1997a, 1997b)), as well as by the kinds of resistant preconceptions and myths described by Britzman and others (1986), which, we felt, might lead students who had got beyond ritualistic reflection into perfunctory engagement in pseudo-reflection.

While there was some evidence of peripheral impact of this kind, as indicated above, in the event we were surprised to discover:

(a) that the student teachers on the *Reflective Practice Project* had very little direct knowledge of the 'standards' by which they would be assessed, tending to trust their tutors to incorporate these into their own lesson planning;

(b) that although each of the student teachers interviewed was very aware of the impact of previous school and home experience on their current professional perspectives and responses, that awareness was such that it could be critically evaluated and drawn upon constructively rather than having an obviously inhibitory effect.

While the list of government-imposed teaching standards themselves had clearly – though not exclusively – been drawn upon by the student teachers' tutors in providing 'scaffoldings' for the students' written lesson evalua-tions, the lack of familiarity and concern with the standards themselves on these students' part did seem to have had an impact in terms of freeing up their reflections and encouraging them to contribute themselves to their 'reflectivity agendas'.

'Reflexivity'

What I have chosen to call *reflexivity* is what many would call – and mean by – reflective practice itself: that is to say, it is a particular form of reflec-tion which takes the reflective practitioner beyond the immediacy of the here and now by locating reflection within wider personal, social and cultural contexts and thus increasing its potential for productivity. It includes considerations of such matters as the teacher's or student teacher's own historicised responses to situations and events ('What is it that makes me react in such a way to such a situation or event?'), to understandings of the impact on students' classroom behaviours of social, cultural and emotional lives experienced previously and currently inside and outside the school walls (see also Moore 1999a, 1999b), and to reflections about how (and why) one is reflecting.

Given the complex nature of and issues related to reflexivity – along with my own preference for this kind of reflective activity – I have chosen to devote the next chapter entirely to this form of reflection. One example, however, drawn from students taking part in the *Autobiography Project*, gives a flavour of this mode of reflection in its early stages, while at the same time reminding us of the relationship of the 'good teacher' to con-ceptualisations of the 'good parent', the 'good pupil' and the 'good son or daughter' (Walkerdine 1990, p. 199), as well as the importance of reflecting upon past and present familial relationships (often, as Britzman and Pitt (1996) remind us, 're-played' in the classroom situation) before we can fully understand classroom interactions and how, or indeed if, we can render them more functional.

During the course of a discussion of teaching-practice experience on one of my student teachers' university-based days, a young student, Ann, began describing to the other students in her group a particularly interesting debate (so she had found it) that had taken place in one of her classes regarding whether or not 12-year-old children should be allowed to have hand-held computer games. The contribution of one particularly vociferous pupil had stuck in the student's mind. This boy had said that his parents were forever telling him that he could not have a computer game because his general behaviour suggested that he was not responsible enough to own one, and that they would only even contemplate letting him have one when he started to act more maturely. His response had been that if his parents *treated* him more like a responsible person, he would act like one. If, on the other hand, they continued to treat him like an irresponsible person, then he would continue to behave like one. The familial argument, from his point of view, seemed to have boiled down to his parents implying that they would buy him a computer game if he started to behave responsibly, and him saying that he would act responsibly if they treated him like a responsible person by (for example) buying him a computer game. It had also been clear from the boy's testimony that his parents had perceived this as a form of threat, and had dug their heels in even harder, telling him angrily that this was a typical example of his irresponsibility and that he would now be lucky if they *ever* bought him a computer game.

At the end of this story, another student in the group, Jane, quite spontaneously chipped in: 'You know, this, in a way, reminds me of what has been happening in Northern Ireland. Sorry . . . I don't know why . . . Just forget it!'

Other students in the group carried the discussion forward, however, and soon began to make some tentative links between the relationship between and behaviours of the parents and the child in the first student's story and the relationship between and behaviours of the British government and the opposing factions – the loyalists and the republicans – in Northern Ireland, finding connections between the kind of impasse reached in the computer-game family's negotiations and those experienced in the wider political arena. I shall not go into these discussions in great depth (or explore the capacity for over-simplification in the comparisons being made), but what emerged was a fascinating discussion of the extent to which people generally continue to adopt parent–child positionings, and to locate themselves within the power relations implicit in parent–child relationships, in all manner of social situations in which they find themselves, both as children and as adults. As one student in the group suggested, half jokingly: 'As a parent myself, this probably explains why I have so much difficulty!' She went on to say, in a more serious vein: 'As a parent, it should be relatively easy for me: I should know a lot more about how children tick. But I suppose in a way I could just as easily slip into the parent position [at times of classroom conflict] as the daughter one – which could be very confusing!' By the end of the session, the students had all spontaneously come up with examples from their own teaching practice of how they might have adopted 'child-like' positionings in relation to their school students, or how they had adopted positionings more like those of the intractable adults in the computer-game story. What was exciting about these exchanges from the point of view of the course tutor was the manner in which reflection about their own behaviours, contextualised within reflections on their own biographies, seemed to feed instantly and quickly into the students' discussions of techniques and strategies for avoiding such (re-)positionings when they proved unhelpful – or indeed for maintaining them when they appeared to have some positive effect!

Forms of reflection: individualisation and collectivity

As has already been indicated, the ten student teachers interviewed in the *Reflective Practice Project* identified several 'sites of reflection' which were linked to a number of overlapping activities that they were happy to describe as reflection about practice. Principal among these discretely defined activities were reflection-in-action; 'in-the-head reflection'; verbally articulated reflection with other professionals; verbally articulated reflection with other student teachers; verbally articulated reflection with non-professionals, including friends and family members; and various forms of written reflection. Each of these reflective activities was seen to have its pros and cons. The students were divided, for example, on the desirability and efficacy of 'reflection-in-action' or 'reflecting on your feet'. For some of them – for some of the time – the situation of being left alone to think about their practice, in the immediate context of the classroom, was both stimulating and important. As one respondent put this:

> I did learn a lot from being left alone: things like classroom management. . . . I'm not a shouting person, so, you know, finding my own way of making myself noticed and that sort of thing. . . . You learn a lot about yourself in that way, because you're constantly being tested by the children. Where are my notes? Where am I going to draw the line? When am I going to pretend that I've drawn the line, when maybe I've actually got a little bit further to go?
>
> (Mizzi: student teacher, *Reflective Practice Project*)

Another student felt that the absence of a critical adult in the classroom – however favourably disposed – had helped her to 'be herself' rather than trying to be someone else or trying to impress someone else, and that the quality and authenticity of her reflection had been enhanced as a result:

> I actually like my classroom, my environment, because I feel that's between me and the pupils: we are learning together. Whereas if someone's in there, it creates a false situation.
>
> (Celia: student teacher, *Reflective Practice Project*)

Even these students, though, were acutely aware of the limitations of such reflection, generally suggesting that they had benefited more – and more enduringly – from 'reflection-*on*-action' carried out at some temporal distance from the experiences and events being evaluated:

> In a way I was learning [through reflection-in-action]: tactics, and so on. . . . But I didn't feel like I was moving. Yes, I was learning more about classrooms, more about the pupils . . . but I wasn't really learning how to . . . to develop myself in a situation. I needed someone else's eye on what I was doing.
>
> (Mizzi: student teacher, *Reflective Practice Project*)

One thing that the student teachers were agreed on was that their *most useful and perceptive* reflections had taken place either on their own, away from the events they were reflecting upon, or in company with other people as part of formal or informal discussions. In the latter case, it was felt to be vitally important that the 'right' respondents were found and that discussions with the 'wrong' people could produce negative and destructive effects. (An example has already been given of one student teacher living at her parents' home during her teaching practice, who was subjected on a daily basis to 'contradictory', common-sense advice and admonishment in connection with how she and her students should be conducting themselves in the classroom.) The student teachers' need for the views of a critical but supportive 'other' to help turn the acquisition of coping and survival strategies into reflection *per se* was voiced in several interviews, both in relation to these kinds of 'situated learning' and with reference to 'in-the-head' reflection carried out in informal, often unstructured ways. For one student, informal, solitary reflection, carried out after the event and with the benefit of hindsight, represented a 'deeper' reflection than that which more directly accompanied action (including lesson planning as well as lesson management), which, he felt, was more competence-based and therefore 'less subtle':

> I think that's much deeper. I think what you do in, say, lesson planning and evaluation you do in five minutes, and say, like, 'He talked. . . . He didn't hand in his homework. . . . I didn't do a recap of the homework.' That's all competency, it's like the hygiene factor. When you sit on a bus, or when you are at home or you go out to the pub, subconsciously it ticks away; and I think that's where you make the fundamental changes, where you say 'OK, I forgot that one particular thing but that wasn't the main thing. The main thing was I hurried the class along too much, or I focused on those three children instead of the whole class.'
>
> (George: student teacher, *Reflective Practice Project*)

If, for this student, solitude was often the most helpful condition for reflection and the pub the preferred social location, other student teachers tended to cite reflection-in-the-company-of-others – what I have called 'articulated' or 'verbalised' reflection – as the most helpful condition for effective reflection. To quote S. Johnston (1994, p. 46), whose research effectively links reflective practice with *research on and into one's practice* (action research), these students had found a particular value in 'formal or informal collaborative groups or networks' (see also Kemmis and McTaggart 1988). These groups varied from student to student, but appeared to be most effective when they were chosen by the student rather than being imposed or 'engineered' by other parties. For some students, the choice was wide-ranging, in certain cases resulting in an eagerness to reflect in company wherever a sympathetic ear could be found. As one respondent, keen for her 'assumptions to be challenged' (Brookfield 1990), told us:

> The thing I find most useful is just talking to the pupils, and talking to classroom teachers. When my tutor [from college] came to see me, I found that enormously helpful: I mean, she sort of said things to me that hadn't even crossed my mind and hadn't crossed the mind of other people that I was with. I think you constantly need to have different perspectives on what you do in the classroom.
>
> (Mizzi: student teacher, *Reflective Practice Project*)

Most of the students, though, were more specific about who their most useful conversation partners were. For some, family – and in particular a parent – had proved most helpful:

> I find talking to my mum is great because she keeps me sane, she'll be like 'calm down, everything's fine'. . . . She's great to have on the other end of the phone. She thinks it's hilarious to think that actually I said at the beginning of the course I was scared of children, that I don't know what I'm doing. . . . [She helped me to realise that] a lot of the kids actually reminded me of when I was at school. I wasn't really very popular at school. And they were actually the ones that used to scare me. For a while, I was having to get over that: not exclude them or anything, but I was a wee bit wary of them. It took me a while. I was thinking I was a child myself, letting a 13-year-old intimidate me.
>
> (Carrie: student teacher, *Reflective Practice Project*)

Other students were more inclined to turn to friends working outside the profession:

> I actually reflect a lot by talking to [my non-teaching friends] about it, which is good for me. It makes me think, it makes me quite passionate

about what I am doing, because I remember things I'd forgotten by the
way they ask questions about it.

(Celia: student teacher, *Reflective Practice Project*)

Most of the students, however, particularly valued discussions with other
students on their course, and the 'safe environment' that such meetings
provided, regretting that this site was all too rarely available to them given
the amount of time spent in school, the amount of work to be got through
on the college-based part of the course, and, as one student put it, 'this
obsession with "standards"':

> I think it would be helpful to have some time, even if not every week . . .
> to come in [to college] to reflect, because although you get professional
> study afternoons in your school, actually that time so far hasn't been
> used as effectively as it could be, because it seems to me that most of
> the time it's somebody sitting in front talking at you. You do get
> group work . . . with [students] from other institutions, but – this
> sounds horrible – in a way they're in competition with you and you
> can't reflect with them. Whereas within your tutor group, and certainly
> your subject area, it becomes easier, because you're with people who
> are at the same level as you.

(Sarah: student teacher, *Reflective Practice Project*)

It is important to note that most of the student teachers' testimonies
seemed to display a healthily positive but critical approach to reflective
practice, suggesting that the conceptualisation of the *reflective practitioner*,
with its perceived emphasis on teachers' learning and professionalism,
held far greater and potentially more enduring appeal for them than the
(government-hijacked) *competent craftsperson* configuration which they
tended to associate with 'spoon-feeding', over-prescription and a lack of
trust in their capabilities. Teachers – certainly (or perhaps even?) at this very
early stage of their careers – clearly see a value in authentic reflection on
their practice, and are able to distinguish such authentic reflection from the
kinds of ritualistic and pseudo-reflection which occur when reflection
becomes colonised by discourses related to competence and 'evidence'. These
testimonies also, however, remind us both of the impact on reflection of the
'larger situation(s)' in which teaching and learning are located and of the
individualisation and idealisation that continue to lie at the heart of much
reflective practice even when it is conducted with some degree of collaboration and mutual support. While (student) teachers may reflect helpfully and
constructively *in the company of others*, for example, the requirement of
'evidence' of reflection (spurious though such evidence may be) inevitably
prioritises individual, privatised reflection; and whatever form reflection
takes, whatever site it is located in, practitioners know that in the end it is
they who will be held responsible for translating their reflective activity

into classroom practice, they who will be held primarily responsible for 'what happens in the classroom'. Inevitably, we return again to the point that reflective activity in the current climate is almost inevitably linked to – and consequently constrained by – a discourse not just of performativity but of the performance of the discrete, individual 'self'.

Sites of reflection and the problem of dislocation

Before we leave reflection for the time being, it is necessary to consider one additional way in which the development of the reflective practitioner is thwarted and marginalised on pre-service courses by the competent craftsperson discourse.

While reflective practice may continue to constitute a dominant discourse, and while teachers and student teachers may be expected and required to develop as *reflective practitioners*, the rhetoric of the discourse is not necessarily matched in practice in terms of the time and support dedicated to it. As we have seen, though originally appearing in lists of competences, reflection on practice has subsequently become marginalised and narrowed in scope both *by* and *within* the dominant competences/standards discourse. In terms of pre-service courses for beginning teachers, this tends to result in the development of reflection being expected and required of students, but there being very little time available to provide support and guidance for it. Reflective practice consequently finds itself being 'fitted in' around everything else, which robs it of the continuing, organic, integrated nature that it both possesses and requires in its most authentic forms. It also tends to produce a quite serious difficulty which I shall call, following the use of the word by one of our students, a problem of 'dislocation'.

This problem of dislocation was raised in one way or another by most of the students taking part in the *Reflective Practice Project*, who suggested that finding the appropriate site for reflective practice was directly related to the fundamental difficulty of life tending to impose its own barriers between 'doing' reflection and subsequently *putting the benefits of that reflection to practical use*. Sometimes, this dislocation was perceived in terms of applying the lessons of the pre-service (PGCE) year to teaching proper:

> I think in some ways it's going to be difficult for me to sort of remember this year when I'm actually in the full thrust of classroom teaching. I hope I don't forget it, because I think there's so much that you do over this year and the theoretical side you should take into teaching. But I think once you're actually there it's going to be difficult.
>
> (Mizzi: student teacher, *Reflective Practice Project*)

More typically, however, the problem was presented as one of relating theory to practice generally, and particularly of articulating what is learned at college and in school-based tutorials with what one actually does in the classroom:

> In school the college becomes irrelevant, and when you're back at college school becomes an irrelevancy. You need the two meshed together somehow.
>
> (Carrie: student teacher, *Reflective Practice Project*)

> There is a dislocation between reflection and practice: like knowing something is right or wrong, but not being able to do it in the classroom for all kinds of reasons you couldn't have thought of in advance.
>
> (Sarah: student teacher, *Reflective Practice Project*)

While some respondents (for example, Sarah) were beginning to see reflective practice itself as one important way of *bridging* these perceived theory/practice, school/college dislocations, for most of the students interviewed the difficulty remained a pressing, if not ultimately insurmountable one that they continued to grapple with throughout their pre-service year – often expressing frustration at the sheer speed and volume of a course that allowed precious little opportunity to 'stand back and look at the bigger picture', as a student, George, put it.

Part III
Positionings

6 The pragmatic turn – coping, surviving and (re-)positioning

A good teacher will . . . recognise that they need to keep an open mind about what works in the classroom and what doesn't. That means that the truly professional teacher will be aware that, however experienced you are, you should continue to learn about your job and remain open to new ideas.
(Lynn: student teacher, *Reflective Practice Project*)

I would say I am a happy medium of traditional and progressive. . . . Traditional – you can see the chairs in rows; but progressive in the sense that I'm . . . keen on allowing students to speak for themselves.
(Edward: secondary-school teacher, *Professional Identities Project*)

Introduction: (re-)positionings

In the previous section, three dominant discourses of teaching and teacher education were identified and elaborated: those of the charismatic subject, the competent craftsperson and the reflective practitioner. It was suggested that while each of these (though particularly the reflective practitioner discourse) may have much to offer teachers and student teachers seeking better understandings of their practice, each also has the capacity – often, indeed, the tendency – to offer as much hindrance as help. This is particularly likely to happen, I have argued, when the discourse seeks to confine understanding within essentialist conceptualisations of the unified, 'ideal' self that take too little account of the wider social and cultural contexts of teaching and learning and too great an account of individual 'responsibility'. It was suggested that:

- these discourses do not operate in splendid isolation from one another;
- teachers' practice and understandings of practice may be expected to exist at the overlaps and intersections of these (and other) discourses;
- teachers are continually involved in adopting professional 'positionings', in which personal values must negotiate accommodations with the sometimes contradictory purposes promoted by the wider practical and ideological-political contexts of their working lives.

I have already quoted Billig *et al.* with regard to this last point:

> Teachers do not have the luxury of being able to formulate and adhere to some theory or position on education, with only another theorist's arguments to question its validity. They have to accomplish the practical task of teaching, which requires getting the job done through whatever conceptions and methods work best, under practical constraints that include physical resources, numbers of pupils, nature of pupils, time constraints, set syllabuses and so on. But these practical considerations inevitably have ideological bases, which define what 'the job' actually is, how to do it, how to assess its outcomes, how to react to its successes and failures, how to talk and interact with pupils, how many can be taught or talked to at once. For example, in the traditional chalk-and-talk lecturing method, a large class size is not so great a practical or ideological problem as it is for a teacher who upholds the value of individual, child-centred learning.
>
> (1998, p. 46; see also Cole and Knowles' description of teaching *practice* in terms of its 'multiple roles and contexts' (1995, p. 131))

In this and the next chapter, I am concerned to explore a little further the notion of teachers' and student teachers' 'positioning' themselves in response to these often competing discourses and ideologies: in response, that is, to the 'cacophony of calls' (Britzman 1991, p. 223) to which they are typically subjected. I shall do this by considering two quite contrasting but by no means mutually exclusive positionings that might be adopted by the teacher or student teacher. The first of these – the 'pragmatic' turn – concerns itself with the adoption of a professional, practical stance that involves the temporary or permanent occupation of what is sometimes referred to in footballing parlance as the 'comfort zone'. Such a positioning, which entails on the practitioner's part the necessary suspension, in the light of wider trends and policies, of some preferred practices (and, in its most extreme form, the suspension of some values and philosophies), is connected very immediately to concurrent classroom practice, and has as its kindred spirit those official or colonised versions of the effective schools movement that have been referred to in Chapter 4.

The second positioning – what I shall call the 'reflexive' turn – is more concerned with developing critical pedagogies and understandings whose practical benefits may be less immediate and less obviously 'visible', and which may at times demand active *avoidance* of the comfort zone of the pragmatic turn. Reflexivity – effectively, the critical and sometimes painful exploration of one's own practice-referenced feelings, responses and behaviours within a range of personal and collective socio-historical contexts – is more closely allied to the project of lifelong learning than the 'here and now', and builds on and develops some of the aspects of reflective practice described in Chapter 5. In that it actively resists attempts at colonisation by the competent craftsperson discourse in a way that the pragmatic turn does not, reflexivity may be seen as inevitably more oppositional than pragmatism to the dominant discourses and ideologies of teaching and teacher education to which I have referred.

I should add that I am not suggesting, in all of this, that teaching is ever 'comfortable' (indeed, the very expression 'comfort zone' is intended to be understood relatively and not too literally). Nor am I being critical of teachers who act pragmatically in relation to mandated policy, or suggesting that we can 'divide' teachers and student teachers into two distinct 'pragmatic' and 'reflexive' camps. My understanding is that pragmatism is always, and probably always has been, a key element of professional practice; that it is perfectly legitimate for us to occupy, on occasion, positions one of whose prime functions may be to help us to cope or to survive; and that the instrumental, pragmatic positionings that we may take will typically happen not *instead of* but *simultaneously with* our more reflexive efforts: indeed, of considerable interest and importance is the relationship and interplay *between* the two turns, as we grapple with our professional identifications and related practices. It is also important to understand that it is not only within the pragmatic turn that professional compromises are made: it is just that the nature, mode and 'siting' of the compromise differs from turn to turn.

Progressivism, traditionalism and pragmatism

In the chapter on competences (Chapter 4), I indicated that teachers we spoke to during the course of the *Professional Identities Project* who self-identified as *effective* also tended to distance themselves from identification as either 'progressive' or 'traditional', seeking to steer a middle course that would draw, eclectically, on elements of each approach – suggesting to us that to be 'pragmatic' was seen by them as an important – perhaps even an indispensable – feature of being 'effective'. These practitioners also shared, however, a particular orientation towards both the effective and the pragmatic 'turns', each of which (rather curiously, perhaps) associated an allegiance to progressivism with *teacher*-centred education (in the sense that through progressivism teachers had been pursuing their 'own ideological interests' at the expense of what was best for their pupils) and traditionalism as an approach which, though flawed, had been too hastily dispensed with and which, for its acknowledged failings, had the interests of all students at its core.

Interestingly, many teachers also tended to locate progressivism as an educational movement that began in an increasingly demonised 1960s and 1970s, linking it variously to the publication of the Plowden Report of 1967, to the burgeoning influence, perceived to have been fuelled by teacher educators at institutions of higher education, of certain elements of Piagetian learning theory favouring the notion of the 'active learner', and to other educational movements of the time including (centrally) the development of comprehensive education. This partial rejection of progressivism, in favour of a welcoming-back of some elements of traditionalism (but more significantly of a return to pedagogical and philosophical pragmatism), may thus also be viewed as part of a wider rejection of the (perceived) libertarian *laissez-faire* attitudes of the post-war decades in favour of a more entrepreneurial, 'harder-edged' cultural orientation of the 1990s and early 2000s. As Alexander (1984) has pointed out, this is a somewhat jaundiced version of events, since authentically progressive education was not nearly as widespread in British classrooms as is often claimed. Nevertheless, the myth of the 'dangerous', 'ideological' 1960s and 1970s persists, and in itself appears to act as a spur to what are sometimes configured as 'less ideologically infused' pedagogies.

The terms 'traditional' and 'progressive' were, of course, being used a long time before the 1960s in debates about the forms that classroom pedagogies should take and the models of learning that should underpin them. Indeed, arguably the best definitions of progressivism and traditionalism in education are to be found in John Dewey's short book *Experience and Education*, which was first published in 1938 and which was into its nineteenth printing by 1955. The Editorial Foreword to this book indicates the existence of a widening 'progressive'/'traditional' divide in educational philosophies and practices in the USA at least thirty years before the Plowden Report was published in the UK.

Dewey's definitions of traditional and progressive pedagogies (the former prioritising teacher-centred, front-of-class, tightly controlled teaching and learning, the latter promoting exploratory or discovery learning, groupwork and class discussion, and a more flexible and responsive curriculum) draw fairly explicit and, for our purposes, very important connections between what might be called the epistemological underpinnings of pedagogy and educational philosophies (that is to say, teachers', schools' and other involved parties' understandings of what knowledge is, including what it is *to know*) and the psychological underpinnings of those same philosophies (that is to say, how we understand the character and workings of the individual learner). As Dewey reminds us, our understanding of 'what it is to know' must have a direct bearing on our understanding of 'what it is to be' (including, in this case, of 'what it is to be *a learner*'), and vice versa. If, for example, we understand knowledge as a body of facts and information to be acquired by the learner, this may sit more comfortably with a model of the learner as primarily a 'receiver' than if we understand the learner as an active, creative meaning-maker. While Dewey makes it clear that such a connection does not inevitably exist, and while he is critical of both overly traditionalist *and* overly progressive approaches to teaching and learning, there is clearly a strong potential for these links. Furthermore, they can operate, as it were, in both directions: that is, our preferred pedagogy can be based upon our preferred understanding of the learning process, but equally our choice of pedagogy and curriculum content can lead us *towards* a certain (perhaps confirmatory) conceptualisation of the learning process. (For Dewey's clear and succinct definitions of traditional and pragmatic approaches to teaching and learning, see Dewey 1938, pp. 2–5.)

'Beyond' traditional and progressive: the pragmatic turn

One of the questions put to teachers and principals during the course of our *Professional Identities Project* was:

> People have sometimes used the terms 'traditional' and 'progressive' as shorthand for locating themselves professionally as teachers. Would you describe your own outlook and practice using either of these terms?

This question typically evoked responses along the lines 'I don't see myself fitting into either category' (to quote one young classroom teacher), or 'I'm a happy medium of traditional and progressive' (to quote another). Furthermore, though not all the teachers in our sample referred to themselves as professional pragmatists, surprisingly few (given that most of them had linked their willingness to be involved in the project to an opportunity to speak candidly about school and government policy) owned up to being ideologically driven in their professional lives, even when their educational values appeared to be at serious odds with those underpinning some of the mandated reforms they were being instructed to put into practice (see Moore *et al.* 2002; Moore, George and Halpin 2002).

It soon became apparent:

(a)   that most teachers were very reluctant to align themselves with either a 'traditional' or a 'progressive' mode of pedagogy, tending to relegate both positions to a pathologised past in which the perceived politicisation and polarisation of pedagogical ideologies had impacted negatively on the classroom experiences and achievements of young people;

(b)   that for most of the teachers and principals interviewed, pragmatism and eclecticism (to put it crudely, the 'happy medium'/'best of all worlds' approach) had been adopted as acceptable alternative professional positionings;

(c)   that an identification of 'good' *with* 'pragmatic' was linked to wider social and political agendas and in particular to a recent avalanche of mandated educational reform which challenged or threatened much received wisdom and through which teachers had to navigate a path in such a way as to remain sufficiently comfortable with their own pedagogic practice. (To put it bluntly, teachers had to find ways of reconciling existing 'personal' beliefs, values and related practices with the sometimes contrasting and conflicting beliefs, values and suggested practices embedded in externally mandated policy.)

Some of those teachers – often more experienced ones who had previously aligned themselves quite strongly to traditional or progressive 'camps' – did continue to categorise themselves in these terms, but did so reluctantly or in a highly circumscribed, circumspect way, as if embarrassed to occupy what might have been seen as a polarised position or as if concerned that in doing so they might be identifying themselves with that (mythical) path- ologised past of educational politicisation and student failure to which reference has already been made. To quote one secondary-school teacher, Arthur, from what might be called the progressive end of the spectrum:

> I am still progressive, yes . . . I suppose so, in my way. In my heart! I never got stupid or carried away about it. . . . And I suppose in a way I'm kind of glad – I mean, I welcome some of the kind of harder-edged initiatives that have been coming in through government policy recently. I still try to be progressive, but it's within a framework of what's . . . a sort of understanding that we have a National Curriculum now, and that it's an entitlement and that all the kids are entitled to have proper exposure to that. So . . . that means there are times when you have to be a bit more traditional, even though you might not always like it – [even though] it might not fit in with your general way of doing things.
> (Arthur: secondary-school teacher, *Professional Identities Project*)

Shirtsleeves and chalkboards: New Labour's model teacher?

By way of looking more closely at how the 'ideal' of the effective/pragmatic teacher might be realised, and by way of confirmation of its popularity in the official domain, we could do worse than turn to the illustrations of classroom life used in government-produced public documentation to sup- port written texts. Such illustrations have become increasingly fascinating since the science of semiotics has been more consciously and deliberately made use of by policy makers and designers in putting their message across to their audiences, and indeed has had a considerable impact on the presentation of school prospectuses, which, in an era of increasing competi- tion between schools for student recruitment, have developed in ways that take many of them far beyond the in-house offerings still widely available throughout the 1970s and 1980s. Front covers, for instance, are now very often carefully selected to encapsulate or epitomise the advertised ethos of the school. For one school, the choice may be a full-colour photograph, taken outside the school buildings, of smiling, happy children in sports- casual school uniform from a range of ethnic backgrounds and with not a teacher, a book or a classroom in sight. For another, the choice may be a solitary, teacherless student in monochrome close-up, in deep academic study in the school library. Another may have gone for a mélange of photographs, each depicting a specific, 'representative' curriculum area – English, Maths, Science, Games, ICT, Drama – with teachers and pupils suggesting a particular kind of working relationship in a variety of organisational contexts: pupils alone at desks in Maths, working collaboratively in Drama, arranged in collaborative groups in English, working in pairs undertaking a Science experiment, and so on. For yet another, there may be no sign at all of any pupil or teacher on the front cover: merely the name of the school, its logo and its motto in two carefully chosen colours.

In the case of government documents, well-chosen photographic images of classrooms have become similarly abundant. Recent publications such as *Excellence in Schools* (DfEE 1997c) or the DfEE/NLT's *Building a Nation of Readers* (DfEE/National Literacy Trust 2000) are positively littered with such images, and provide a sharp contrast to the entirely image-free documents that accompanied the original National Curriculum for England and Wales in the late 1980s, with their geometrical, one-colour-plus-black-and-white front covers – the result, perhaps, of a movement of interest and concern (repeated in increasing government interest in *pedagogy* in, for example, the National Literacy and Numeracy Strategies) away from what the curriculum 'states' (the *written* curriculum) to what the curriculum 'looks like' (or should look like) in practice (the curriculum as *taught* and as *experienced*).

One of the most interesting of these recent publications (from the point of view, that is, of the illustrations rather than of the written content) is the *Teacher Training Agency Corporate Plan 2002 to 2005*, the front cover of which offers a perfect visual summary of the new pedagogic discourse of eclectic pragmatism. The image used – a photograph – encapsulates a desire to bring together the best of all past approaches in order to move forward into a better, synthesised future: a desire and a strategy which, indeed, might be traced back to classical 'thesis–antithesis–synthesis' modes of Western academic rationalism.

In the picture, an ethnically mixed class of boys and girls who could be upper primary or lower secondary are enthusiastically taking part in a lesson with a young teacher – we are to assume, I imagine (bearing in mind his youthfulness and the fact that this is a Teacher Training Agency document), a *student* teacher. The image contains a number of interesting elements indicative of the pragmatic approach: there is, for example (see also MacLure 2003), a chalkboard that is clearly in use (despite this being the much-vaunted computer age), and the children sit at quite strikingly old-fashioned-looking desks which bring to mind the school desks with built-in porcelain inkwells that some of us will remember from the 1950s and 1960s. The teacher, however, is standing animatedly in front of the chalkboard, facing the children – almost as though he has just emerged from it – using it as a reference-point, and adopting voice and hand gestures to communicate interactively with the pupils. The children are clearly excited and engaged, some *almost* out of their chairs to answer a question the teacher has apparently asked, or perhaps to contribute their own take on what he has to say. This is a contained, orderly enthusiasm, however – the children's arms raised in time-honoured fashion, pleading to be incorporated into the lesson. Though these young people are sitting at traditional desks, furthermore, the desks themselves have been arranged so that groups of four children sit around them – suggestive, perhaps, of group-work, or at least of a recognition of the place of social interaction in the learning activity. While the snapshot picture is of oral exchanges, a reminder of the enduring *written* basis of school work (what Green (1993) has called 'the insistence of the letter') is indicated by the work-books open on the children's desks and by the associated paraphernalia of rulers and writing implements. The pupils themselves are smartly and formally dressed, all in the same red cardigans or jumpers and apparently all wearing neckties. The young teacher is also smart – but in more of a 'smart casual' way. He wears dark trousers and a trendy, open-necked white shirt with the sleeves rolled up, Tony Blair-style, for action (reminding us, perhaps, that effective teachers can also be young and 'hip'). While he is unambiguously in control of the class, that control is indicated in the image through his *orchestration* of the children's (apparent 'active') learning rather than, as may have been the case in years gone by, his ability to make – and keep – the class silently at work.

The extent to which this photograph is authentic or posed we have no immediate way of knowing. For the purposes of analysis here, however, it does not really matter. The point is, it has been chosen by a government agency concerned with the training of new teachers to put on the front cover of one of its official publications. We can be reasonably secure in assuming that it is unlikely to portray a model of classroom practice and behaviour with which that government agency is anything but entirely satisfied. The image selected is one of both orderliness and active engagement, of both formality and informality, of both oracy and literacy, of both teacherly control over collective endeavour and pupils' control over their own engagement – a happy mix of tradition and progressivism.

Three kinds of pragmatism: the contingent, the principled and the discursive

The (student?) teacher in the above example may be seen as the embodiment of some universal pragmatic teacher of the twenty-first century, and indeed to represent a model of 'Third Wayist' pedagogy – more of which a little later on. However, it was very clear in our own research studies, and a particularly strong feature of our interviews with teachers in the *Professional Identities Project*, that not all teachers – even those most extrinsically and consciously espousing pragmatism – were 'being pragmatic' in the same way. Nor, moreover, were they universally 'comfortable' with their pragmatic orientations.

For some teachers we spoke to, pragmatism was clearly linked to existing pedagogies of eclecticism (Girard 1986; Larse-Freeman 1987) related to notions of pedagogic 'effectiveness' and based on a view that the best instruction needs to seek out and utilise the best of a *variety* of instructional approaches regardless of any 'ideological' content they might have. Other teachers, however, had clearly taken the concept of pragmatism a stage further, focusing not so much on the 'instrumental' aspects of pragmatism (the conscious and explicit relation of the pragmatic approach to specific teaching *methods*) but rather on pragmatism itself as an appropriate pedagogical orientation in its own right. That is to say, some teachers appeared to have adopted a *discourse of pragmatism* – perhaps an *ideology of pragmatism* – as an appropriate lens through which to consider education and pedagogy in their wider contexts and as an appropriate framework through which to construct or reconstruct their pedagogical 'selves'.

These differing articulations of the pragmatic stance suggested a taxonomy of pragmatism, comprising two related but differentiated kinds of pedagogic pragmatism – what we came to call 'contingent' and 'principled' pragmatism (Moore and Edwards 2002) – along with one qualitatively different kind of pragmatism, which we chose to call 'ideological' or 'discursive' pragmatism. (An additional form of pragmatism – 'strategic pragmatism' – was also identified in the research, principally in relation to school principals and educational management and 'leadership'. I do not intend to explore this form of pragmatism here, given that my current focus is on classroom teachers; however, further details are to be found in Moore, George and Halpin 2002 and Moore and Edwards 2002.)

I want to suggest that each kind of pragmatism (and again, these were not mutually exclusive, often coexisting within the same developing professional identity) had led the practitioner towards an orientation whereby they were able to occupy as it were a floating practical/ideological platform that shuttled back and forth between progressive and traditional orientations, enabling possible future re-migrations to these positions but also providing a 'third place' which had the capacity to become a more lasting pedagogical home. For some (particularly those I shall refer to as principled pragmatists and as discursive pragmatists), occupation of this middle ground was relatively comfortable, and indeed may have been undertaken in order to circumvent the problems of occupying (or continuing to occupy) a more 'extreme' pedagogical, ideological or philosophical position in the face of external opposition. For others (in particular, those I have identified as contingent pragmatists), occupation of the middle ground was far less comfortable, though still a necessary price to pay for professional survival.

'Contingent pragmatism': temporary settlements

Contingent pragmatism is the term we used in our analysis to identify the way in which teachers often embrace teaching approaches and philosophies *according to specific circumstances that may change with time or location*. These may be the circumstances of their own particular school's intake and location, or of their wider private and professional lives, or of particular policy pressures such as those imposed by national literacy or numeracy strategies or 'results-based funding'. In such cases, teachers may often feel *constrained or resigned* to be pragmatic, adopting pragmatism as a kind of 'coping strategy' (Woods 1985; Troman and Woods 2000), or may change their self-identification as a good or effective teacher, pinning this to prevailing conceptualisations within the official domain. The *Professional Identities Project* suggested that such pragmatism could involve the temporary suspension of previously held values and philosophical or pedagogical orientations, whereby these are, to quote one newly qualified teacher, 'put on one side', perhaps to be taken up again as and when circumstances change.

Examples of this kind of pragmatism were particularly apparent when we talked to teachers about recent trends towards more strictly enforced and traditional school uniforms in English schools, and away from mixed-ability teaching to increased setting of students according to notions of ability. We were particularly interested in attitudes to these issues, since we felt that, in addition to suggesting a particular 'political' orientation, the latter would provide us with information about the teachers' epistemological positionings, while the former might tell us a lot about how teachers saw themselves *vis-à-vis* relations of power between teachers and students.

The following example, drawn from an interview with a secondary-school teacher in his early fifties, provides an illustration of contingent pragmatism as well as of its potentially troubling nature. The interviewee – Bill – was an English teacher and assistant principal at an inner-city school that had recently moved away from mixed-ability teaching towards the increased setting of students according to ability. It had also changed from being a non-uniform school to one in which the wearing of school uniform was compulsory. Bill's attitude towards each of these developments remained touched by ambivalence. While the decision to adopt school uniform had, he told us, been taken very democratically, involving teachers, parents and pupils, he had openly opposed it at the time, on the grounds that the existence of school uniform was likely to create more problems – including more staff–pupil conflicts – than it would solve. Even though this view was based on Bill's own experience of having moved from a uniform school to a non-uniform school, he had, by the time of the interview, come to accept – if somewhat tentatively – that 'probably, overall, [introducing uniform] was the right thing'. His subsequent elaborate defence of his position, however, suggested a continuing lack of comfort with this personal shift of view and, indeed, with his shifting ground over mixed-ability teaching. It also prompted questions as to how far these shifts of attitude had been genuinely brought about by a moral imperative that prioritised democratic processes, or how far they had simply been *legitimated* by such an imperative in order to make them less uncomfortable:

> I think we had to go for uniform because of the rivalry, the competitiveness – and parents overtly wanted it. . . . I think probably overall it was the right thing. You know, I think it was because of a sense of identity. We made the uniform friendly. Most of the parents like it. Some of the kids didn't, but most of them did. . . . I think it's very hard to know in the long run. You know, our intake has gone up, and we are much more popular. That might be one of the reasons. . . . I think it might lead to an improvement in exam results, and a good [government inspection report] – you know – because those things do have an effect, quite a large effect, out there. But I'm still not . . . Again, I suppose it's like the mixed-ability thing: I'm willing to go along with whatever we agree democratically. But I was not one of the people necessarily in favour.
>
> (Bill: secondary-school teacher, *Professional Identities Project*)

Bill's self-conscious and slightly reluctant change of view (clearly, Bill was not the universal pragmatist portrayed on the cover of the TTA's corporate plan!) was typical of the 'contingently pragmatic' responses of many of the classroom teachers we spoke to, and a reminder of the extent to which discourses of good teaching are linked both to feelings we have towards our professional 'selves' in the wider life of the school *and* to other social discourses. While the apologetic, somewhat unconvincing nature of his response speaks of half-hearted acceptance rather than full-blown allegiance to an item of policy change, it seeks to justify what has clearly been an uncomfortable, enforced change of approach within the terms of a pre-existing, comfortable and highly valued one – in this case, an allegiance to 'democracy'. It also implies that the acceptance of this particular change is something of a temporary settlement, flagged by the parenthetical but significant 'I think probably . . . But I'm still not . . .'

Whether Bill's settlement – which appeared to provide a degree of comfort that allowed him to get on with the principal task of teaching to the best of his ability within the pulls and constraints of a not-always-sympathetic *system* – would *remain* temporary or become permanent was uncertain. Much will depend, in these cases, on the individual teacher. As far as Bill was concerned, the changes that he had reluctantly accepted, although they may have been prompted by changes in the wider social and educational systems, were changes that had been initiated within the school itself, and it was partly for this reason that he had accepted them with equanimity if not with enthusiasm. Other teachers, including other teachers at

Bill's school, presented themselves more as *victims* of imposed change, however, particularly where they felt that these were being enforced by powerful systems that rendered opposition futile, and that they were being pushed away from their own versions of the good teacher towards other versions with which they felt far less comfortable. Such teachers (Moore, Edwards, Halpin and George 2002) also adapted pragmatically to contingencies, but with a far greater degree of reluctance and discomfort than Bill, and with a far greater feeling of their own cherished pedagogical values – and even their own educational philosophies – being undermined in the process. As another teacher at Bill's school put this in relation to the changes he felt forced upon him by, among other things, increased formal testing of students:

> I have become less progressive: I have become reactionary, I find . . . I have become less liberal . . . in my thoughts about education. As a teacher, I have become more abrasive.
>   (Graeme: secondary-school teacher, *Professional Identities Project*)

To return to an earlier point, we might say that while Bill seemed to support the view that teachers are often aware of ideological contradictions in their work and 'feel themselves involved in difficult choices and . . . having to make compromises' (Billig *et al.* 1988, p. 46), some of these other teachers, *like* Graeme, rather brought to mind Britzman's observation that 'there are always *antagonistic* discourses that urge particular dispositions at the cost of others' (Britzman 1991, p. 223, my italics).

Principled pragmatism: beyond here and now

Britzman's suggestion (1991, p. 223) that 'no teaching identity is ever single or without contradictions' and Billig *et al.*'s argument (1988, p. 46) that teachers' ideological conceptions are not always 'neatly packaged and consistent' offer a helpful introduction to considerations of a different kind of professional pragmatism, which I am calling 'principled pragmatism'. By 'principled pragmatism' I refer to those cases wherein teachers adopt introduced changes into their existing practice more deliberately and proactively than is the case with contingent pragmatism, and are happy, in hindsight, to justify them within the wider contexts of their work. Such pragmatism is usually more comfortably accomplished than contingent pragmatism, and is possibly more durable.

An illustration of this kind of pragmatism is offered in the testimony of a young secondary-school teacher, Edward, who worked in a different school from Bill and Graeme (see also Moore, Edwards, Halpin and George 2002). Edward came across in interview as self-consciously eclectic and pragmatic, both in his *pedagogy*, through which he proactively and without prejudice sought out and used a variety of instructional approaches, and in his educational *views*, including views about recent educational reforms such as the greater devolution of budgets to schools or the imposition on English schools of a National Curriculum.

Some of Edward's pragmatism was of the 'contingent' variety described above – it appeared thrust upon him, with varying degrees of coercion, by circumstances outside his immediate control and carried with it conceptualisations of the good teacher that did not necessarily chime with those he already possessed. Edward cited, for example, the constraints of available financial and material resources as forcing him towards a more 'traditional', front-of-class approach to teaching than the one he had begun with, which, given those constraints, had limited his time for the preparation for and marking of his students' work. While he had not, he said, ruled out the possibility of a return to a more 'progressive' mode of teaching, that would only happen if the economic circumstances, nationally or locally, changed sufficiently to make it practicable.

It was precisely Edward's willingness to accept local and temporal constraints in respect of his professional practice, however, that simultaneously reflected and created the possibility for that other kind of pragmatism – 'principled pragmatism' – that I have identified, which is characterised by the fact that its case can be argued by the teacher *beyond specific reference to the here and now.*

An example of this kind of principled-pragmatic response was provided by Edward's interesting explanation of sitting his students in rows (in opposition to his previous practice of sitting them in small groups around tables) and the promotion within his classroom of 'democracy'. Observing that he saw himself as 'neither "progressive" nor "traditional"', Edward went on to say:

> I try to look back on each of those approaches and use parts of them both. . . . I would say I am a happy medium of traditional and progressive. . . . Traditional – you can see the chairs in rows; but progressive in the sense that I'm . . . keen on allowing students to speak for themselves.
>
> (Edward: secondary-school teacher, *Professional Identities Project*)

Though sitting his students in rows may have originated – at least partly – in his perceived need to rethink classroom management in the context of externally imposed economic constraints, it was clear from his testimony that Edward had come to see – or perhaps to find – a *value* in this different approach, arguing that, contrary to what one might expect, the physical 'isolation' and compulsory ordering of his students had not compromised his agenda for developing democratic processes and practices within his classroom, or for promoting student voices: on the contrary, he even suggested that the increased amount of 'control' effected by the arrangement provided a better context and climate for the development of classroom 'conversations' (cf. the fictional Mr Thackeray, described in Chapter 3 above) which, he felt, most of his students had hitherto been unused to and had consequently been rather poor at.

While it could be argued that Edward – like Bill, perhaps – was simply seeking a justification for an action which he initially (and perhaps still) found undesirable in his own or others' eyes, inserting an indefensible resort to traditionalism into an acceptable discourse of democracy, his undisguised enthusiasm for the change tended to argue against such an interpretation. In striking contrast to Bill (who did not suggest that school uniform or setted classes had contributed to democracy; merely that they had been introduced by way of a democratic *process*), Edward's movement in this case may have been contingent and approach-based at its inception, but had evidently 'become' principled and attitude-based over time – comprising, perhaps, a move away from the kinds of 'temporary', 're-orientation' change described by McLaughlin (1991), in which the teacher or school absorbs 'the language of reform but not its substance' (Ball 1997, p. 261), towards a more durable 'colonisation' change (ibid.) that involves a major shift in 'the cultural core of the organization' – incorporating, in this case, the culture and value-system of the individual classroom teacher.

'Discursive pragmatism': Third Wayism in the classroom

I want to suggest that each of these two kinds of pragmatism is qualitatively different from a third kind that we came to identify in our study as *discursive* or *ideological* pragmatism. Unlike contingent and principled pragmatism, discursive pragmatism is descriptive not so much of the particular pragmatic response itself, but rather of a particular orientation *towards* pragmat*ism*. It is an orientation already evident, in a small way, in Edward's suggestion that 'I try to look back on each of those approaches and use parts of both of them': an orientation, that is, whose presupposition is that pragmatism has a value *in its own right* – that it is an appropriate, 'balanced', 'rational' approach to professional life. Within this orientation, a pragmatic response is likely to be found on the teacher's part across a far wider range of changes than was the case with Edward, who for all his 'pro-pragmatic' stance was still firmly resistant to the possible impacts of some imposed policy changes such as the UK government's 'back to basics' agenda – which, he felt, had undermined teachers' professional judgement, over-simplified the educational issues, and promoted mechanistic, 'uninventive' modes of teaching and learning.

An example of this third kind of pragmatism can be found in the following extract from one of our interviews with a primary-school principal, Helen:

> There are a lot of good things about the child-centred 'seventies educational climate that we've been keen to hang on to, but we also grasped

some initiatives which . . . are actually taking education back towards a more traditional approach. . . . I think that the problem with education too often in the past is that it . . . polarised politically. . . . And because New Labour haven't polarised it, in a sense it's a bit more difficult to make those distinctions. I think that people [now] are much more pragmatic in the methods they use. So things like pupil grouping don't become a political issue so much. You are actually looking at the evidence, you are looking at the research and what works best for the kids, what are the pros and cons.

(Helen: primary-school principal, *Professional Identities Project*)

Helen's *educational* (re-)orientation, as illustrated both here and elsewhere in her testimony, appears to be based not so much on cherished or even 'new' educational *values*, or on the conflicts and accommodations between these values and the 'imposed' values of mandated reform, but rather on a notion that:

- children's education has previously suffered at the hands of ideological conflicts between and among educators and policy makers;
- the current UK government has adopted a (desirable) 'ideologically neutral' approach to education;
- this approach is based on disinterested considerations of 'evidence' rather than on unquestioned, ideological 'stands'.

The suggestion that student grouping is 'not a political issue' is a somewhat curious one, which only achieves credence *within* the discourse and ideology of pragmatism. Effectively, it sidelines issues of gender, race, class and power relations in the classroom, condemning these to the reconfigured wastelands of ideology and to the unhelpful practices of the ideological bandits who operate there. With its clear links to 'Third Wayism' (Blair 1998) in the wider political field, such observations as Helen's illustrate how discursive pragmatism operates as yet another force for *conservatism*, representing what Toynbee (2001) calls an '*escape* from self-definition' in which politics as previously understood, characterised by argument, passion and debate, is effectively 'killed off' in favour of a *pseudo*-politics of contrived consensus. Pragmatism in this context becomes a desirable orientation and achievement in itself: an ideology at whose centre, paradoxically, is a critical, rhetorical *opposition* to ideology and, therefore, by implication, to the very conviction-politics whose robes it often borrows.

Pragmatism as dogmatism

In the educational context, the 'pragmatic turn' is not, of course, necessarily or inevitably a development to be resisted – certainly, for example, when allied to the kind of careful, open-minded approach suggested by the student teacher quoted at the start of this chapter. In terms of developing more sophisticated *understandings* of the teaching experience, whether as practitioners or as researchers, it can also help move us

> beyond the assumption that students' thinking can be adequately captured by static dichotomies such as traditional versus progressive, conservative versus liberal, or custodial versus humanistic.
>
> (Goodman 1988, p. 121; see also Boler 1999)

As with the other discourses, however, I want to suggest that the pragmatic turn does become problematic when adopted as a new dogma, ideology or discourse (that is, when it becomes *discursive*) that deflects pedagogic activity away from its political, socially oriented aspects too far towards an emphasis on the methodological and the practical – to adapt a metaphor of Kress's (Kress 1989, p. 7), when it represents the invading army of a 'military power' (in this case, usually the competences discourse) 'whose response to border skirmishes is to occupy the adjacent territory' (that of the teacher as social activist). If we accept Dewey's dictum (1938, p. 10) that 'any theory and set of practices is dogmatic which is not based upon critical examination of its own underlying principles', we may need to be particularly concerned when pragmatism – adopted *as* a 'theory and set of practices' – excuses itself from such internal investigation purely on the grounds of its own self-validating fundamentalism: that is to say, on the basis that it is inevitably and intrinsically good since it avoids the taking up of (inevitably bad) 'extreme' positions.

An allied danger is that the adoption of such a position makes political *opposition* something of a dirty word, in the process deflecting pedagogic activity away from its political, socially oriented imperatives and from its concerns with the means by which learning is promoted and developed towards bland technicism where all that is important is the production of an appropriately skilled (or unskilled) workforce. As Hartnett and Carr have argued, it is fundamental to the teacher's role that it has a strong social and political dimension – that it is not merely about 'raising standards' (of, for example, the most basic of literacies and numeracies) but that it is concerned with critiquing and promoting the good life:

> Teachers are . . . central to a principled democratic theory of education. Society is dependent upon the quality of their judgements, values, knowledge and sensitivities, in particular in social contexts, to negotiate acceptable solutions to issues of authority in education; to sustain the development of democratic values in the wider society; and to creating a social environment in which children can deliberate about, and reflect critically upon, the nature of the good life and the good society. It is teachers who should be a centre of resistance to totalitarian, centralist and utopian thinking and control within society. They are a critical

pivot between the state, parental power, institutional power and the development of democratic values and attitudes in each new generation.

(1995, p. 43)

Discursive pragmatism and the 'de-politicisation' of teachers

As I have already suggested, the pragmatic turn can, in the context of formal education, bring advantages to both teachers and pupils – particularly when it is indicative of a more balanced approach to teaching that seeks to select the best practice available and to reject discredited practice. It can, however, when it takes the discursive or ideological turn, also lead to a de-politicising agenda, whereby:

- teachers become more 'accepting' of and less resistant to government policy on education (including policy that, in their hearts, they may be *politically opposed to*);
- they become more inclined to 'position' themselves both professionally and philosophically in terms of the local, instrumental rather than wider, social effects of key educational issues (see also Coldron and Smith 1999);
- they become less likely to mobilise locally or nationally for active, collective political opposition, tending to divert their energies to the 'internal' politics of their own institutions (McLaren 1996).

In exploring these possibilities a little further, we need do no more than return to the forms of pragmatism identified in the classroom teachers in our *Professional Identities Project*, where a relatively high degree of the pragmatic responses – especially where the pragmatism was 'contingent' – were characterised by reluctance, resignation and (Smyth *et al.* 1999) a sense of 'being done to'. As I have already indicated, these less enthusiastic forms of pragmatic response often led to justifications of the acceptance and implementation of unliked policy through its framing within discourses that were more acceptable, or through an insistence on locating debates around the issues in local (contingent) *circumstances* rather than addressing wider social *issues* ('I oppose school uniform/streaming/front-of-class teaching/the literacy strategy in principle, but I can appreciate their usefulness in this particular school/classroom/socio-economic location' etc.). It also resulted in an increased unwillingness on the part of many of the teachers we interviewed to debate such key educational and social issues as:

- the relevance and status of social justice in the school curriculum;
- the degree of importance of 'basic' literacy and numeracy skills in relation to social, creative and thinking skills;
- the choice of 'content' in school curriculum subjects;

- the desirability or otherwise (on social rather than narrowly 'academic' grounds) and the corresponding effects of 'setting' or 'streaming' students according to 'ability';
- the pros and cons of school uniform.

On these issues, many teachers seemed reluctant to take – almost guilty about taking – an oppositional stance, and any 'resistant' positioning seemed to have become, by and large, apologetic or weak. Certainly, opposition to the official line on such matters was not on the collective public agenda of most of the classroom teachers we spoke to, who at best talked in somewhat furtive, besieged terms of 'subverting' the new orthodoxies of setting, of focusing on numeracy and literacy skills, of returning to 'traditional' pedagogies, and of continuing to present a largely Anglo-centric school curriculum. To quote one primary-school teacher, Kaz, who had elsewhere told us that children ought to be 'encouraged to question and think about things', and that an emphasis on 'the basics' was likely to result in a 'loss of the whole . . . broad education':

> The children seem to really like the literacy hour. They like the routine of it. They like to sit and read a book and do their phonics and then have their activities.
>
> (Kaz: primary-school teacher, *Professional Identities Project*)

As with Bill, Kaz appeared to be 'justifying' her part in the implementation of a potentially controversial policy change by embedding it in a more universally acceptable discourse: in this case, rather surprisingly, perhaps, given that the curriculum is seldom, if ever, constructed around 'what children like', the discourse of customer satisfaction. Like Bill and other teachers we interviewed, Kaz used a pragmatic orientation to seek out a 'comfort zone' in which, feeling very much like a lone and disempowered operator rather than a member of a collective workforce, she would not have to wrestle internally with potentially discomforting issues, or feel obliged to engage in public debates wherein any opposition to the new orthodoxies of setting, mechanistic testing, league tables, corporate identities, and maximally detailed national curricula is immediately pathologised as obstructive. While pragmatic, eclectic approaches to pedagogy may have much to recommend them in steering teachers away from dominant discourses of competence and charisma, traditionalism and progressivism, the good teacher as conceived within the pragmatic *discourse* is also, necessarily, the teacher who *complies*.

7 The reflexive turn – exploring private and professional selves

> It is essential a teacher understands the human condition, and I believe the way to do that is to know myself.
>
> (Dan: student teacher, *Reflective Practice Project*)

> During my reflections on what I think constitutes 'a good teacher', I also looked at the influence from my family. These memories and experiences also have a large bearing on my feelings towards motivating pupils to learn and to want to learn.
>
> (Celia: student teacher, *Reflective Practice Project*)

> In the postmodern world multiple rather than singular forms of intelligence are coming to be recognized . . . multiple rather than singular forms of representation of students' work are being advocated and accepted. . . . Many ways of knowing, thinking and being moral, not just rational, 'logical' ones, are coming to be seen as legitimate.
>
> (Hargreaves 1993, p. 22)

The reflexive turn: including the self in the reflective process

In the previous chapter, consideration was given to one kind of practitioner 'positioning': that is, the strategic, essentially instrumental adoption of the pragmatic stance. In this chapter, I want to look at a contrasting, perhaps even an oppositional positioning: that of reflexivity. While the pragmatic turn may help teachers and student teachers with regard to immediate and continuing survival – and I have not intended to understate or underestimate the value, legitimacy or importance of such a course – I believe that the reflexive turn (which, if the testimony of the student teachers in our *Reflective Practice Project* is anything to go by, is quite capable of being nurtured and developed *alongside* the pragmatic turn) offers practitioners the best hope, however uncomfortable the approach may prove in the short term, of long-term professional happiness and improvement of classroom practice.

The concept of reflexivity is one that increasingly occurs in writing and research about the social sciences in general and about education in particular, and is often referenced to research practice itself (Alvesson and Skoldberg 2000; Davies 1999; Shacklock and Smyth 1998). Since reflexivity can have a number of different meanings, it is important to begin this chapter by reminding ourselves how the term is being interpreted for the purposes of this particular book, and developing points introduced in Chapter 5 regarding the ways in which reflexivity differs from other forms of reflective practice.

In one way, the meaning I have adopted is close to that of Giddens, who has talked of the 'reflexive project of the self, which consists in the sustaining of coherent, yet continuously revised, biographical narratives' (Giddens 1991, p. 5). I am aware that such a conceptualisation may be seen as tending to acknowledge, confirm or celebrate the *delusory*. (I am thinking, for instance, of the kinds of life-narratives described by Convery (1999), wherein teachers construct, in interview, stories of the development of their professional selves which may be based more closely on self-images with which they can feel comfortable than with self-critique.) However, the fundamental *intention* of the reflexive project with which I am concerned is that it should be authentically and constructively critical, that it should be challenging rather than confirmatory, and that it should 'use the past' (Mitchell and Weber 1996) by way of promoting better understandings of the present and perhaps promoting more rewarding futures.

This particular version of the reflexive turn is linked to:

- the notion that, whether professionally or more generally, we need to perceive and understand our 'selves' as comprising multiple rather than singular identities;
- an understanding that discourses such as that of the competent craftsperson with its universalising turn, or the charismatic subject discourse with its essentialist turn, or variants of the reflective practice discourse that over-emphasise individual over collective responsibility, operate against such a perception and understanding;
- the need for flexible responses to meet the demands of specific and perhaps changing situations and circumstances (the contingent) as well as taking full and constructive account of our own individuality (the idiosyncratic). (As McLaughlin and Talbert (1990, p. 1) ask: 'How is it that two teachers with the same educational background and professional aspirations who are teaching in the same objective school context – in schools with similar levels of resources and student and community characteristics, for example – can develop substantively different instructional goals, practices, and student learning outcomes?' They conclude (ibid., p. 2): 'Research prompts us . . . to see effective teaching as the product of individual attributes and the settings in which teachers work and learn to teach');

- an emphasis on accommodation rather than assimilation (opening ourselves to the possibility of modifying our own understandings and behaviours rather than limiting our understandings and behaviours to what
  we have pre-decided, or seeking to force situations and other people
  into conforming to our unquestioned world-view);
- in terms of the pedagogical project, an emphasis on 'navigation' (for
  example, helping young people to acquire and develop the skills and
  orientations they will need to make their way successfully, both individually and collectively, through an uncertain future) rather than control
  (for example, focusing on the reproduction of conformity and the status
  quo).

Unlike the notion of self implied in the competences discourse, in the
charismatic subject discourse and, to a lesser extent, in much of what
passes for reflection in the reflective practitioner discourse, these notions of
self prioritise individual and collective flexibility and collaboration along
with informed understandings of the multiple contexts within which one
operates. In doing this, they introduce, in place of the notion of the unified,
ideal, 'Cartesian' self (favoured by the competent craftsperson and charismatic subject discourses), the material, constructed self: that is, the self as a
'text' which is formed at the intersections of various discursive practices
and which can be 'read' both by others and 'by the self itself'.

These alternative notions of the self, and of the manner in which it is
constructed, have given rise to new modes of practice in initial teacher education as well as to new forms of theoretical inquiry, in which teachers and
student teachers are encouraged to interrogate and critically reflect upon not
only their pupils' behaviours or what has 'happened' in the classroom (in
terms of failure and success), but also their own behaviours – on the ways
in which they have responded to situations, interacted with other people
and experienced emotional responses. Such practice, which re-emphasises
the significance of intra- as well as inter-personal relationships in classroom
practice, starts from the premise that teachers are, indeed, 'made' – though
not quite in the sense inscribed within the competences discourse. When
they come to teaching, for example, teachers already bring with them a
history and a culture through which they have negotiated and – however
impermanently – 'fixed' meanings, orientations and understandings about
such things as how learning works, what schools and education are for
and how teachers should conduct themselves, which are immediately subject to revisitations once the practice of teaching begins. Teachers also
bring, whether they want to or not, emotional, historical 'baggage' which,
in the highly charged atmosphere of the school classroom, can intrude on
practice and experience both positively and negatively (negatively when, for
example, the classroom becomes the social space for the playing out or
repetition of family-related repressions, irresolutions and role anxieties). As
Smyth argues:

[D]eveloping teachers and improving their teaching involves more than giving them new tricks. We are beginning to recognize that, for teachers, what goes on inside the classroom is closely related to what goes on outside it. . . . Teachers learn in the way they do not just because of the skills they have or have not learned. The ways they teach are also grounded in their backgrounds, their biographies, in the kinds of teachers they have become.

(1995, p. vii)

In making a not dissimilar point, Hartnett and Carr remind us that it is not only teachers who have a past, who are 'constructed', but also the systems and institutions within which they work – suggesting that the real work of reflexivity is to explore the one context *within the context of the other*:

Teachers do not work and reflect in a social vacuum. They act within institutions, structures and processes which have a past and a social momentum.

(1995, p. 41)

The reflexive project in the field of school teaching and teacher education encourages teachers, appropriately supported by their tutors (Combs 1972; Wragg 1974), not only to reflect critically on continuing experiences *in themselves*, but to contextualise these experiences within previous experiences as a way of developing more helpful teaching strategies and orientations (Quicke 1988; Schon 1988; Cole and Knowles 1995; Thomas 1995). Part of that activity, aimed at helping practitioners to understand more clearly 'the way in which a personal life can be penetrated by the social and the practical' (Thomas 1995, p. 5) and to make sense of 'prior and current life experiences in the context of the personal as it influences the professional' (Cole and Knowles 1995, p. 130), involves encouraging individual teachers and student teachers to critique difficulties they may be experiencing in the here and now within the context of previous roles and experiences they have encountered 'outside' the classroom situation in, for example, their family life or their own schooling, rather than ignoring or denying such encounters. Inevitably, this also introduces issues of *desire* (Hargreaves 1994; McLaren 1996; Boler 1999) into understandings of practice: 'What do I want from these interactions?' 'What do others want of me?' 'What am I afraid of?' 'What do I want to do about the things I don't like here?' – and perhaps the hardest and yet most glibly answered of all: 'Why did I choose to become a teacher [in the first place]?'

There are, of course, obvious dangers in an approach that invites teachers to interrogate their own behaviours textually. Chief among these are:

(a) that practitioners and their tutors may engage in ill-informed 'amateur psycho-analysis' that ends up benefiting nobody or even worsening an already difficult situation;

(b) that the reflexive approach may slip into the very pathologisations implied by the dominant discourses we have already considered, and provide yet another way of obscuring the 'macro blot' (Bernstein 1995, p. 56).

In relation to the first of these potential difficulties, teachers and teacher educators might be well advised to take heed of Sigmund Freud's observation in relation to his students of psycho-analysis, that 'It will be enough if [the student] learns something *about* psycho-analysis and something *from* it' (1968, p. 173, my italics). The point has already been made that the invitation to reflexivity of the kind I am suggesting is not an invitation to psycho-analysis (we must assume, after all, that our students are not likely to be in need of such therapy). It is, rather, founded on a suggestion that teachers do not only need to know 'how to teach'; they need also to learn something – perhaps something about themselves – *from the teaching activity*. More recently, Anna Freud has taken this notion a step further in relation to pedagogic activity and reflexive/reflective practice, suggesting that teachers have a *duty* to attempt to understand their own actions and reactions in order to avoid the possible negative consequences on their pupils of a failure or a refusal to do so. To quote Britzman and Pitt's summary of Anna Freud's (1979) position:

> [T]eachers' encounters with students may return them involuntarily and still unconsciously to scenes from their individual biographies. Such an exploration requires that teachers consider how they understand students through their own subjective conflicts. . . . The heart of the matter, for Anna Freud, is the ethical obligation teachers have to learn about their own conflicts and to control the re-enactment of old conflicts that appear in the guise of new pedagogical encounters.
>
> (Britzmann and Pitt 1996, p. 118)

Concerning the second danger, that reflexivity may lead to the same kinds of pathologisation, negativity and 'personalisation' of problems as sometimes occurs in relation to discourses of competence, charisma and reflection, it is particularly important to remember that there is a great deal of difference between, on the one hand, *understanding* our emotions and learning to live with them (one of the key features of the reflexive turn) and, on the other, denying or directly subjugating them. To quote one primary-school teacher, Mike (*Professional Identities Project*), 'Sometimes, it's really tough, and you have to let it get raw: forget the strategies and techniques for a while, and just accept that sometimes it's just you and them and it *can* be a battle' – echoing the suggestion of one of the student teachers on our *Reflective Practice Project* that 'sometimes you have to make judgements about how much rein to allow your emotions and how much to bottle them up'.

As Boler (1999) reminds us, while some emotions may be actively encouraged in schools (typically, those related to 'empathy', obedience, respect and tolerance), others (for example, anger, rejection, or emotions leading to behaviour that may be deemed confrontational) tend to be outlawed. While there may be perfectly good and ultimately acceptable reasons for this, problems do arise when emotional issues become locked exclusively into matters of obedience and 'discipline', and rendered 'safe' through their colonisation or incarceration by rationalistic (and rationalising) discourses such as those of competence and reflection.

An interesting parallel to the development of the reflective practitioner discourse, which I have not had time to explore in this text, is that of the development of the 'reflective pupil', linked by Boler to some recent conceptualisations of 'emotional intelligence'. Within the terms of this discourse, 'misbehaving' pupils, rather than being subjected to punishments resulting in, say, an immediate loss of privilege, are 'counselled' in order for them to understand why their behaviour is 'inappropriate', to reflect upon the impact of their behaviour on others, and to 'modify' their future behaviour accordingly. When the desire of teachers is similarly subjugated by discourses of 'reason' (and the reflexive turn is by no means immune to such subjugations), being in touch with one's fears, angers, frustrations and, indeed, the joy of teaching, can, rather than leading to happier, more effective practice, all too easily result in debilitating self-consciousness of the kind experienced by one student teacher on the *Autobiography Project*, who complained in one of his diary entries:

> Sometimes you can think a bit too much about what motivates and demotivates you until you don't seem to be able to see the wood from the trees any more. Teaching in my opinion is mainly about doing things, it's about practising and experiencing and trying things out and learning from that, not necessarily in ways that are articulated or that you are even consciously aware of. Thinking too consciously about a lot of stuff has I feel resulted in making it hard for me in the past to be spontaneous, and that hasn't been a positive thing. Maybe I'm just not ready for that kind of reflection yet?
>
> (Justin: student teacher, *Autobiography Project*)

Each of these potential dangers calls for care and common sense, I would suggest, rather than for a blanket dismissal of the reflexive approach. We must never forget that two of the other discourses we have considered – those of the competent craftsperson and the charismatic subject – are also replete with dangers, not least in their reluctance fully to acknowledge either the emotive, autobiographical aspects of classroom interactions or the socio-historical contexts within which classroom practice occurs: omissions which often cut off central avenues of explanation for perplexed teachers when things go wrong. Experience, furthermore, suggests that the incorporation of the 'reflexive turn' *with* those of (say) the competent craftsperson and the reflective practitioner can, if properly handled, have very beneficial effects, not least for student teachers experiencing classroom difficulties and for those who, in terms of seeking and responding to advice, seem to have reached an impasse of the kind 'I have tried everything, and everything has failed' described elsewhere in this book. As has already been indicated, this is not a question of *substituting* the competences and reflective practitioner discourses with the reflexive turn, but rather of adopting it 'outside' those discourses in a way that makes it easier and more profitable for students to 'enter', to understand and to negotiate them; that is to say, a contextualising function that helps replace morbid, unconstructive 'self'-criticism ('Something *in me* is wrong') with constructive, reasoned, 'action' criticism ('Something *that's happening* needs my attention').

Reflexive reflection: moving beyond the basics

In exploring in a little more detail where the reflexive project might come from, where it might take us, and how reflexivity might differ from what is sometimes included in the notion of 'reflection', I want to take a course of action that students are often recommended not to take, and to look at some dictionary definitions of these two terms – not with the intention of finding a neat answer to my questions but rather by way of moving towards more helpful working understandings of the terms. This involves a process of drawing out, from the multiplicity of meanings typically attributed to each term, some elements that are common to both and some that are not.

The *Chambers English Dictionary* (1990) – which I have selected for no better reason than that it happens to be the one usually sitting on my desk – includes in its definitions of 'reflect' 'to give an image of in the manner of a mirror', 'to consider meditatively', 'to cast a light'. Among the definitions of 'reflexion' are 'change of direction when an electromagnetic wave or sound-wave strikes on a surface and is thrown back', 'the action of mind by which it is conscious of its own operations', 'a thought or utterance arising from contemplation'. Definitions of 'reflex', meanwhile, include 'illuminated by light from another part of the same picture', 'reflected light', and, with reference to the single-lens *reflex camera*, 'one in which the image is reflected on to a glass screen for composing and focusing'.

In terms of the reflective practitioner discourse discussed in the previous chapter, it will be immediately clear that there are certain similarities here in the way that the two concepts of reflection and reflexivity *might* be used in the educational context. Both include the notion of pondering on things, of thinking about how and why things have happened ('to consider meditatively', 'a thought or utterance arising from contemplation'), and both incorporate a sense of 'illuminating' a particular situation, problem or practice. Both are also concerned with the notion of a 'change of direction' brought about by a particular action which brings one thing or property into contact with another, as exemplified by the student teacher who 'tries something out' in the classroom – a particular strategy, a text, a classroom arrangement, a manner of self-presenting – as a result of which they not only change the course of the originally planned lesson or suite of lessons but allow for some more lasting change in their own practice, perception, understanding or self-awareness. In 'reflecting' upon this change of direction, the student teacher will be as concerned to contemplate – and perhaps even to give permission to – their *own* development as they will to contemplate and take full advantage of the class's or individual pupil's development.

Some of the additional definitions given for 'reflexion' and 'reflex', however, provide us with a useful entry-point into an understanding of what reflexivity might mean in the context of professional practice, and the ways in which it is significantly different from what sometimes passes for reflective practice itself. One of these definitions, the 'action of mind by which it is conscious of its own operations', highlights an essential characteristic of reflexivity, that it is not just about the ability to reflect on what has happened and what one has done but about the ability to *reflect on the way in which one has reflected*. (Why, for example, has one approached an issue in one way or from one direction rather than another? Why has one highlighted certain things in the reflection rather than others?) This idea finds its expression in a body of recent work that foregrounds the importance and benefits of 'learning about learning' (Flutter *et al.* 1998; Watkins *et al.* 2000), and can also be found in Bourdieu's suggestion that the 'habitus' – those normally 'hidden dispositions' that typically guide our actions and choices without our conscious awareness of what is happening – can be made 'visible' and therefore worked upon towards the possibility of change by what Bourdieu calls the 'awakening of consciousness and socioanalysis' (Bourdieu 1990, p. 116; see also Moore 2000).

Two of the other definitions of 'reflexivity' and 'reflexive' also provide particularly useful *metaphors* in relation to our understanding of the reflexive turn, and it is on these that I want, briefly, to focus. They are the notions of:

- a *part* of a picture being illuminated by light *from another part of the same picture*; and
- an image being 'held' as a reflection, where it can be worked upon creatively before becoming 'fixed'.

The concept of a part of a picture being illuminated by light from another part of the same picture, usually applied to painting or photography, offers a particularly useful insight into the *context* within which reflexivity operates and is cited, as well as the *manner* in which the operation of reflexivity is carried out. The notion of an image being 'held' that is to be actively and creatively 'worked upon' also provides a useful metaphor in terms of its recognition that images are, in a sense, 'produced' by the viewer rather than simply being 'received' or recorded: that the viewer, that is to say, may not appear in the image as an 'object' but is nevertheless always present – we might say, omnipresent – in terms of its composition and its interpretation.

As was pointed out in Chapter 5, one of the difficulties with straight-forward reflection is that the limits of reflection are often constrained by what is immediately 'visible' to the person undertaking the reflection. In terms of reflection on classroom practice, for example, the limits or scope of the reflection may be set by what occurs inside the classroom, rather than (say) the reflective practitioner looking for explanations of events that might exist independently of the classroom situation. Similarly, the manner of reflection may be constrained by a rather narrow set of questions (increasingly, those embedded in the competences and standards discourse) such as: 'Who learned what?'; 'How did my classroom management strategies work?'; 'Did my planning take appropriate and full account of the need to differentiate?'; 'Was I adequately prepared in terms of my subject knowledge?'

While it must be stressed, again, that there is nothing wrong with these kinds of question or this kind of reflection, reflexivity moves the critical practitioner *beyond* such forms of self-evaluation towards its location (to refer back to the dictionary definition) in a much bigger picture: a picture that may include the practitioner's own history, dispositions, prejudices and fears, as well as the wider social, historical and cultural contexts in which schooling itself is situated. In other words, within *reflexivity*, that which is being evaluated or reflected upon (that 'part of the picture') is not treated as if it were the whole of the picture, but is made sense of by reference to what is happening in the rest of the larger picture. As John Elliott, himself a leading proponent of reflexive-reflective practice, argues:

> the practitioner reflects upon the taken-for-granted beliefs and assumptions which underpin his/her practical interpretations of professional values and their origins in his/her life experiences and history. (S)he begins to reconstruct his/her constructs of value and discovers that this opens up new understandings of the situation and new possibilities for intelligent action within it.
>
> (1993c, p. 69)

This suggests, as a prerequisite for reflexivity, that the practitioner is aware of the existence of that bigger picture in the first place, as well as of its potential significance and value. Furthermore, as Hartley (1997, p. 79) has argued, it includes an understanding of – and a willingness to engage with – issues of *desire* in that bigger picture: 'the desire of the teacher to teach' and 'the desire of the learner to learn'. Hartley agrees with McWilliam's assessment (McWilliam 1995) that this is 'a "risky" discourse', recognising that 'its initial effect is to disrupt and to look beneath the cool surface of the smug sensibilities of classroom competences on the part of both teacher and pupils'; however, he implies long-term benefits in such disruptions, both for the teacher and for the taught.

Techniques of reflexivity

It will be evident from all this that processes of contextualisation and recontextualisation are central to the reflexive project: not only contextualisations and recontextualisations that relate to personal and collective histories, moreover, but those, too, that are concerned with ideologies and discourses – including those dominant discourses of 'good teaching' that have been considered in previous chapters. To be reflexive about one's practice requires a certain 'holding' of the practice itself, both in its constituent parts and *in toto*: a holding that can be 'located' within different discursive practices to offer multiple readings. When a lesson goes well or badly, for example – for whatever specific reason(s) – the inquest can be conducted not just within the competent craftsperson discourse *or* the charismatic subject discourse *or* the reflective practice discourse, but within the competent craftsperson discourse *and* the charismatic subject discourse *and* the reflective practice discourse. That is to say, the situation, the experience, can be understood in a variety of ways through its being framed and reframed within the competing, overlapping discourses within which our practice occurs and, indeed, through experimentation with the focus of what is to be understood.

It is precisely this capacity and willingness to 'carry away' our experiences, responses and initial understandings and to analyse them from a variety of perspectives, entertaining a variety of explanations, that characterises the reflexive approach and that gives an indication of how, even as it problematises and complexifies, it offers the practitioner hope and support. What is curious is that it does so precisely by inserting the personal both into the analysis and interpretation of specific situations and events *and* into its wider social and historical contexts, rather than merely dwelling on a personal account that is *de*-contextualised or unhelpfully located (in, for example, misplaced or misunderstood concerns about our behavioural 'impact' on others) – a process which helps to 'de-personalise' often very personally experienced classroom difficulties and successes, encouraging the (student) teacher towards more constructive/productive responses to their reflections and evaluations than might be the case if they thought only about the 'here and now' of each perceived success and failure. To quote M. Johnston:

Discourse that is [truly] reflective will include more than an inward look at the personal, because the personal is embedded historically and morally in socially shared meanings that can be examined.

(1994, p. 11)

In summary, we might say that whereas some forms of reflection tend to focus on the immediate, to be self-referential, and to feed directly into plans, tactics and strategies (an essentially instrumentalist orientation), reflexivity focuses more on the broader picture of the social contexts of classroom interactions, including the teacher's and their students' biographies and experiences, and hence is part of a 'slower', longer-term route to improved practice through developing self-understandings that may feed into teaching in ways that are often not planned in advance. As I have sought to imply, reflexivity may be undertaken in a number of ways, making use of a variety of techniques, but all with the notion of exploring – and sharing – personal biographies at their heart. Some of these techniques are described very usefully in Mitchell and Weber's book *Reinventing Ourselves as Teachers*. They include activities such as:

- remembering and talking about our own good and bad school experiences as children;
- using school photographs as a way into self-study;
- considering our own and others' attitudes to the teacher's physical presence in the classroom – the way teachers 'look' and dress;
- exploring images of teachers and teaching in popular film and fiction;
- exploring video-recordings of ourselves in teaching situations.

As Mitchell and Weber say of this practice:

The idea of reinvention . . . implies an approach to professional identity that is ongoing – we are perpetually becoming teachers, so to speak. The term also connotes playfulness, pleasure, and fantasy – things we may not usually associate with professional identity but that are essential to it in a rather serious way.

(1996, p. 8)

Though presented here in an immediately attractive way, this focus on 'becoming', situated within a closer, more honest study of what (and how) one has 'become', can also, as Boler (1999), Hartley (1997) and McWilliam (1995) have variously pointed out, be a very uncomfortable business. It is, nevertheless, a vitally important business in the reflective process, focusing our attention on key questions that are too easily overlooked in the discourses of the competent craftsperson and the charismatic subject (to which we might add the teacher as eclectic/pragmatist) or in colonised versions of the reflective practitioner discourse. Such questions include, centrally, for the reflective practitioner:

- Why am I reflecting in this way and on these particular things? In what alternative ways might I reflect, and on what alternative events, experiences and issues?
- Why am I *responding and reacting* in certain ways to certain events, and what might be the connection between these responses and reactions and my previous and current life experiences including those of family, school and learning?
- What light can be cast on the picture of my practice in this part of the picture, with reference to things that are happening in the bigger picture – including both my personal history/biography and considerations of the larger socio-economic conditions and relations of power within which teachers' educative practice is located?

Reflection, reflexivity and the o/Other: 'someone else's eye'

The point has already been made that one of the advantages of reflexivity is its capacity to provide a context within which better sense can be made of other discourses, and of one's 'positioning' in relation to these discourses. Indeed, my own sense of the importance of reflexivity has come largely from encounters with the *difficulties* experienced by teachers and student teachers in relation to the dominant discourses of teacher education, and the inability of such discourses to help them move beyond practice-related difficulties. (In some cases, indeed, the dominant discourses of the competent craftsperson and the charismatic subject appear to have exacerbated or contributed to such difficulties.) Even with relatively successful and untroubled teachers and student teachers, however, reflexivity can have a significant part to play in moving the practitioner to a position which is simultaneously more critical (both of 'self' and of 'system') and more confident. It is interesting in this respect to return to the testimonies of some of the student teachers taking part in the *Reflective Practice Project*, some of which have been cited in the previous chapter.

In their discussions of their developing reflective practice, the ten students in our case-study sample, it will be recalled, identified a number of factors that helped their reflections, as well as a number of factors that inhibited them. These inhibiting factors, I suggested, appeared to be less directly related to problems with the competent craftsperson and charismatic subject discourses and more concerned with practical matters such as lack of time, the presence of anxiety and stress, and the sheer volume of new experiences to reflect *upon*. To refer back to some of these testimonies:

I think I have only just started reflecting properly. I am really only starting to get my head around looking at me properly, looking at my environment properly.

(Celia: student teacher, *Reflective Practice Project*)

Thursdays I had five lessons out of a seven-period day, and I used to be really, really tired at the end of it, and I finished teaching at 4 o'clock and would find it very difficult to reflect on even what had happened in the last period because I was so tired. And that is one of the things I don't like about having to do reflections, because there are times when you are absolutely dog tired and all you're thinking about is going home and sleeping. Because that's what I've begun to do: go home at the end of the day and sleep for a couple of hours. And I think if you're not careful you'll lose it. I mean, you'll lose your memory of what's happened.

(Sarah: student teacher, *Reflective Practice Project*)

Most of us hadn't been in school for a long time, and suddenly to be in a class, you need time to assimilate these things. . . . And I think it's too quick in a way. It doesn't give you the time to reflect in that kind of structured way.

(Mizzi: student teacher, *Reflective Practice Project*)

I have suggested that another of the potential inhibitors of reflective practice often cited in the literature and indeed borne out in our own previous *Autobiography Project* – that of the persistence of pre-existing, common-sense views of effective teaching – was not identified by our *Reflective Practice* respondents as an issue, and did not identify *itself* through the course of our interviews. These student teachers, by contrast, appeared to recognise (or at least to have *begun* to recognise) the impact of their past life experiences on their current perceptions and practices, and were generally open to questioning and challenging any assumptions they had brought with them on to the course (Brookfield 1990, p. 177; M. Johnston 1994) – often beginning with a recognition of the idiosyncratic aspects of reflection itself:

The thing with this thing called reflective practice is that . . . it boils down to your life experience so far, and I think part of that, the way you do reflective practice, comes from where you've come from and what your most recent experiences in life as a whole are.

(Sarah: student teacher, *Reflective Practice Project*)

Some of the students connected their own 'assumption hunting' (Brookfield 1990) to an awareness of the potential for reflection to become ritualistic and meaningless – for it to become absorbed into existing structures

(Mezirow 1991) which simply *reinforced* their current thinking and perception, becoming a shelter within which to hide from more challenging explanations of circumstances and events. As one of the students observed:

> We were talking about this. I can't remember what the theory was about, but if you've got a roller-skate on the stairs, you go up the stairs and you think 'I must get rid of that roller skate, because someone is going to trip up on it', and you come down the stairs and you go up the stairs, and by the third or fourth time you don't see it any more. I think that's what happens with teachers. You get stuck in this same old pattern of whatever, and that's when you do stop reflecting properly – or if you keep reflecting, you've got the words 'reflecting', 'observing', 'evaluating', but you've lost sight of what they're about.
>
> (Celia: student teacher, *Reflective Practice Project*;
> see also Ruddock 1985)

A further interesting feature of our sample was that none of the student teachers appeared to be hampered in developing as reflective practitioners *by* the life experiences they recognised and talked about, and, even in the cases of students who had arrived on course with views that would run counter to how they would be taught to understand and operate by their tutors, none appeared to have any lasting difficulty in adapting, modifying or finding and 'correcting' assumptions that might be described as unhelpful or erroneous. One respondent, for example, George, who felt that he had been 'saved' by a 'strict disciplinarian' of a teacher when he had been a school pupil, and whose initial thoughts on 'what makes a good teacher' had been written in what might be seen as somewhat confrontational terms based on a transmissive, custodial model of behaviour and learning, appeared to experience surprisingly little difficulty in modifying his outlook and approach in the light both of his training and of his professional experience. Having told us in interview that he had started off wanting to imitate the authoritarian, 'charismatic' style of his own saviour-teacher and that his initial classroom encounters had also been strongly influenced by 'hygiene factors' such as tight, detailed lesson planning and the strict following of school sanction mechanisms, he went on to say: 'I understand much more about the reflective model now', indicating that at the start of his teaching practice he had been far too easily drawn into 'a competitive mode' but that now he took a broader view of things, taking account of his pupils' home circumstances, trying a wider range of approaches in terms of classroom management, and generally becoming 'more empathetic'. Authentic reflection on his practice had also, he said, helped him to realise that his pupils were all different from one another and that they therefore, to some extent, required different approaches from him. Accepting that this change of approach was likely to be 'more painful', he felt, nevertheless, that it was worth the effort in order to become a better teacher in the long run, quoting one of his tutor's observations that 'The people who think they know it all [from the start] will be the first to fail.'

These levels of self-awareness, adaptability and willingness to challenge previously held assumptions were a feature of all the student teachers in our sample, leading us to hypothesise that such qualities were a major contributory factor to their success in the classroom and that, conversely, the lack of such qualities was a major contributory factor to the difficulties experienced by some of the 'failing students' in our previous study. For most of the students in the *Reflective Practice Project*, certainly, no major disagreements existed between previously held assumptions and what their tutors and their classroom experiences were telling them. Without exception, the student teachers in our sample had – at least by the time we came to interview them – very pupil-centred approaches to education, couched within a critical awareness of the role of the social and economic circumstances within which education and schooling are located. For some, therefore, any assumptions that were hunted out and challenged were of a relatively minor nature, which caused no real awkwardness or discomfort – as in the following example of a respondent who had changed her view of teachers' work to include diligence and careful planning where before there had been only charisma and wisdom:

> I hadn't realised how much planning went into things – how organised you had to be. . . . My assumption [as a pupil] was that the teachers were just really clever. I had no understanding of the hours and hours of preparation and marking in evenings and weekends that had gone into it.
>
> (Felicia: student teacher, *Reflective Practice Project*)

For others, adjustments were more difficult but still embarked upon with determination. One respondent, for example, had underestimated the amount of patience – both towards her pupils and towards herself – that she would require in the classroom, recognising that her own 'perfectionist' personality was making it difficult to make progress in this area, but determined to modify her outlook and behaviour accordingly.

While the student teachers in our sample still, not surprisingly, tended to focus on immediate lesson and school issues and experiences in their various sites and forms of reflection, there was evidence that they were all beginning, in varying degrees, to expand their reflective horizons into the reflexive way of examining their developing practice. For some of them, this move had been accompanied – and perhaps precipitated – by a growing awareness of the limitations of the *kinds* of reflective practice they had been hitherto engaged in. One respondent (Sarah) spoke of the 'danger of reflective practice, [in that] it's all down to the [student] teacher' (see also Moore 1999b). This student felt that she had outgrown the forms of reflection she had initially been encouraged towards, with their emphasis on evaluations of specific lessons and their focus on performativity, going so far as to suggest that those kinds of reflection had acted as a barrier to more sophisticated, wider-ranging forms. Her movement towards increased reflexivity had included deeper considerations of pupil difference and of her own need to adapt to these differences as well as to regularly changing circumstances, in addition to making serious efforts to understand what lay behind those surface differences and situational changes. For another respondent (Felicia), reflexivity had led to considerations of 'the feasibility of teaching everyone *en masse* in a place like London' and to a growing interest in the impact on learning of her pupils' backgrounds as well as the impact on her teaching of her own background. Another student (George) suggested a *continuum* of reflective development, in which one moved, as one's confidence and comfortableness grew, from fixations on competence issues and one's own personality towards 'objective reflection' on specific lessons and incidents, and finally to a growing awareness of one's reactions and professional *behaviour*. For this respondent, an early focus on poor lessons and personal 'performance' had been superseded by more constructive considerations of 'self-improvement' and of 'who you are – what your background has made you'.

This willingness to engage both with reflection *and* with debates *about* reflection may well have had something to do with the nature of the sample itself: these were all successful rather than struggling students, and it seems reasonable to conclude that their capacity to be accommodating, as well as the close pre-course match between their views and those espoused *on* the course, had contributed to that success or at least had produced favourable conditions for it. What we did find, however, was that, even with these successful students, previous experience did sometimes act in an inhibitory way – albeit less directly and to a far less influential extent – as with the 'at risk' students we had considered in our previous *Autobiography Project*: specifically, in the various manifestations of uncomfortable feelings of 'exposure' described by the students, whereby someone or something – either a tangible, 'external' presence or a voice or voices that had become 'internalised' – operated in a disquieting and not always helpful way in the reflective process.

While all the students taking part in the *Reflective Practice Project* valued the voices of the critical friends and support networks they had chosen – the need for 'someone else's eye', referred to by one student – not all were, by any means, as comfortable with what they saw as unwanted, invasive critics, whose eyes and voices often produced awkward, negative and unconstructive feelings, and whose origins they were often unwilling or unable to discuss. For some of the students, this uncomfortable, inhibitory feeling of being watched or exposed manifested itself as an acute sense of being brought face to face for the first time with 'oneself' – and, in particular, with one's 'shortcomings'. To return to one student's take on this, already quoted:

That exposure . . . I mean, I have never been in that kind of situation before. It's a big thing. . . . My kind of strengths and weaknesses are kind of really there, in front of me.

(Mizzi: student teacher, *Reflective Practice Project*)

For a number of the students, there was a strong sense of seeing themselves as the pupils might be seeing them, including, in some cases, a very powerful desire to be *liked* by the pupils; while for others the difficulty presented itself as an ambition to measure up to absent-but-ever-present teachers they had had at school, or had seen teaching impressively at their practice schools – the charismatic subject discourse, we might say, rearing one of its uglier heads:

With teaching, it's not just how you see yourself, it's about how you see how other people see you: how you see yourself being seen. . . . What you inevitably end up doing is looking at the pupils and judging yourself through them. The children are in your head all the time.

(Mizzi: student teacher, *Reflective Practice Project*)

I wanted to be liked by the children. . . . At the start, I was intimidated by them and my aim then was to fight back: if I get them to like me, they won't intimidate me, they'll like me.

(Carrie: student teacher, *Reflective Practice Project*)

For all respondents on the *Reflective Practice Project*, this sense of exposure was accompanied by a sense of *fear* of exposure (to quote one student teacher, Sarah, 'There are certain people you're not going to ever admit to that things are going wrong'): a mixture, perhaps, of wanting to be able to 'be oneself' with pupils and colleagues – of *exposing oneself*, in a sense; of being 'found' – and of being afraid *to* be found, with all one's shortcomings there for everyone to see. In some cases, this led to a decision that true exposure could only be countenanced once a certain degree of 'self-improvement' had been achieved (George), or in the temporary adoption of a classroom 'persona' (Celia):

It's a bit of a persona in a way and not really wanting that persona to be too far away from who I am, because then it feels like you are having a role all day long and I think that's very hard work, having to actually pretend to be someone different.

(Celia: student teacher, *Reflective Practice Project*)

Though voiced by seemingly very confident people, such confessions may be seen to reveal the sometimes fragile nature of the human psyche and the way in which that fragility is put under particular pressure or particularly exposed in the teaching situation. They may also cast some light on the difficulties experienced by some 'failing' students (including some of those in our earlier study), as well as helping us to understand what makes the 'meaning schemes' (Mezirow 1991) of some adult learners more durable and resistant to modification than others.

Reflection and the o/Other: 'Che vuoi?'

> The subject is always fastened, pinned, to a signifier which represents him [*sic*] for the other, and through this pinning he is loaded with a symbolic mandate . . . is given a place in the intersubjective network of symbolic relations.
>
> (Zizek 1989, p. 113)

To develop this line of inquiry a little further, I want to refer, briefly, to the work of Slavoj Zizek, who takes key ideas of the psycho-analyst Jacques Lacan (see Lacan 1977, 1979) and applies them to the everyday situations and experiences within which we all find ourselves.

In his book *The Sublime Object of Ideology* (1989), Zizek focuses on issues of personal/professional identity and identification, drawing a Lacanian distinction between 'imaginary' identification and 'symbolic' identification. According to this distinction, imaginary identification ('imaginary' here is not to be confused with the more common usage of the word to imply 'fictitious' or 'not real') relates to 'identification with the *image* in which we appear likeable to ourselves': the image, that is, of 'what we would like to be' (Zizek 1989, p. 105). Symbolic identification, on the other hand, concerns the way in which we perceive ourselves within and in relation to the 'symbolic order' of language, ritual, custom and representation – of society, indeed – within which we operate and within which we perceive and understand all 'experience'. In Zizek's words, this symbolic identification is effectively an identification with the 'place' (within the symbolic order) from which we are being observed, 'from where we look at ourselves so that we appear likeable, worthy of love' (p. 105).

With reference to the discourse of the charismatic subject, described in Chapter 3, this conceptualisation connects with Harris and Jarvis's accounts (2000, p. 2) of the practitioner 'who has emotional needs that can only be satisfied by situations in which students have to be grateful for extra support', or of 'individuals who are more interested in their own image than in student learning'. Zizek's argument, however, is, as will become apparent, of equal importance in considerations and understandings of teachers and student teachers who eschew the charismatic discourse in favour of the reflective-reflexive one.

Zizek suggests that the 'interplay' between the two forms of identification – the imaginary and the symbolic – constitutes (1989, p. 110) 'the mechanism by means of which the subject is integrated in a given socio-symbolic field' (we might include, for example, in addition to the over-arching socio-symbolic world into which the infant human is integrated, the socio-symbolic fields of teaching and learning or of formal schooling into which the adult teacher is (re)-integrated). Although each form of identification has, at its root, the individual's desire to satisfy and to be loved, and to find out what action/behaviour is *required* in order to satisfy and be loved (a question formulated by the phrase 'Che vuoi?'), in the case of imaginary identification the subject seeks to emulate, perhaps through the kind of role-playing referred to by one of the students in our sample, qualities that they feel they have discovered in other individuals (for us, for example, other teachers) in order to achieve the desired effect. In the case of symbolic identification, however, the question inevitably arises: 'For *whom* is the subject enacting this role? *Which gaze* is considered when the subject identifies himself [*sic*] with a certain image?' (ibid., p. 106).

What this suggests is that in addition to copying models of 'good practice' found in 'other people', the practitioner will be making a judgement of what that good practice is, not from some ideal, primordial, disinterested point of view, but from a particular perspective within the symbolic order, which may be the perspective of a particular set of shared social practices and beliefs but might equally (and simultaneously) be the perspective of a specific individual or group of individuals. (Constant references to parents and their views, for example, might be seen as a symptom of a deeper anxiety in the student teacher, who feels continually spotlighted under the paternal or maternal gaze.)

For Lacan and Zizek, difficulties arise as a result of a 'gap' between 'the way we see ourselves' (imaginary identification) and 'the point from which [we are] being observed to appear likeable to [ourselves]' (symbolic identification) (Zizek 1989, p. 106) – typically linked, in the professional field, to the requirement for a 'symbolic mandate': for example, 'I have been mandated to be a teacher, but what must I be – what am I expected to be – within the terms of the symbolic order, the 'Other', and within the terms of my own image of self, in order to *justify* my role as teacher, in order to be able to *explain* my mandate to myself and to others?' Zizek's argument is that it is precisely an ability to move beyond such questions, or to come to view them as unnecessary (i.e. 'There *is* no mandate to support the role I seek to assume'), that is necessary if the difficulty caused by such questions is to be removed. Similarly, it is an *inability* to move beyond such questions – an obsessive pursuit of the answer to the question 'What do others – what does *the* Other – desire of me, beneath it all, beneath the demands that are being made upon me and that I am meeting but still without being liked?' – that results in continued anxiety, in a sense of failure and lack of self-worth and, ultimately, in failure itself. As this is configured within psycho-analytic terms:

> [T]his mandate is ultimately always arbitrary: since its nature is perfor-
> mative, it cannot be accounted for by reference to the 'real' properties
> and capacities of the subject. So, loaded with this mandate, the subject
> is automatically confronted with a certain '*Che vuoi?*', with a question
> of the Other. The Other is addressing him [*sic*] as if he himself possesses
> the answer to the question of why he has this mandate, but the question
> is, of course, unanswerable. The subject does not know why he is occu-
> pying this place in the symbolic network. His own answer to this '*Che
> vuoi?*' of the Other can only be the hysterical [*sic*] question 'Why am I
> what I'm supposed to be? Why have I this mandate? Why am I . . . (a
> teacher, a master, a king . . .)?' Briefly: '*Why am I what you (the big
> Other) are saying that I am?*'
>
> (Zizek 1989, p. 113)

As Zizek concludes (ibid.), 'the final moment of the psychoanalytic process is, for the analysand, precisely when he [*sic*] gets rid of this question –
that is, when he accepts his being as *non-justified by the big Other*'.

If the tension caused by a gap between imaginary and symbolic identification and by the questions posed by the 'Other' may be seen, at first glance,
as a relatively insignificant issue in terms of the practical and reflective
development of the student teachers in the *Reflective Practice Project*, there
is sufficient evidence in the data – in, for example, stories of moving away
from 'needing to be liked for who I am' to 'focusing more on my pupils'
development, and hoping they may come to like and respect me as a result',
or of adopting classroom 'personae', or of overcoming feelings of professional inadequacy, or of being concerned about 'how you see yourself
being seen' – to suggest that this particular field of inquiry might offer
useful insights not only into understanding the nature of successful teaching
but also – and more pertinently, perhaps – into understanding how better to
support beginning teachers who appear to have many of the necessary attributes for pedagogic success but still find themselves failing in the classroom
under the weight of anxiety and of what one of the student teachers in the
earlier *Autobiography Project* referred to as 'over-personalisation'. In terms
of the (succeeding) student teachers in the *Reflective Practice Project*, we
might say that, for whatever reasons, they had learned – either before join-
ing the course or during it – not just to be pragmatic and eclectic in terms
of classroom *practice* but (another thing altogether) to be 'comfortable
with a *self* that is complicated and inconsistent' (Laupert 1985, p. 193, my
italics), and, furthermore, that this was something of a prerequisite for the
development of authentic reflection on their practice leading to improvement *in* that practice. We might not unreasonably hope that a deeper understanding of how they have achieved such relative comfort, or of the impact
of previous and continuing experiences *on* that achievement, will provide
us with invaluable help not only in offering appropriate support in the

development of their own reflective practice, but in working with student teachers for whom such an achievement comes far less easily and whose accomplishment is likely to require far more pain.

Personal and collective responsibility: the importance of contexts

So far, I have argued that teachers and student teachers might benefit – and that consequently their pupils might benefit – from interrogating in an informed, constructive way their own classroom behaviours in the context of previous and continuing life-roles and experience: in effect – though not in a 'detached', depersonalising way that denies desire – being open to the idea of examining themselves and their classrooms as deconstructible *texts*. I have indicated that such an approach, properly and sensitively handled, perhaps with the invited support of a mentor, can help (student) teachers to locate for themselves diagnoses of – and possible solutions to – apparent breakdowns in classroom communication, but that the approach and its associated techniques have the potential to support and enrich all teaching and all classroom situations. It is this notion of self-help, of offering teachers the tools and the opportunities to work through their professional diffi-culties through recourse to their own developing professional*ism*, that is at the heart of the reflexive project so configured. As Beyer (2002, p. 244) has argued with reference to parallel developments in teacher education in the USA, '[t]eacher education cannot be instituted through processes that are exclusively driven by external standards' – reminding us of a similar exhor-tation by Young (1998, p. 59) in relation to teacher education in England, concerning the necessity to move away from 'increased control to a policy of *extending the process of public learning*' (my italics).

I am also suggesting that students need to move beyond the identification and acknowledgement of the kinds of issues embedded in the psycho-analytical perspective towards a kind of 'reflexive *sociology*' (Wacquant 1989) which further locates those issues within wider social circumstances and arrangements through a recognition of the impact of such circum-stances and arrangements on the experiencing, perceiving social individual: that is to say, we need to include in our reflexive effort not merely our 'own' histories (decontextualised from the larger histories), but rather our own histories-in-context. As Boler puts this, arguing for what she calls a 'pedagogy of discomfort' (1999, pp. 178ff.), we need to move further towards practices that

> invite students and educators to examine how our modes of seeing have been shaped specifically by the dominant culture of the historical moment.

Recognising the potential dangers of such a move, which includes an imperative to question the very ethical, moral and discursive premises upon which our practice is habitually based, Boler continues:

> A pedagogy of discomfort invites students to leave the familiar shores of learned beliefs and habits, and swim further out into the 'foreign' and risky depths of the sea of ethical and moral differences.
>
> (1999, p. 181)

Elsewhere, Hartnett and Carr have invoked a similar agenda for teacher education in resistance to increasing pressure for teachers and teacher educators to move (yet further) *away from* the personal, the emotional and the critical/political towards the universal, the technicist and the rationalist – an agenda which likewise demands of the student teacher (and of the teacher of the student teacher) a critical evaluation both of the wider social context and of their own positioning within it:

> [T]eachers from their initial training have to grapple with complex moral and political issues. These include an examination of the assumptions and limitations of their own education and how this might inhibit access to education and to democratic values by other groups; insight into diverse cultural values and differences and how these differences are often translated into educational failure; an understanding of schools as social institutions whose norms and practices might create obstacles to education and solidify the differences between cultures; an understanding of how to connect with, and establish a rapport with, a wide range of cultural, class, ethnic and gender groups.
>
> (1995, pp. 43–4)

Relating the adoption of a pedagogy of discomfort to another marginalised discourse – that of the teacher as researcher and theorist – and to another imperative, to allow *desire* into our classrooms and curricula, Boler suggests:

> A pedagogy of discomfort begins by inviting educators and students to engage in critical inquiry regarding values and cherished beliefs and to examine constructed self-images in relation to how one has learned to perceive others. Within this culture of inquiry and flexibility, a central focus is to recognize how emotions define how and what one chooses to see, and, conversely, not to see.
>
> (1999, pp. 176–7)

As Boler adds (ibid.), very importantly:

This inquiry is a collective, not an individualized, process [that] requires that educators and students learn how to notice how one's sense of self and perspectives are shifting and contingent.

Reflexivity in practice

If we share the view of Boler (and of Hartley and of McWilliam, cited earlier) that what is on offer through the reflexive endeavour is potentially dangerous as well as potentially liberating, it would be foolhardy to promote the kinds of reflexive practice outlined in this chapter without some evidence of their possible – even their likely – *value*. In particular, bearing in mind that we are mainly considering student teachers here, it seems relevant to cite examples of what Boler calls 'the first sign of success of a pedagogy of discomfort', which comprises 'quite simply, the ability to recognize what it is that one doesn't want to know, and how one has developed emotional investments to protect oneself from knowing' – a recognition which, Boler argues, offers 'the greatest hope of *revisioning* ourselves' (1999, p. 200, my italics).

To this end, I want to conclude this chapter – and effectively this book – with reference to some of the testimonies provided by student teachers taking part in the *Autobiography Project* – in each case, testimonies of students who were experiencing severe difficulties at one time or another both in managing certain pupils and classes and in managing their own highly charged, very emotional reactions to these difficulties. These students, as with other concerned students at the time, complained that existing sources and modes of advice – lists of competences, school- and college-based mentoring, notes and debriefings of lesson observations, auditing more experienced teachers' classes – had all failed to help them sort out their difficulties, leading them to a tendency to self-pathologisation and self-blame.

One of the central rationales for the revised *Autobiography Project*, it will be remembered, was that a view that our students could often gain a great deal of benefit through 'getting in touch with' and 'textualising' their own histories, and through *con*textualising their actions within those histories; to try, in this way, to stand back a little from their own actions, and to address those actions critically rather than merely 'experiencing' them: in some cases, indeed, to move a little away from understanding their work within notions of the charismatic (or uncharismatic, 'failing') self, towards a perception of self in terms of experiences and roles. Interestingly – as the following testimony extracts from the two students Stan and Elspeth seem to suggest – such development appeared to have the capacity to strengthen feelings of 'selfhood' through the very process of 'depersonalising' disturbances and reinterrogating them from the viewpoint of pedagogic 'functionality':

When things started going wrong, I felt as if I was losing all confidence in myself as a person. Even at home with my partner I began to feel as if she was putting me down all the time and undermining me – my confidence. It was as if I didn't really know who I was any more, and . . . all the things I'd previously believed in, to do with people and education, it just didn't seem to make sense any more. I just couldn't see a way out of it. . . . Thinking back in an 'objective', reflective way to my own previous home life and schooling and to my relationships outside the classroom, I think that really made quite a huge difference. Not straight away. In fact, at the start it just seemed to make things worse. But later, I started to see things in terms of what people do rather than who they are, and at the kind of circumstances and social situations that push them into doing this or that. . . . I realised that what was going wrong was not my fault. Actually, it wasn't the fault of any single person in the classroom.

(Stan: *Autobiography Project*)

What did I learn from the autobiographical activities? A lot. More than I'd probably care to let on, if the truth was known. Mostly, I learned a lot about myself: what it was in my 'history' that was contributing to making me behave and respond to things the way I sometimes did, and to the way I was even seeing things. Basically, I stopped seeing it all as a battle of wills or personalities, and that really helped me to get on with things.

(Elspeth: *Autobiography Project*)

Stan's observation that in the beginning this kind of reflexive-reflection had a negative impact is an important one, and it needs to be said that not all of the students taking part in the revised *Autobiography Project* (participation in which was entirely voluntary) were as positive as, in the end, these two students were. Some still found the activities of little or no use to them in their professional development, and others – albeit a very small minority – suggested that we had overstepped the bounds of our competence and authority in proposing such activities in the first place. We had also been keenly aware from the outset that getting in touch with one's history in the way that we were suggesting was not likely to result in some kind of 'hallelujah' or 'eureka' moment for our students, or the discovery of some past event whose very unearthing would immediately change their ways of experiencing things. We hoped, however (and believed), that the reflexive activity would provide additional useful contexts both for the development of other skills (related to communication, competence and evaluative reflection) and for making sense of what was happening in the classroom.

That this was not a vain hope is borne out by a number of testimonies of students taking part in the revised project, including the following two lengthy responses with which I have chosen to conclude this chapter – in each case, importantly, the testimonies of students who, at the time of 'signing up' to the project, had been experiencing profound professional difficulties and who had been on the verge of abandoning the course:

> I was getting angry, and was told that this was exacerbating my problems [with this particular class]. I'd tried to sort this out in my lesson evaluations. I felt I was getting angry because the kids were misbehaving and just refusing to do what I was asking of them. I'd tried being patient, but that hadn't got me anywhere either. With two particular kids, I was rapidly developing a 'relationship' that I would describe as dysfunctional. Not only would they refuse to do anything I told them, but they also continually interfered with other children in the class – but the worst thing was that they started ignoring my presence. In the end, I had them removed from the class, but that just seemed to cause resentment among the rest of the class. I must say that the only thing that really helped in the end was when I took the advice to focus on my own anger and ask 'Why am I getting so cross here?' After all, this was only two children not working – and I knew my anger was not out of frustration at them not getting on, or anything like that. It was personal. Thinking about other situations that made me angry like this or had done in the past, and just going through with someone some of the feelings of power and powerlessness I had experienced myself as a child in a working-class home meant that when I went home in the evening I was able to think more clearly and get things in perspective and focus more on actual strategies. It also helped me to stop hating these two and to remember that they were probably behaving the way they did because of the lives they had. I won't say my anger has gone away entirely, but I'm definitely getting better at controlling it and I do have the kids back in the class now and generally enjoy a much better relationship with the class as a whole. In a strange way it's also helped me to appreciate the politics of the situation. I feel much more clued up now about the way society itself can operate against the interests of some kids, and against teachers who try to do something about it.
>
> (Norbert: *Autobiography Project*)

> The trouble was I was taking everything personally, and just taking it home with me. I know we were always told not to do that, but it's easier said than done. Instead of after a lousy lesson or a rotten day going away and carefully, rationally thinking what would I do next time to make things work better, I was just wallowing in feelings of inadequacy and dreading the next day – so much so that I went in expecting more trouble, and obviously the kids sensed it and obliged me. The reflexive writing we were asked to do did help, though I was very

dubious about it at the start and I don't know how useful it would have been if I'd been forced to show it to anyone rather than volunteering it like this. Just talking through things 'with myself' did help me to appreciate that the kids' behaviour, although I experienced it as being directed against me, was really about something much bigger, and instead of acting confrontationally I had to be sympathetic in my heart and firm and sensible in my manner. Part of what I realised was that I'd had this feeling of kind of being watched all the time – as if there was some expectation of classroom performance that I was constantly not living up to. It helped talking about this too, and realising I wasn't the only one experiencing things this way. Another bit, related to that, was that I actually wanted the kids to be 'more personal' to me, if that makes any sense. I think I needed to be liked and respected, and strange as it seems now I'd never actually understood that myself – how my need was contributing to the overall problem.

(Marlene: *Autobiography Project*)

What these testimonies suggest is that when student teachers are encouraged and allowed to develop reflexivity in this particular way, not only can the dangers of pathologisation be substantially reduced, but the students can be enabled to take a more positive view both of themselves and of the possibilities that are available to them. Indeed, I would suggest that the prioritisation of this kind of agency – directed politically outwards rather than clinically inwards – puts them in a far better position not just to deal sensibly with classroom difficulties but to engage, as 'transformative intellectuals' (Giroux 1988), in wider projects aimed both at 'changing the conditions of their own work . . . and struggling towards a larger vision and realization of human freedom' (Giroux and McLaren 1992, p. xiii).

There are important issues here too, however, about responsibility as well as about blame and guilt. What the reflexive process, in the pedagogy of discomfort mode, does not do is absolve the individual practitioner of responsibility; nor does it deny the possibility, even the inevitability, of guilt. It does, however, avoid holding the teacher overly responsible for classroom difficulties, even as it adopts a self-critical stance. As Boler (1999, p. 187) suggests, a path must be sought in this respect between the polarities of destructive guilt on the one hand and unhelpful 'innocence'/self-justification on the other. Just as 'the student who assumes the "guilty" position often stops participating in discussion, feels blamed, possibly defensively angry, and may refuse to engage in further complex self-reflection or critical inquiry', so 'guilt cannot be done away with altogether' since 'not all actions are acceptable or ethical' (ibid.). Stressing the need to learn how, by way of a 'historicized ethics', to 'inhabit a more ambiguous sense of self not reduced to either guilt *or* innocence', Boler concludes:

The challenge within educational environments is to create a space for honest and collective self-reflection and inquiry rather than closing off discussion. At the same time, such inquiry needs to avoid letting ourselves 'off the hook' from responsibilities and ethical complexities.

(1999, p. 187)

8 Afterword: reclaiming teaching

Our vision of the coming century is one in which the pursuit of learning is valued by individuals and by authorities all over the world not only as a means to an end, but also as an end in itself. . . . Hence, much will be expected, and much demanded, of teachers, for it largely depends on them whether this vision can come true. . . .

The importance of the role of the teacher as an agent of change, promoting understanding and tolerance, has never been more obvious than today. It is likely to become even more critical in the twenty-first century. The need for change, from narrow rationalism to universalism, from ethnic and cultural prejudice to tolerance, understanding and pluralism, from autocracy to democracy in its various manifestations, and from a technologically divided world where high technology is the privilege of the few to a technologically united world, places enormous responsibilities on teachers who participate in the moulding of the characters and minds of the new generation.
(Delors *et al.* 1996, pp. 141–2; see also Hartnett and Carr 1995, pp. 43–4)

[Included in] ten practices for principals that impact student learning:

- ensuring that fifty per cent of all problems students are asked to solve have no obvious 'right' answers;
- ensuring that the curriculum requires students to 'find' and define problems as frequently as they are required to solve them;
- using models from real-world products to set standards of excellence;
- eliminating practices that promote competition among students.
(Betts 1999, p. 31)

Reclaiming teaching

In the previous chapter, reflexivity was introduced not so much as a 'discourse' (both its somewhat marginalised position and its anti-discursive nature tend to preclude it from achieving such status at the present time) as something that teachers can engage in to help modify, fend off, get into perspective, critique or even resist some of the dominant discourses – in particular, that of the competent craftsperson, within which teaching is, currently and largely, sited and which tend to narrow our field of vision in relation to what good teaching might look like and how we might achieve it. That we do resist, and very forcefully resist, the competences discourse (which is not the same as denying the need to be competent, or suggesting that there is nothing of any merit in identifying, sharing and being assessed according to our competence across a range of areas) is imperative if we are to have any hope of reclaiming teaching – of reclaiming our *profession* – from politicians and bureaucrats fearful of the potential power of education to challenge or overturn the status quo. Whatever else we may say of it, reflexivity provides one avenue for teachers to take charge of their own learning and development on their own terms, in ways that specifically and systematically include the idiosyncratic, contingent aspects that are so crucial in their work (and in their understanding of their work) but which tend to be largely overlooked in the reductionist discourses of official policy.

While those of us working in England and Wales, and perhaps in some other parts of the world, may feel that the reflexive goals and strategies described in the previous chapter are light years away from current education agendas in the public policy domain – agendas constructed around conformity, performativity, 'auditing' and competition between individuals – the quotations with which this chapter began serve as important reminders that there is a world (a very large world) outside these shores, and that the reflexive project, though marginalised and often scorned here, is receiving wide and growing support elsewhere, along with co-traveller initiatives such as movements towards more future-oriented curricula, more democratic classrooms, lifelong learning, authentic assessment, and social justice.

Though currently marginalised in England and Wales, these initiatives are not, however, moribund here, and are almost certain to enjoy increasing official support in Britain as, in line with most of our European neighbours, we begin to take democracy – including the necessary *evolution* of democracy – more seriously (Moore 2002; Hartnett and Carr 1995). When that happens, as it must if we are to survive as a nation, politicians will find ready support in those programmes of initial and continuing teacher education which, in addition to debating 'the often technical minutiae of local issues about teacher education', have refused to break with more serious debates concerning 'the historical, intellectual and moral issues about the nature of the good society and of the good life, and the role of teachers, schools and education in helping to imagine, construct and maintain them' (Hartnett and Carr 1995, p. 41).

In this regard, it must be acknowledged that, despite government efforts to neutralise them, approaches which continue to take a constructively critical orientation, which recognise the complexity and diversity of classroom life and 'professional identity', and which question taken-for-granteds about what education is and should be for, what is and is not 'acceptable classroom behaviour', and what ends are and should be served by curriculum, assessment and pedagogical practices, still thrive where they can in the vast majority of teacher-education courses. They are there, for instance, in a persistent, if ever-more-difficult-to-fit-in, practice of encouraging student teachers to write and talk in very personal, evaluative ways not only about what happens in the classroom, but about memories of their life experiences outside the immediate teaching context (reflections which deliberately seek to contextualise idiosyncratic and contingent difficulties within constructive criticisms of systemic problems, and which form part of a genuine dialogue between students and their tutors); they are there in the form of block lectures and seminars that critique rather than merely 'teach how to teach' the National Curriculum or the National Literacy Strategy; they are there in resistance to the reduction of all things educational to the check-list, the competence and the word (Kress 1989); and they are there in teachers' own resistance, sometimes, unfortunately, experienced negatively, to being instructed to do things that they feel, often very profoundly, are likely to do their students harm. (If teachers may, currently, be experiencing a certain enforced 'de-politicisation', as I have suggested, this does not mean that they have abandoned cherished values and beliefs, or that they have surrendered empowering conceptualisations of the 'good life'.)

Reclaiming learning

Resistance is also there, however, in combating the relentless drive of attention away from *what learners do* towards *what teachers do*. This is not to say that what teachers do is not important, but rather that an over-emphasis on this can make us lose sight of what – and who – education is really for: notably, not reducing young people to grades and levels *en route* to 'feeding' the national economy, but helping them to develop as critical, independent, social and sociable thinkers and actors, who may rectify rather than reproduce the mistakes of the past, and pulling off that rather difficult pedagogic trick of helping young people both to achieve academic and creative success *and* to develop as critical, confident, independent and socially responsible citizens.

An interesting feature of the photographic illustrations chosen for the Plowden Report, which sets it in stark contrast to much that is current in the field of public-policy documentation related to education, is that in a large number of those illustrations the teacher is absent. Even in those in which teachers are present, they are typically engaged in what might be described as communal, collaborative activity with the children. We are clearly not to make of this that teaching – or the quality of it – was not considered important by Plowden, but rather that the model of good teaching being promoted in the report is in harmony with the model and theory of learning that underpin it. The good teacher here, that is to say, is precisely the teacher who does not 'take over', dictate, instruct, but who supports, responds, advises, assesses needs and assists development: a communicative, competent, reflective practitioner who also enjoys a high degree of professional autonomy and respect and whose success as a teacher may be judged in terms of the extent to which they expand their students' expectations and possibilities.

This emphasis on what *learners* do should lead also to better understandings of why they do what they do – itself leading to more effective, and indeed more reflective, teaching. If reflexivity helps us to understand ourselves as teachers – what motivates us, what pleases us, what concerns us, what we desire, how our out-of-school lives affect our in-school responses – it should also help sensitise us to the difficulties, challenges, hopes, dreams, desires and reluctance experienced every day by 'our' students.

All of which brings us back to the quotation from the UNESCO Commission Report of 1996 with which this short chapter opened. This quotation has been included not just to remind us that good teaching is, in the final analysis, always related to what we see as the 'good life' and 'good learning' (i.e. that it is always related to the lasting impact it has on our students), but to remind British readers, too, how out-of-step our educational policy makers currently are with much of the rest of Europe and the English-speaking world. In England, even in the Internet age, we continue to find policy founded upon the 'back-to-basics, back-to-Victorian-values' agenda constructed by Margaret Thatcher's Conservative government and subsequently taken over and developed by the current 'New Labour' government under Tony Blair: an agenda which continues to over-emphasise basic numeracy and basic 'literacy' (which is not, actually, literacy at all, in any sense of the word) – taught through a return to 'traditional' teaching (i.e. front-of-class, even if the shirt sleeves are rolled up), increased setting and streaming, and the endless, debilitating testing of young people. At the same time, other nations are beginning to construct new educational agendas – often including or structured around new national curricula – that are more genuinely geared towards an uncertain, intriguing, yet-to-be-constructed future rather than backwards to a glamorised past, that prioritise the child rather than the curriculum, and that are more concerned with the creation of democratic, culturally inclusive classrooms than with cultural and behavioural conformity.

It is important for teachers in Britain to know this: for our governments and our civil servants cannot continue indefinitely to attempt to buck the trend, to convince themselves and us that we are the only nation that knows best. Sooner or later, even if on purely financial grounds, our own government must radically change its education policy; must stop pouring money down the drain of the design, production and marking of test papers that tell us nothing and that don't even 'raise the standards' they claim to, and begin to divert resources to making schools more pleasant, co-operative, democratic and socially just environments – both physically and in terms of curricula and pedagogies. When that change comes, teachers must –

and, I have no doubt, will – be ready for it. To make sure that we are, however, it is vital that we do not allow ourselves to become so far drawn into current dominant agendas and discourses – to have our practice so effectively 'colonised' by them – that we are left bereft of ideas when these agendas and discourses are finally abandoned and when our professional freedom is returned.

References

Abbott, J. (1999) 'Battery Hens or Free Range Chickens: What Kind of Education for What Kind of World?', *The Journal of the 21st Century Learning Initiative*, January, 1–12

Afonso, C. (2001) 'Understanding Student Teachers' Perceptions of the Teaching and Learning of English as a Foreign Language through their Analysis of Computer-Generated Materials', unpublished Ph.D. thesis, King's College, University of London

Alexander, R. (1984) *Primary Teaching* London, Holt, Rinehart & Winston

Alexander, R. J., Craft, M. and Lynch, J. (eds) (1984) *Change in Teacher Education* New York, Praeger

Allen, G. (1994) *Teacher Training: The Education Bill 1993/4, Research Paper 94/58* London, House of Commons Library

Alvesson, M. and Skoldberg, K. (2000) *Reflexive Methodology: New Vistas for Qualitative Research* London, Sage

Amiguinho, A. (1998) 'Formação de professores: à procura de projectos institucionais globais', *Aprender* 21, 34–42

Arnold, M. (1909) 'The Function of Criticism', in *Essays Literary and Critical* London, Dent, pp. 1–25

Ash, A. and Moore, A. (2002) 'Key Factors in the Promotion and Obstruction of Reflective Practice in Beginning Teachers' Ideology of Pragmatism'. Paper presented at the 27th Annual Conference on Teacher Education and Reform, University of Warsaw, Poland, 24–28 August 2002

Ball, S. (1997) 'Policy Sociology and Critical Social Research: A Personal Review of Recent Education Policy and Policy Research', *British Educational Research Journal* 23(3) 257–74

Ball, S. (1999) 'Global Trends in Educational Reform and the Struggle for the Soul of the Teacher!'. Paper presented at the Annual Meeting of the British Educational Research Association, University of Sussex, Brighton, September 1999

Barthes, R. (1972) *Mythologies* London, Cape

Barthes, R. (1975) *S/Z* London, Jonathan Cape

Barthes, R. (1983) *Selected Writings* Oxford, Fontana/Collins

Belsey, C. (1980) *Critical Practice* London, Methuen

Bernstein, B. (1996) *Pedagogy, Symbolic Control and Identity: Theory, Research and Critique* London, Taylor & Francis

Betts, B. (1999) 'Ten Practices for Principals that Impact Student Learning', *The International Educator*, February, 31

Beyer, L. E. (2002) 'The Politics of Standardization: Teacher Education in the USA', *Journal of Education for Teaching* 28(3) 239–45

Billig, M., Condor, S., Edwards, D., Gane, M., Middleton, D. and Radley, A. (1988) *Ideological Dilemmas: A Social Psychology of Everyday Thinking* London, Sage

Blair, T. (1998) *The Third Way* London, Fabian Society

Blandford, S. (1997) *Middle Management in Schools: How to Harmonise Managing and Teaching for an Effective School* London, Pitman

Boler, M. (1999) *Feeling Power: Emotions and Education* New York and London, Routledge

Bourdieu, P. (1971) 'Intellectual Field and Creative Project', in M. F. D. Young (ed.) *Knowledge and Control* London, Collier-Macmillan, pp. 161–88

Bourdieu, P. (1977) *Outline of a Theory of Practice* Cambridge, Cambridge University Press

Bourdieu, P. (1979) *Algeria 1960* Cambridge, Cambridge University Press

Bourdieu, P. (1990) *In Other Words* Cambridge, Polity Press

Bowring-Carr, C. (1997) *Effective Learning in Schools: How to Integrate Learning and Leadership for a Successful School* London, Pitman

Britzman, D. (1986) 'Cultural Myths in the Making of a Teacher: Biography and Social Structure in Teacher Education', *Harvard Educational Review* 56(4) 442–56

Britzman, D. (1989) 'Who Has the Floor? Curriculum, Teaching and the English Student Teacher's Struggle for Voice', *Curriculum Inquiry* 19(2) 143–62

Britzman, D. (1991) *Practice Makes Practice* Albany, NY, SUNY

Britzman, D. and Pitt, A. (1996) 'Pedagogy and Transference: Casting the Past of Learning into the Presence of Teaching', *Theory into Practice* 35(2) 117–23

Broadfoot, P. (2000) 'Culture, Learning and Comparison: Lawrence Stenhouse's Vision of Education for Empowerment', *BERA Stenhouse Lecture 1999*, Southwell, BERA

Brookfield, S. D. (1990) 'Using Critical Incidents to Explore Assumptions', in J. Mezirow and Associates, *Fostering Critical Reflection in Adulthood: A Guide to Transformative and Emancipatory Learning* San Francisco, Jossey-Bass

Bruner, J. (1996) *The Culture of Education* Cambridge, MA, Harvard University Press

Burr, V. (1995) *An Introduction to Social Constructionism* London, Routledge

Calderhead, J. (1991) 'The Nature and Growth of Knowledge in Student Teaching', *Teaching and Teacher Education* 7(5/6) 531–5

Calderhead, J. and Robson, M. (1991) 'Images of Teaching: Student Teachers' Early Conceptions of Classroom Practice', *Teaching and Teacher Education* 7(1) 1–8

Calderhead, J. and Shorrock, S. B. (1997) *Understanding Teacher Education* London, Falmer

Carnell, E. and Lodge, C. (2002) *Supporting Effective Learning* London, Paul Chapman

Clandinin, D. J. (1985) 'Personal Practical Knowledge: A Study of Teachers' Classroom Images', *Curriculum Inquiry* 15(4) 361–85

Clift, R., Meng, L. and Scott, E. (1994) 'Mixed Messages in Learning to Teach English', *Teaching and Teacher Education* 10(3) 265–79

Cohen, L. and Manion, L. (1977) *A Guide to Teaching Practice* London, Methuen

Coldron, J. and Smith, R. (1999) 'Active Location in Teachers' Construction of their Professional Identities', *Journal of Curriculum Studies* 31, 711–26

Cole, A. L. and Knowles, J. G. (1995) 'Methods and Issues in a Life History Approach to Self-Study', in T. Russell and F. Korthagen (eds) *Teachers who Teach Teachers* London, Falmer

Combs, A. W. (1972) 'Some Basic Concepts for Teacher Education', *Journal of Teacher Education* 23 (Fall), 286–90

Connelly, F. M. and Clandinin, D. J. (1985) 'Personal Practical Knowledge and Modes of Knowing: Relevance for Teaching and Learning', in E. Eisner (ed.) *Learning and Teaching the Ways of Knowing* Chicago, University of Chicago Press, pp. 174–98

Connelly, F. M. and Clandinin, D. J. (1986) 'On Narrative Method, Personal Philosophy and Narrative Unities in the Story of Teaching', *Journal of Research in Science Teaching* 23(4) 293–310

Convery, A. (1999) 'Listening to Teachers' Stories: Are we Sitting too Comfortably?', *Qualitative Studies in Education* 12, 131–46

Corey, S. (1953) *Action Research to Improve School Practice* New York, Columbia University Press

Council for the Accreditation of Teacher Education (CATE) (1992) *Circular 9/92* London, CATE

Cummins, J. (1996) *Negotiating Identities: Education for Empowerment in a Diverse Society* Los Angeles, CABE

Dalton, M. (1999) *The Hollywood Curriculum: Teachers and Teaching in the Movies* New York, Peter Lang

Davies, C. A. (1999) *Reflexive Ethnography: A Guide to Researching Ourselves and Others* London, Routledge

Delors, J. *et al.* (1996) *Learning: The Treasure Within: Report to UNESCO of the International Commission on Education for the Twenty-first Century*, Paris, UNESCO

Department for Education and Employment (DfEE) (1997a) *Teaching: High Status, High Standards* London, DfEE

Department for Education and Employment (DfEE) (1997b) *Annex A to Teacher Training Circular 1/97: Standards for the Award of Qualified Teacher Status* London, DfEE

Department for Education and Employment (DfEE) (1997c) *Excellence in Schools* London, The Stationery Office

Department for Education and Employment (DfEE) (1998) *Requirements for Courses of Initial Teacher Training* London, DfEE

Department for Education and Employment (DfEE)/National Literacy Trust (2000) *Building a Nation of Readers: A Review of the National Year of Reading, September 1998 to August 1999* London, National Literacy Trust on behalf of the DfEE

Department of Education and Science (DES) (1981) *Teacher Training and the Secondary School* London, DES

Dewey, J. (1938) *Experience and Education* New York, Macmillan

Eagleton, T. (1983) *Literary Theory: An Introduction* Oxford, Blackwell

Eisner, E. (1985) *The Educational Imagination* New York, Macmillan

Elliott, J. (ed.) (1993a) *Reconstructing Teacher Education* London, Falmer

Elliott, J. (1993b) 'The Relationship between "Understanding" and "Developing" Teachers' Thinking', in J. Elliott (ed.) *Reconstructing Teacher Education* London, Falmer, pp. 193–207

Elliott, J. (1993c) 'Professional Education and the Idea of a Practical Educational Science', in J. Elliott (ed.) *Reconstructing Teacher Education* London, Falmer, pp. 65–85

Fairclough, N. (1992) *Discourse and Social Change* Cambridge, Polity Press

Farber, P. and Holm, G. (1994) 'A Brotherhood of Heroes: The Charismatic Educator in Recent American Movies', in P. Farber, E. Provenzo and G. Holm (eds) *Schooling in the Light of Popular Culture* Albany, NY, SUNY Press

Feiman-Menser, S. (1990) 'Teacher Preparation: Structural and Conceptual Alternatives', in W. R. Houston (ed.) *Handbook of Research on Teacher Education* New York, Macmillan, pp. 212–33

Felman, S. (1987) *Jacques Lacan and the Adventure of Insight: Psychoanalysis in Contemporary Culture* Cambridge, MA, Harvard University Press

Flinders, D., Noddings, N. and Thornton, S. (1986) 'The Null Curriculum: Its Theoretical Basis and Practical Implications', *Curriculum Inquiry* 16(1) 33–42

Flutter, J., Kershner, R. and Rudduck, J. (1998) *Thinking about Learning, Talking about Learning: A Report of the Effective Learning Project* Cambridge, Cambridgeshire County Council and Homerton College, Cambridge

Foucault, M. (1971) *L'Ordre du discours* Paris, Gallimard

Foucault, M. (1980) *Power/Knowledge* Chicago, Harvester

Foucault, M. (1992) *The Archaeology of Knowledge* London, Routledge

Freud, S. (1968) 'Introductory Lectures on Psycho-Analysis, Part Three', in *Standard Edition*, vol. 17 (trans. J. Strachey) London, Hogarth Press

Freud, A. (1979) *Psycho-analysis for teachers and parents* (trans. B. Low) New York, W. W. Norton

Freud, S. (1991) *The Essentials of Psycho-Analysis* London, Penguin

Gallop, J. (ed.) (1995) *Pedagogy: The Question of Impersonation* Bloomington, Indiana University Press

Gergen, K. (1990) 'Metaphor, Metatheory and the Social World', in D. Leary (ed.) *Metaphors in the History of Psychology* Cambridge, Cambridge University Press

Giddens, A. (1991) *Modernity and Self-Identity: Self and Society in the Late Modern Age* Cambridge, Polity Press

Gill, J. (1883) *Introductory Textbook to School Education, Method and School Management* London, Longmans Green

Girard, D. (1986) 'The Eclectic Way', *English Teaching Forum* 24(1) 11–14

Giroux, H. (1988) 'Critical Theory and the Politics of Culture and Voice: Rethinking the Discourse of Educational Research', in R. Sherman and R. Webb (eds) *Qualitative Research in Education: Focus and Methods* London, Falmer, pp. 190–210

Giroux, H. A. and McLaren, P. (1992) Introduction to W. B. Stanley *Curriculum for Utopia: Social Reconstruction and Critical Pedagogy in the Postmodern Era* Albany, NY, SUNY Press

Goodman, J. (1988) 'Constructing a Practical Philosophy of Teaching: A Study of Preservice Teachers' Professional Perspectives', *Teaching and Teacher Education* 4, 121–37

Goodson, I. F. and Walker, R. (1991) *Biography, Identity and Schooling* London, Falmer

Goudie, E. Mun Har (1999) 'Student Teachers' Experiences of the Art and Design Curriculum: A Transformative Pedagogy', Unpublished Ph.D. thesis, Institute of Education, University of London

Green, B. (ed.) (1993) *The Insistence of the Letter: Literacy Studies and Curriculum Theorizing* London, Falmer

Green, B. (1995) 'Post-curriculum Possibilities: English Teaching, Cultural Politics and the Post-modern Turn', *Journal of Curriculum Studies* 27(4) 391–409

Greene, M. (1988) 'Qualitative Research and the Uses of Literature', in R. Sherman and R. Webb (eds) *Qualitative Research in Education: Focus and Methods* London, Falmer

Halpin, D., Moore, A., Edwards, G., George, R. and Jones, C. (1998–2001) *Educational Identities and the Consumption of Tradition: ESRC Project R000237640* London, Institute of Education, University of London

Hamilton, D. (1993) 'Texts, Literacy and Schooling', in B. Green (ed.) *The Insistence of the Letter: Literacy Studies and Curriculum Theorizing* London, Falmer

Handal, G. and Lauvas, P. (1987) *Promoting Reflective Teaching: Supervision in Action* Philadelphia and Milton Keynes, Society for Research into Higher Education/Open University Press

Hare, W. (1993) *What Makes a Good Teacher?* Winnipeg, Manitoba, The Althouse Press, University of Western Ontario

Hargreaves, A. (1993) 'Professional Development and the Politics of Desire', in A. Vasquez and I. Martinez (eds) *New Paradigms and Practices in Professional Development* Teachers College Press, New York

Hargreaves, A. (1994) *Changing Teachers, Changing Times: Teachers' Work and Culture in the Postmodern Age* London, Cassell

Harland, J. (1996) 'Evaluation as Realpolitik', in D. Scott and R. Usher (eds) *Understanding Educational Research* London, Routledge

Harré, R. and Gillett, G. (1994) *The Discursive Mind* London, Sage

Harris, A. (1996) *School Effectiveness and School Improvement: A Practical Guide* London, Pitman

Harris, A. and Jarvis, C. (2000) 'Including the Excluding Image: Researching and Teaching Cultural Images of Adult Educators'. Paper presented at SCUTREA 30th Annual Conference, 3–5 July 2000, University of Nottingham

Hartley, D. (1997) *Re-schooling Society* London, Falmer

Hartnett, A. and Carr, W. (1995) 'Education, Teacher Development and the Struggle for Democracy', in J. Smyth (ed.) *Introduction to Critical Discourses on Teacher Development* London, Cassell, pp. 39–54

Hay McBer (2000) *Research into Teacher Effectiveness: A Model of Teacher Effectiveness* London, DfEE/The Stationery Office

Hollingsworth, S. (1989) *International Action Research: A Casebook for Educational Reform* London, Falmer

Hopkins, D., Ainscow, M. and West, M. (1994) *School Improvement in an Era of Change* London, Cassell

Institute of Education (1972) *Education and the Training of Teachers: Statement on the James Report* London, Institute of Education, University of London

Jenkins, R. (1992) *Pierre Bourdieu* London, Routledge

Johnson, B. (1989) 'Developing Preservice Teachers' Self-Awareness: An Examination of the Professional Dynametric Program', in J. A. Braun Jr (ed.) *Reforming Teacher Education: Issues and New Directions* New York and London, Garland Publishing

Johnson, K. (1994) 'The Emerging Beliefs and Instructional Practices of Pre-service English as a Second Language Teachers', *Teaching and Teacher Education* 10(4) 439–52

Johnston, M. (1994) 'Contrasts and Similarities in Case Studies of Teacher Reflection and Change', *Curriculum Inquiry* 24(1) 9–26

Johnston, S. (1994) 'Is Action Research a "Natural", Process for Teachers?', *Educational Action Research* 2(1) 39–48

Jones, L. and Moore, R. (1995) 'Appropriating Competence: The Competency Movement, the New Right and the "Culture Change" Project', *British Journal of Education and Work* 8(2) 78–92

Kemble, B. (ed.) (1971) *Fit to Teach* London, Hutchinson Educational

Kemmis, S. (1985) 'Action Research and the Politics of Reflection', in D. Boud, R. Keogh and D. Walker (eds) *Reflection: Turning Experience into Learning* London, Kogan Page, pp. 139–63

Kemmis, S. and McTaggart, R. (1988) *The Action Research Planner* Geelong, Deakin University Press

Kress, G. (1989) *Linguistic Processes in Sociocultural Practice* Oxford, Oxford University Press

Lacan, J. (1977) *Ecrits* London, Tavistock Publications

Lacan, J. (1979) *The Four Fundamental Concepts of Psycho-Analysis* London, Penguin

Landon, J. (1886) *School Management* London, Kegan, Paul, Trench

Larse-Freeman, D. (1987) 'From Unity to Diversity: Twenty-five Years of Language-teaching Methodology', *English Teaching Forum* 25(4) 2–10

Laupert, M. (1985) 'How do Teachers Manage to Teach? Perspectives on Problems in Practice', *Harvard Educational Review* 55, 178–94

Laurie, S. S. (1882) *The Training of Teachers and Other Educational Papers* London, Kegan Paul, Trench

Levin, D. M. (1987) *Pathologies of the Modern Self: Postmodern Studies in Narcissism, Schizophrenia and Depression* New York, New York University Press

Loughran, J. (1996) *Developing Reflective Practice: Learning about Teaching and Learning through Modelling* London, Falmer

Loughran, J. and Russell, J. (eds) (1997) *Teaching about Teaching: Purpose, Passion and Pedagogy in Teacher Education* London, Falmer

MacBeath, J. and Mortimore, P. (2001) *Improving School Effectiveness* Buckingham, Open University Press

Macdonell, D. (1986) *Theories of Discourse: An Introduction* Oxford, Blackwell

McIntyre, D., Hagger, H. and Burn, K. (1994) *The Management of Student Teachers' Learning* London and Philadelphia, Kogan Page

McKernan, J. (1991) *Curriculum Action Research: A Handbook of Methods and Resources for the Reflective Practitioner* London, Kogan Page

McLaren, P. (1996) *Critical Pedagogy and Predatory Culture* Albany, NY, SUNY Press

McLaughlin, M. W. and Talbert, J. E. (1990) 'The Contexts in Question: The Secondary School Workplace', in M. W. McLaughlin, J. E. Talbert and N. Bascia (eds) (1990) *The Contexts of Teaching in Secondary Schools: Teachers' Realities* New York, Teachers College Press.

McLaughlin, R. (1991) 'Can the Information Systems for the NHS Internal Market Work?', *Public Money and Management*, Autumn, 37–41

Maclure, J. S. (1986) *Educational Documents: England and Wales 1816 to the Present Day* London, Methuen

MacLure, M. (2003) *Discourse in Educational and Social Research*, Open University Press

Maclure, S. (1990) *A History of Education in London 1870–1990* London, Allen Lane

McNiff, J. (1988) *Action Research: Principles and Practice* London, Routledge

McWilliam, E. (1995) '(S)education: A Risky Enquiry into Pleasurable Teaching', *Education and Society* 13(1) 15–24

Maguire, M. (1995) 'Dilemmas in Teaching Teachers: The Tutor's Perspective', *Teachers and Teaching* 1(1) 119–31

Marland, M. (1975) *The Craft of the Classroom* Oxford, Heinemann Educational

Marsh, C. (1990) *Reconceptualising School-Based Curriculum Development* London, Falmer

Medgyes, P. (1990) 'Queries from a Communicative Teacher', in R. Rossner and R. Bolitho (eds) *Currents of Change in English Language Teaching* Oxford, Oxford University Press, pp. 103–10

Mezirow, J. (1991) *Transformative Dimensions of Adult Learning* San Francisco, Jossey-Bass

Mitchell, C. and Weber, S. (1996) *Reinventing Ourselves as Teachers: Private and Social Acts of Memory and Imagination* London, Falmer

Moore, A. (1992) 'Forcing the Issue: An Evaluation of Personal Writing Initiatives with Student Teachers', Department of Educational Studies, Goldsmiths College, University of London

Moore, A. (1996) '"Masking the Fissure": Some Thoughts on Competences, Reflection and Closure in Initial Teacher Education', *British Journal of Educational Studies* 44(2) 200–11

Moore, A. (1998a) 'English, Fetishism and the Demand for Change: Towards a Postmodern Agenda for the School Curriculum', in G. Edwards and A. V. Kelly (eds) *Experience and Education* London, Paul Chapman, pp. 103–25

Moore, A. (1998b) 'Forcing the Issue: An Evaluation of Personal Writing Initiatives with Student Teachers: Updated and Revised', Goldsmiths College, University of London

Moore, A. (1999a) 'Unmixing Messages: A Bourdieusian Assessment of Tensions and Helping-strategies in Initial Teacher Education', in M. Grenfell and M. Kelly (eds) *Pierre Bourdieu: Language, Culture and Education* Berne, Peter Lang, pp. 301–12

Moore, A. (1999b) 'Beyond Reflection: Contingency, Idiosyncrasy and Reflexivity in Initial Teacher Education', in M. Hammersley (ed.) *Researching School Experience: Ethnographic Studies of Teaching and Learning* London, Falmer, pp. 134–52

Moore, A. (1999c) *Teaching Multicultured Students: Culturism and Anticulturism in School Classrooms* London, Falmer

Moore, A. (2000) *Teaching and Learning: Pedagogy, Curriculum and Culture* London, RoutledgeFalmer

Moore, A. (2002) 'Citizenship Education in England and Wales: Democracy, Community and Control'. Paper presented at the Second International Knowledge and Discourse Conference, June 2002, University of Hong Kong

Moore, A. and Ash, A. (2002) 'Developing Reflective Practice in Beginning Teachers: Helps, Hindrances and the Role of the Critical o/Other'. Research paper presented at the British Educational Research Association Annual Conference, September 2002, University of Exeter

Moore, A. and Atkinson, D. (1998) 'Charisma, Competence and Teacher Education', *Discourse* 19(2) 171–82

Moore, A. and Edwards, G. (2002) 'Teaching, School Management and the Ideology of Pragmatism'. Paper presented at the second Knowledge and Discourse Conference, June 2002, University of Hong Kong

Moore, A., Edwards, G., Halpin, D. and George, R. (2002) 'Compliance, Resistance and Pragmatism: The (Re)construction of Schoolteacher Identities in a Period of Intensive Educational Reform', *British Educational Research Journal* 28(4) 551–65

Moore, A., George R. and Halpin, D. (2002) 'The Developing Role of the Headteacher in English Schools: Management, Leadership and Pragmatism', *Educational Management and Administration* 30(2) 177–90

Moore, A. and Klenowski, V. with Askew, S., Carnell, E., Larsen, J. and Jones, C. (2003) 'Revising the National Curriculum: Teachers' and Pupils' Perspectives at KS2 and 3': Report of DfES-funded research study *An Evaluation of Recent Changes to the National Curriculum* London, HMSO

National Society (1879) *The Teacher's Manual of the Science and Art of Teaching* London, National Society's Depository

National Union of Teachers (NUT) (1976) *Teacher Education: The Way Ahead* London, National Union of Teachers

Ofsted (2002) *Good Teaching: Effective Departments: Findings from HMI Survey of Subject Teaching in Secondary Schools, 2000/2001* London, Ofsted

Ofsted/TTA (1996) *Framework for the Assessment of Quality and Standards in Initial Teacher Training 1996/97* London, Ofsted

Oliver, D. W. with Gershman, K. W. (1989) *Education, Modernity and Fractured Meaning: Toward a Process Theory of Teaching and Learning* Albany, NY, SUNY

Pajares, F. (1992) 'Teachers' Beliefs and Educational Research: Cleaning Up a Messy Construct', *Review of Educational Research* 62(3) 307–32

Parker, I. (1992) *Discourse Dynamics: Critical Analysis for Social and Individual Psychology* London, Routledge

Penley, C. (1989) *The Future of an Illusion: Film, Feminism and Psychoanalysis* Minneapolis, University of Minnesota Press

Pickering, J. (1997) *Raising Boys' Achievement* Stafford, Network Educational Press

Plowden Report (1967) *Children and their Primary Schools* London, Central Advisory Council for Education: HMSO

Pollard, A. (2002a) *Reflective Teaching: Effective and Evidence-Informed Professional Practice* London, Continuum

Pollard, A. (ed.) (2002b) *Readings for Reflective Teaching* London, Continuum

Popkewitz, T. S. (ed.) (1987) *Critical Studies in Teacher Education: Its Folklore, Theory and Practice* London, Falmer

Quicke, J. (1988) 'Using Structured Life Histories to Teach the Sociology and Social Psychology of Education', in P. Woods and A. Pollard (eds) *Sociology and Teaching* London, Croom Helm

Reid, W. A. (1993) 'Literacy, Orality and the Functions of Curriculum', in B. Green (ed.) *The Insistence of the Letter: Literacy Studies and Curriculum Theorizing* London, Falmer

Ricoeur, P. (1994) *The Rule of Metaphor: Multi-disciplinary Studies of the Creation of Meaning in Language* London, Routledge

Rose, J. (2001) 'The Impact of Action Research on Practitioners' Thinking: A Supporting Case for Action Research as a Method of Professional Development', Unpublished Ph.D. thesis, Goldsmiths College, University of London

Rousmaniere, K., Dehli, K. and de Coninkl-Smith (eds) (1997) *Discipline, Moral Regulation and Schooling* New York, Garland

Ruddock, J. (1985) 'Teacher Research and Research Based Teacher Education', *Journal of Education for Teaching* 11(3) 281–9

Sammons, P. (1999) *School Effectiveness: Coming of Age in the Twenty-first Century* Abingdon, Swets & Zeitlinger

Schon, D. A. (1983) *The Reflective Practitioner* New York, Basic Books

Schon, D. A. (1987) *Educating the Reflective Practitioner* San Francisco, Jossey-Bass

Schon, D. A. (1988) 'Coaching Reflective Teaching', in P. P. Grimmett and G. L. Erickson (eds) *Reflection in Teacher Education* Vancouver, British Columbia, Pacific Educational Press

Selleck, R. J. W. (ed.) (1968) *The New Education: 1870–1914* London, Pitman

Shacklock, G. and Smyth, J. (eds) (1998) *Being Reflexive in Critical Educational and Social Research* London, Falmer

Skilbeck, M. (1984a) *School-Based Curriculum Development* London, Harper & Row/Paul Chapman

Skilbeck, M. (ed.) (1984b) *Readings in School-Based Curriculum Development* London, Harper & Row

Slee, R. and Weiner, G. (eds) (1998) *School Effectiveness for Whom?* London, Falmer

Smith, A. (1996) *Accelerated Learning in the Classroom* Stafford, School Network Educational Press

Smyth, J. (ed.) (1995) *Introduction to Critical Discourses on Teacher Development* London, Cassell

Smyth, J., McInerney, P., Hattam, R. and Lawson, M. (1999) *Critical Reflection on Teaching and Learning: Teachers' Learning Project, Investigation Series* Flinders Institute for the Study of Teaching/Dept of Education, Training and Employment South Australia

Standish, P. (1995) 'Post-modernism and the Education of the Whole Person', *Journal of Philosophy of Education* 29(1) 121–36

Stephens, P. and Crawley, T. (1994) *Becoming an Effective Teacher* Cheltenham, Stanley Thornes

Teacher Training Agency (TTA) (1998) *National Standards for Qualified Teacher Status* London, Teacher Training Agency

Thomas, D. (1995) 'Treasonable or Trustworthy Text: Reflections on Teacher Narrative Studies', in D. Thomas (ed.) *Teachers' Stories* Buckingham, Open University Press

Toynbee, P. (2001) 'This is Blair's New Road Map, but it Leads Nowhere', *Guardian*, 28 February; polly.toynbee@guardian.co.uk

Troman, G. and Woods, P. (2000) 'Careers under Stress: Teacher Adaptations at a Time of Intensive Reform', *Journal of Educational Change* 1(3) 253–75

Tunstall, P. (2003) 'Definitions of the "Subject": The Relations between the Discourses of Educational Assessment and the Psychology of Motivation and their Constructions of Personal Reality', *British Educational Research Journal* 29(4) 505–20

Valli, L. (ed.) (1992) *Reflective Teacher Education* Albany, NY, SUNY Press

Van Manen, M. (1991) *The Tact of Teaching: The Meaning of Pedagogical Thoughtfulness* London, Ontario, The Althouse Press

Wacquant, L. J. D. (1989) 'Towards a Reflexive Sociology: A Workshop with Pierre Bourdieu', *Sociological Theory* 7

Walkerdine, V. (1982) 'A Psycho-semiotic Approach to Abstract Thought', in M. Beveridge (ed.) *Children Thinking through Language* London, Arnold, pp. 129–55

Walkerdine, V. (1990) *Schoolgirl Fictions* London, Verso

Watkins, C., Carnell, E. and Lodge, C. (2000) *Learning about Learning: Resources for Supporting Effective Learning* London, Routledge

Watkins, C. and Mortimore, P. (1999) 'Pedagogy: What do we Know?', in P. Mortimore (ed.) *Understanding Pedagogy and its Impact on Learning* London, Paul Chapman, pp. 1–19

Weber, S. and Mitchell, C. (1996) 'Drawing Ourselves into Teaching: Studying the Images that Shape and Distort Teacher Education', *Teaching and Teacher Education* 12(3) 303–13

Weinstein, C. S. (1989) 'Teacher Education Students' Preconceptions of Teaching', *Journal of Teacher Education* 40(20) 53–60

Wideen, M., Mayer-Smith, J. and Moon, B. (1998) 'A Critical Analysis of the Research on Learning to Teach: Making the Case for an Ecological Perspective on Inquiry', *Review of Educational Research* 68(2) 130–78

Williams, R. (1976) *Keywords* London, Fontana

Wolf, A. (1995) *Competence-Based Assessment* Buckingham, Open University Press

Woods, P. (1979) *The Divided School* London, Routledge & Kegan Paul

Woods, P. (1985) 'Conversations with Teachers: Some Aspects of Life History Method', *British Educational Research Journal* 11, 13–26

Woods, P. (1996) *Researching the Art of Teaching: Ethnography for Educational Use* London, Routledge

Wragg, E. C. (1974) *Teaching Teaching* Newton Abbot, David & Charles

Young, M. (1998) 'Rethinking Teacher Education for a Global Future: Lessons from the English', *Journal of Education for Teaching* 24(1) 51–62

Zeichner, K. M. (1983) 'Alternative Paradigms of Teacher Education', *Journal of Teacher Education* 34(3) 3–9

Zizek, S. (1989) *The Sublime Object of Ideology* London, Verso

Index